Praise for *Mindblowing Sex in the Real World*

"Mindblowing Sex is a breath of fresh air. Sari Locker is a find!"

—**Warren Farrell,** Ph.D., author of *The Myth of Male Power*
and *Why Men Are the Way They Are*

"An advice manual addressed to teenaged and twenty-something generation Xers, unique in being authored by a sexologist woman of their generation's own real world of HIV and safe sex—pragmatic gravity nicely balanced with a touch of vernacular flippancy—no-holds-barred."

—**John Money,** Ph.D., editor of *Handbook of Sexology*

"Mindblowing Sex in the Real World is without peer—it is savvy, vivacious, witty, and absolutely up to the minute! This book is a standout!"

—**Leah C. Schaefer,** Ed.D., past president, Society for the
Scientific Study of Sex

MINDBLOWING
SEX
IN THE
REAL WORLD

MINDBLOWING SEX IN THE REAL WORLD

HOT TIPS FOR DOING IT IN THE AGE OF ANXIETY

SARI LOCKER

HarperPerennial

A Division of HarperCollinsPublishers

HarperCollins books may be purchased for educational, business, or sales promotional use. For information please write: Special Markets Department, HarperCollins Publishers, Inc., 10 East 53rd Street, New York, NY 10022.

FIRST EDITION

Designed by Alma Orenstein

Library of Congress Cataloging-in-Publication Data

Locker, Sari.
    Mindblowing sex in the real world : hot tips for doing it in the age of anxiety / Sari Locker. — 1st ed.
       p.   cm.
    Includes index.
    ISBN 0-06-095099-4
    1. Sex instruction for youth.   2. Young adults—Sexual behavior.
3. Generation X.   I. Title.
HQ35.L555   1995
306.7'07—dc 20   95-16846

95 96 97 98 99 ❖/RRD 10 9 8 7 6 5 4 3 2 1

CONTENTS

Acknowledgments   vii

1. Welcome to Sex in the Real World   1

2. Who, What, When, Where, Why, and
How Far to Go   19

3. Speaking of Sex   47

4. Understanding and Loving Your Body   69

5. All the Right Moves: Sexual Positions and

Sexual Techniques   87

6. Mindblowing Sex *with* Condoms?!?   109

7. Coming to Your Senses: Using All Five Senses
to Enhance Sex   145

8. The Wide World of Sex: Understanding Sexual
Diversity and Accepting Your Erotic Potential   165

9. Sexual Healing: Resolving Sexual Difficulties   203

10. Playing It Safe: Birth Control, STD's,
and Sexual Health   221

Final Words: Mindblowing Sex for Real People 243
*Helplines: Free Information and Referrals
About Sexuality* 245

Index 247

ACKNOWLEDGMENTS

The first time is always the most memorable, so I thank the following people for helping me with my first book.

I thank Marty Berman for his professional encouragement and guidance. Many thanks to Mel Berger, my superb literary agent at William Morris Agency. Also thanks to his assistant Claudia Cross. Thanks to Henry Reisch, Jim Griffin, and Richard Hofstetter.

I am enormously grateful to Nancy Peske, my mindblowing editor, for her intelligent and creative contributions to the content and style of this book. Thanks to my new editor Jennifer Griffin for her dedication to this project. Thanks to others at HarperCollins for their invaluable efforts on behalf of this book: Susan Weinberg, Joe McKeown, Alma Orenstein, Craig Herman, Clio Manuelian, Suzanne Noli, and Joseph Montebello.

I thank other people who brought their knowledge and creativity to help shape this book: Kera Bolonick, Dr. Bel-Michele De Mille, Jennifer Glaisek, Michael Langsdorf, Paul Levy, and Christopher Rose. Thanks to the artistically brilliant photographer Darryl Estrine.

Thanks to my colleagues and mentors in the Society for the Scientific Study of Sex. I was deeply influenced by SSSS, since I joined them at age eighteen. Thanks for showing me the way, especially to Dr. Leah Schaefer, Dr. Konstance McCaffree, Dr. Warren Farrell, and Dr. Marty Klein.

Thanks to my radio audience and the staff at WBAI 99.5 FM for giving me the opportunity to talk about sex on the radio in the middle of the afternoon. Thanks to my students all around the country in colleges, high schools, and singles groups who are interested in my perspectives on sex and who teach me about theirs.

I am especially grateful to my best friends who are a constant source of motivation in my life. Thanks for your insights and thoughtful help with this book, and for always being there for me: Erica Lichtenbaum, Daniel Kaufman, and Amanda Carlson.

Thanks to my extraordinarily supportive and loving family: Dr. Morris Siegel, Gertrude Siegel, Jonathan Siegel, Jodi Siegel, and Jeffrey Lind. Special thanks to my mother and first sex educator, Molly Lind, whose love and understanding help me every day. Thanks to my father, Dr. Laurence Locker, whose encouragement teaches me to always strive for the best. And thanks to the first person with whom I ever shared my bedroom: my wonderful sister Aliza Locker.

Most of all, thanks to the twentysomethings who generously shared their sex stories for this book.

MINDBLOWING
SEX
IN THE
REAL WORLD

CHAPTER 1

Welcome to Sex in the Real World

Redirecting the Sexuality of Our Generation

What ever happened to the joy of sex?

It seems I read its obituary somewhere between stories about Magic Johnson, Madonna, and condom distribution in the public schools.

People over forty revel in all this controversy—talk of danger, promiscuity, and youth—glad, it seems, that they're not involved. They say they'd hate to be young and single again in this age of AIDS and sexually explicit culture. Too dangerous. Too confusing.

But what about us? The twentysomethings or MTV Generation or Generation X or whatever tired label they try to slap on us. We're still here.

Not only do we want to have sex, we want it to be *mind-blowing*.

Today sex does have added layers of danger and confusion. So I offer you this guide, as a road map to the pitfalls and pleasures of being young and sexual in a time when a lot of people think that's impossible.

Maybe you're wondering how a twenty-four-year-old can know so much about sex. Well, since 1988 I have taught thousands of people about sexuality in the workshops that I conduct in colleges, high schools, and singles groups all across the country, on my own call-in radio show in New York City, and on many national TV talk shows. From listening to these individuals' stories, I found out what they say they want and need to enjoy their sexuality, to find fulfilling relationships, and to face the realities of being single and sexually active today.

Yet I am writing this book as more than just a professional sex educator. I am a young adult myself, who grew up much the same as other kids from our generation. When I was little, I played with Barbies, roller-discoed, watched *The Love Boat* and reruns of *The Brady Bunch,* and struggled to solve the Rubik's cube and conquer Space Invaders. Fortunately (perhaps unlike most other kids) I had a sexually literate mother, so my earliest sex education came from talking with her about sex. She explained the basics and talked to me about loving my body and interpreting the sexual feelings that I would have at different stages of my life. Whenever I didn't understand a dirty joke that I had heard in elementary school, I'd ask Mom to explain it to me. During my impressionable preteen and early teen years, I learned a tremendous amount about sex from sexy pop images found in places like MTV, *Penthouse,* soap operas, Dr. Ruth, steamy movies, and books. In high school, my sex education was limited to two days on the biology of sex ("Can you draw a picture of the fallopian tubes?") and a scary lecture about AIDS.

During my freshman year of college at Cornell University, my friends and I had detailed sexually graphic conversations in the hallway of my dorm some time between the midnight pizza and the 4 A.M. laundry. But soon our late night talks turned away from sharing stories about our newest sexual experiences and turned toward debates about sexual politics. The politics of abortion, date rape, gay rights, and feminism were blasted all across campus through posters, protests, and endless conversations in and out of class. Once we were bombarded by sexual politics, that was all anyone wanted to talk about anymore. Even during my graduate school program in sex education at the University of Pennsylvania, lessons on how to teach about the "sensitive" political issues of sex overshadowed lessons on how to teach about the personal issues of sex.

Besides the sexual politics in school that got in the way of learning about the personal issues of sex, the messages about sex that we received from society when we were growing up also clouded our understanding of how to deal with the day-to-day personal issues of sex.

Today's society tries to ignore the fact that young adults deserve sexual pleasure, presenting us instead with a sexual paradox. On one hand, we have been given many sexually repressive messages: "Just say no." "Sex equals death." We have been haunted by AIDS, teen pregnancy, sexually transmitted diseases, and date rape. On the other hand, we have been given many sexually stimulating messages, particularly from the media. Howard Stern, *Basic Instinct,* Kelly Bundy, 2 Live Crew, and the Artist Formerly Known As Prince all enticed us to believe what a naughty thrill sex could be.

What our society did not allow us to know is that behind the sexual politics, and somewhere between the sexual repression and the explicit eroticism, exists the realities of sex and relationships. Sex is a lot more complex than most of us were ever told. This book will expose sex as everything that it can be. Sex can be natural, warm, spiritual, kinky, confusing, messy, silly, awesome, predictable, depressing, earth-shattering—and that's just for starters. Sex doesn't have to end in disease or hurt, nor does it always flow as spontaneously as it does in the movies.

Since most of us were denied education about the complex realities of sex, I wondered what my peers still wanted and needed to learn. Besides seeking information from my workshop participants and radio listeners, I also interviewed and surveyed young adults about what's working for them sexually and what's not. Throughout the book, you'll read their quotes. I found one overwhelming similarity in their responses. Above all, people wanted to sort out the complexities of sex, and learn how to make it better and more pleasurable.

Growing up, the frightening myths that we heard about sex were almost as pervasive as the rumor that Pop Rocks killed Mikey, the kid in the Life cereal commercials. Today, most of us know that hair won't grow on our palms from masturbating. We know that douching with Coca-Cola is not an effective means of contraception. We know that we're supposed to use condoms. We know our sexual plumbing. But when it comes to obtaining true sexual pleasure, many of us are still in the dark.

Jerry, a twenty-eight-year-old man I interviewed, expressed this best when he said, "The first time I had sex it was like I was having sex in a black hole. I was fifteen, and I didn't have the slightest idea of what I was doing. It didn't even feel that great. It wasn't until recently—more than ten years later!— that I started to understand sex. Finally, instead of having sex in a black hole, it's like I'm having sex in the Garden of Eden."

As Jerry expressed, the lack of complete, unbiased information about sex has made it difficult for many young people to enjoy their sexuality. Research has shown that only about 30 percent of girls enjoy their first sexual experience and fewer than 10 percent have an orgasm during that experience. One quarter of sexually active college women still have never had an orgasm. Studies also found that they never learned enough about their sexual response to know how to stimulate their clitoris during sex. About 60 percent of the young men interviewed found that their first intercourse was not as enjoyable as they had expected: it was either faster than they had hoped for, because they had not learned to control their ejaculation, or uncomfortable because their partner was not enjoying it, or upsetting because they lost their erections due to anxiety over first-time "performance."

Many men and women in our generation have been faking their enjoyment of sex, sometimes even to themselves. People should not merely be going along with the moves, wondering if their orgasm felt as good as it should, wondering if sex could be more fulfilling, wondering if they really wanted to be doing it with the person they just did it with.

▼ ▼ ▼ ▼ ▼ ▼ ▼ ▼ ▼ ▼ ▼ ▼ ▼ ▼
Stop faking it and start making it!
▲ ▲ ▲ ▲ ▲ ▲ ▲ ▲ ▲ ▲ ▲ ▲ ▲ ▲

Sex is a skill and now is the time to learn all about it. My fear is that if we don't figure out how to be happy with our sexuality *now*, we will end up like the generation before us, crying to Oprah and Sally about our sexual problems. We deserve to help ourselves today. Sex is one of the most important, wonderful aspects of our lives.

Now is the time for us to claim our sexual rights, to redefine the sexuality of our generation as important to us—as meaningful—as pleasurable. We don't need to feel sorry for ourselves or be pitied by the older generation because we missed the age of free love. We don't need to feel like losers because everyone on TV seems to be doing it better than we are. Nor do we need to be captivated by sexual politics instead of talking about the realities of S-E-X. What we do need, and what I hope this book will provide, is information that can help make sex blissful, comfortable, pleasurable, exciting—and completely mindblowing.

We all deserve to have mindblowing sex. Learning how to have mindblowing sex is a process, which I will explain. When you follow the process you can improve your sex life. Of course, there is no guarantee that every sexual encounter will be terrific. In the real world, sometimes your sexual experiences are not all that you had hoped they would be. But by learning ways to develop and understand your sexuality, you can create a much more fulfilling sex life.

What Is Mindblowing Sex?!

Mmmm. Mindblowing sex. Sounds incredible. Everybody wants it! You wish you had the script and the director to have the kind of sex that you see in hot movie sex scenes. You compare notes with your friends to figure out how they have great sex. You grab a magazine off the newsstand because the cover reads, "How to Have the Best Sex of Your Life." You hang on every word of the "expert" on a TV talk show. And, of course, isn't that why you're reading this book?

You're waiting, wanting, needing to understand how to have sex that will make your heart pound, your mind whirl, your body go wild, and your partner beg for more.

Well, you can stop searching so desperately, because there is no magic key to unlocking the door to mindblowing sex. Yet, with some knowledge and experience, you'll be able to find it for yourself.

In the workshops that I teach, I've asked the participants to tell me their definition of "mindblowing sex." On my radio show, I've listened to people tell me the stories of the difficulties they experience attaining the type of sex lives that they'd love to have. What I have come up with is a theory based on a composite of common factors from the definitions of mindblowing sex and from the sexual problems and pitfalls that people fall into when they are looking for mindblowing sex.

As I will explain, there are four steps in the process of achieving mindblowing sex:

1. The first step is learning the three basic elements of good sex: the Emotional, the Natural, and the Technical.
2. The second step is achieving balance with those elements.
3. The third step is applying the Intellectual element of sex, which leads you to master decision making and good choices about sex.
4. The fourth step is finding out and expressing what you like within the Personal Creativity and Pleasures of mindblowing sex.

Step One: Learning the Three Basic Elements of Good Sex

There are three basic areas where we can grow sexually: the Emotional, the Natural, and the Technical.

▼ ▼

The first step in the process of achieving mindblowing sex is learning what constitutes each of the three elements of good sex: the Emotional, the Natural, and the Technical.

▲ ▲

Each of the elements is described below.

1. The "Emotional" element of sex means being aware of and accepting the feelings involved in sex. More specifically, this element includes:
   ▸ being aware of the emotions, desires, and moods you

are experiencing before, during, and after sex

▸ accepting whether you need to feel love to enjoy sex

▸ being able to talk about your emotions with your partner and being able to ask your partner about his or her emotions

▸ trusting your partner and being honest with your partner

▸ feeling "safe" and comfortable when you are intimate with someone—not fearful of "being smothered" in a close relationship and not "smothering" the other person

▸ feeling good about yourself and loving yourself, which will help you be able to feel good about, and become intimate with, another person

2. The "Natural" element of sex means accepting and enjoying your sexual self, your body, and your preferences. More specifically, this element includes:

▸ accepting your gender and the way you choose to portray your maleness or femaleness

▸ accepting your sexual orientation

▸ enjoying your nude body

▸ not being self-conscious about the way your body looks and moves during sex

▸ not being self-conscious about the sounds or smells that you may make during sex

▸ accepting that masturbation is healthy and natural and can be fun

▸ letting yourself go and feeling free and confident during sex

▸ letting yourself feel pleasure and have fun during sex

3. The "Technical" element of sex means understanding the mechanics of sex. More specifically, this element includes:

- ▸ knowing about your sexual organs, your sexual response, and your orgasms
- ▸ knowing what sexual positions you like
- ▸ knowing where and when you like to have sex
- ▸ knowing how long you like sex to last
- ▸ knowing what tempo and rhythm you like during sex
- ▸ knowing what you like in the great variety of sexual styles and behaviors
- ▸ knowing how to use birth control and condoms
- ▸ knowing how to prevent STD's
- ▸ knowing how to take care of your sexual health

Step Two: Achieving Balance in the Three Basic Elements of Good Sex

People who complain about having difficulty achieving pleasure in sex are often people who have not yet reached a balance of the three basic elements of good sex, which are equally critical to achieving mindblowing sex.

▼ ▼

The second step in the process of achieving mindblowing sex is learning how to be an Emotionalist, a Naturalist, and a Technicalist all rolled up in one.

▲ ▲

People who are strong in only one category will probably end up with dissatisfaction in their sex lives. For instance, a pure Technicalist would want sex with no emotions, no protection, no connection: just lusty, seductive, sweaty, primal sex with no strings attached. Twenty-two-year-old Technicalist Tim said it this way: "What makes sex so good is that you get to do nasty things to people and they appreciate it!" However, at some point, true Technicalists usually end up faking their enjoyment of sex, feeling as if they are just going through the motions and not getting any deeper than that. It's not enough to have mastery of a well-rehearsed repertoire of sexual positions and to be proficient at having orgasms. And unless you are a member of the Spur Posse, having sex just to keep score of the number of your conquests becomes meaningless. Technicalists often find that sex is confusing, awkward, or clumsy because they have not built up the Naturalist element in themselves. They may feel empty after sex or never reach intimacy because they have not built up the Emotionalist in themselves.

For pure Emotionalists, caring, honesty, trust, and communication may seem like enough to have mindblowing sex. As twenty-four-year-old Emotionalist Steve explained, "The best sex is when I feel connected and in tune with my girlfriend." Yet Emotionalists will usually find that that connection alone is not enough. They may become self-conscious because they are not strong Naturalists. They may have difficulty with orgasm and feel awkward trying new sexual positions or behaviors because they lack the knowledge and skills of the Technical element.

A pure Naturalist, like Sandi, twenty-eight, said that she enjoys sex when she "just lets nature takes its course." She and other Naturalists may find that sex does not occur so simply and naturally. Even if sex feels natural, like an instinct, that good feeling alone does not make sex good. Naturalists must develop the ability to communicate with their partners, like the Emotionalists, and must acquire some Technical information and skills.

The following example illustrates how two people need to achieve sexual balance in order to be sexually gratified.

A twenty-six-year-old woman, Linda, called in to my radio program to ask my advice on how she could become more satisfied with her sex life. Linda said that for the past six months she'd been with a twenty-eight-year-old boyfriend,

Lewis. When I asked her what her problem was, she said, "It's just not good sex." Then I asked her to explain what she meant. Linda complained that Lewis only kisses her twice before he enters her. He only touches her body a little. Sex only lasts for a few minutes. He doesn't wait for her to have an orgasm. He never looks into her eyes during sex. Then he falls asleep afterward thinking that everything was fine.

Doesn't that sound like unfulfilling sex? Perhaps for Linda sex would be better if Lewis would get into positions so she could have her orgasm; if they'd have lots of sex play before sex; if they'd talk after sex. Lewis might be able to have better sex with more variety and excitement, more intimacy, and a more natural connection to Linda.

You can understand from my explanation of finding balance in the three basic elements of good sex, how Linda and Lewis can improve their sexuality. Lewis needs to work more on his Technical element in order to help her gain satisfaction in their sex life. Also, he needs to develop his Emotional and Natural elements to be more intimate, sensitive, and communicative. Linda needs to develop her Technical element in order to know how to please herself during sex. She also needs to find balance in her Emotional element, so she can learn to initiate the conversations about how she feels about their sex life, make suggestions for improving it, yet not feel that sex always has to be overflowing with emotion. If Linda and Lewis want to have good sex, and eventually mindblowing sex, they need to develop and balance all three elements.

Step Three: The Intellectual Element

Besides having sex that will make you feel fulfilled emotionally, technically, and naturally, the next step is being able to develop your intellectual ability to handle sexual decisions. The following outline of the Intellectual element of sex will show how it can help you master sexual decision making skills.

The "Intellectual" element of sex means knowing how to make choices based in reality and practicality. Moreover, it means:

▶ sticking to your values and making good choices about sex
▶ understanding and knowing how to deal with the consequences of all of your actions
▶ choosing and using birth control to prevent unintended pregnancy and using condoms to protect against sexually transmitted diseases
▶ knowing when and how to communicate about practical issues of sex
▶ being levelheaded and mature when making decisions about sex
▶ having good judgment about who to have sex with and where and when to have sex
▶ understanding that sex does not necessarily lead to love and love does not necessarily lead to sex
▶ taking responsibility and being accountable for your choices (even if you were influenced by alcohol, drugs, power, lust, or any other external factor)

Once you get to this step in the process, you need to be careful not to think *too* much about the consequences of sex. Rachel, twenty-four, illustrates how someone can put too much emphasis on the Intellectual element. She said, "I would only have sex if I was sure that the person would use the kind of condoms I like. But then again, I'd worry that even condoms may not protect me from all disease. Maybe I would make the person get tested before sex. But probably, we'd want to have sex spontaneously, so I don't know if we'd have time to get tested. But I would never be with anyone who didn't abide by my values about using protection." When the Intellectual element outweighs all the other elements, people overanalyze every decision, try to make strict rules for sex, worry about diseases and pregnancy, and feel obsessed with not making any mistakes. They still need to maintain the balance of the other elements. They need the Emotionalist's ability to relate to their partner and to feel closeness or intimacy. They need the Naturalist element to feel relaxed with another person and with themselves. They need the Technical element to have enough information about sexual practices and sexual variety.

The Intellectual element should keep each of the other three elements in check. For example, someone who is considering having sex purely for physical "Technicalist" reasons, may stop to intellectually consider the pros and cons. If this person uses his or her Intellectual capacity, the person would probably not regret his or her sexual experiences or end up being faced with the negative consequences of sex. The person would understand that sex just for Technical reasons may have negative repercussions.

▼ ▼

Sex should feel good, but it should also be good for you.

▲ ▲

If people are having sex for Emotional reasons, like thinking that sex will make them feel filled with love, then checking it with their Intellectual element should help them grasp reality to know the difference between love and lust.

The Naturalists who may want to do it spontaneously need to be able to make responsible decisions about sex based on their Intellectual element, knowing that choices about having sex should be thought through before doing it.

When you master the third step in the process toward

achieving mindblowing sex, you should find that you are making better decisions and having fewer regrets in your sex life.

Once you have achieved a sexual balance of the three basic elements of good sex and you can intellectually deal with sex, then you are well on your way to going over the top in order to have mindblowing sex.

Step Four: Experiencing the Personal Creativity and Pleasures of Mindblowing Sex

When you have balanced the basics and can make good decisions about sex it will be easier to choose from the vast menu of sexual behaviors and potential sexual partners. At that point, you may enjoy experimenting to find out what variations of sex will bring you the most pleasure. Then you can add your personal creative expressions of pleasure to sex to create mindblowing sex.

▼ ▼

Adding the fourth step—the extra components of "Personal Creativity and Pleasure"—will create mindblowing sex.

▲ ▲

Everyone has his or her own sexual style and preferences. From who you choose to have sex with to where you do it to what positions you like, it's all about personal creativity and pleasue. The more you have sex, the more you'll find out what will give you fulfillment and with whom you are sexually compatible.

By finding a balance of the Emotional, the Natural, the Technical, and the Intellectual, finding a compatible partner, and making careful, creative personal sexual choices, you may even see fireworks, hear bells, feel like you're riding a roller coaster, or have the deepest, most powerful connection of your life.

Everybody learns about sex from having sex!

Just because you will learn more about sex from experiencing sex, it does not mean that you have to get out there and have sex and try everything. Besides learning from doing, you can also learn from reading about all kinds of sexual variations and methods to enhance sex. That's where this book will come in handy.

How This Book Will Help You Achieve Mindblowing Sex

Each chapter of this book will help you develop the elements of mindblowing sex. Think about what elements you could strengthen: Can you express how you feel about sex (Emotional)? Do you accept how your body feels during sex (Natural)? Do you understand the mechanics of sexuality (Technical)? Do you have good judgment about the realities of sex and relationships (Intellectual)? Can you come up with creative ways to enhance your own sexuality (Personal Creativity and Pleasure)? When you read each chapter, you can focus on the sections of that chapter that will enhance your sex life the most.

Chapter 2 explains sexual decision making to help guide you through choices about why to have sex, who to have sex with, when to have sex, and what to do sexually. This chapter will help you develop your Intellectual element. It will also help you see how to maintain balance to base your decisions on your emotional expressions, technical knowledge, and natural abilities. The chapter will help you set sexual guidelines for making well thought out decisions that you will seldom regret. Finally, chapter 2 gives you advice on how to accept the decisions you make, and how to grow and move on if you have regrets.

Chapter 3 explains how to communicate about sex, which will help you develop your Emotional and Intellectual elements. Talking about sex is more than just knowing when to say yes and no. This chapter will help you learn to express your sexual desires and expectations and your emotions. The chapter goes even further to explain more detailed forms of sexual communication, like how to read a prospective lover's body language, and how and when to say, "I love you."

Chapter 4 offers insight into understanding and accepting your body and sexual response to help you strengthen your Technical and Natural elements. This chapter will explain how you feel desire, what gets you aroused, and how erections and orgasms function. It also uncovers answers to questions such as what is the G-Spot and can men have multiple orgasms. The chapter also helps you explore how you feel about your body and how to improve the way you feel about your body. This chapter provides tips for you to get the most out of sex by being able to accept your body and your lover's body.

Chapter 5 explains a great variety of sexual positions. Learning about these can help you develop your Technical element and add to your own Personal Creativity and Pleasure. While sometimes people can figure out what positions they like by just moving around, many times reading about the variety of ways people can do it provides the spark to ignite sexual creativity. This chapter may give you some new things to try.

Chapter 6 is about how to creatively and intelligently deal with condoms. To prevent sexually transmitted diseases, condoms are a necessity, so this chapter shows you how to have mindblowing sex with them by giving you ways to add variety, enhancing your Personal Creativity and Pleasure. After you read chapter 6, you'll get plenty of ideas about how to enjoy sex with condoms. Then you may actually *want* to use condoms to add to sexual fulfillment.

Chapter 7 looks at the sensual side of sex, how to use all five senses to make sex more erotic. You can intensify your sexual experiences by varying what you see, hear, feel, taste, and smell during sex. Using your mind to tune in to all of your senses can really *blow* your mind. As the old saying goes, "Sex is between your ears, not your legs." This chapter can add to all of the basic elements of good sex and can definitely enhance your Personal Creativity and Pleasure.

Chapter 8 also adds to your own Personal Creativity and Pleasure by providing you with sexual options and more hot tips for creating mindblowing sex. It discusses the many varieties of sexual behaviors in which people engage. It seems like the old man-on-top-sex-in-marriage has become the most far out kind of sex today. People are now moving toward a wider, more legitimate sphere of sexual choices. There is a growing acceptance of all sexual orientations, behaviors, and lifestyles, including a greater acceptance of gays, lesbians, bisexuals, transvestism, sadomasochism, prostitution, stripping, cybersex, group sex, and more. Our mission is to figure out what is right for each of us, and that doesn't necessarily mean trying everything. Mostly, it means learning the realities of all kinds of sex. The discussion on sexual diversity and erotic potential will help you figure out what is right (or wrong) for you.

Even after learning all about how to have mindblowing sex, there will still be times in everyone's sex lives when they have to deal with some of the imperfect, negative aspects of sex. Thus, *Chapter 9* explains how you can overcome sexual difficulties, like inability to have an orgasm, loss of sexual desire, loss of erections, or premature ejaculation. The chapter will also give advice on when you should consult a sex therapist, or how you can try to solve your problem on your own. This will help you develop your Natural element and Technical element.

Chapter 10 gives you information about sexual health, birth control, unintended pregnancy, sexually transmitted diseases, and AIDS. Learning about these subjects will help you develop your Intellectual and Technical elements. To enjoy the positive, pleasurable, creative aspects of mind-blowing sex, you also need to master the responsibilities of sex.

Finally, this book provides a list of important resources that you can use to find more answers to any other questions you may have in your quest to find meaningful, sexy, and, of course, safer sex. All of the information in this book should help you have mindblowing sex!

CHAPTER 2

Who, What, When, Where, Why, and How Far to Go

Setting Sexual Guidelines

Can you have casual sex? Should you be in love to make love? How can you decide who to have sex with? Will you use condoms every time you have sex? Do you want to have a threesome? Would it turn you on to get into S/M? Do you want to film your own sex video?

Making decisions about sex is not simple. Your heart may tell you one thing while your mind may tell you another. Then, when you get turned on and all of your blood rushes to your genitals, you may think something completely different. That is why it's important to decide on your own personal sexual guidelines ahead of time and stick to them. Don't make a last-minute decision you'll regret and beat yourself up for it later.

Deciding on your guidelines requires you to look at your

choices from all angles of the basic elements of good sex. Do you have the the Emotional understanding or stability to respond well and not regret the decision? Do you have the Natural ability to enjoy that sexual choice? Do you have the facts about the Technical elements of the sexual choice? Will you use your Intellectual ability to use good rational judgment?

Think through as many of the possible negative and positive outcomes as you can. Then, set sexual guidelines that will lead you to the most positive consequences. Take all the time you need to make a clear, rational decision. If you stick to your guidelines, you'll find that you'll have an easier time when you get in a confusing or sexually charged situation because you will already know what you'll want to do.

▼ ▼
Think about your choices. Plan ahead. Be decisive.
▲ ▲

Sticking to Your Sexual Guidelines

It won't always be easy to stick to your sexual guidelines. If you make spontaneous decisions, they may be based more on your hormones, on your loneliness, on the way you feel about the other person's power or good looks, on your alcohol or drug consumption, or simply on blind lust.

Twenty-seven-year-old Mike explains how his snap decisions and outside influences lead to regrets: "I was at the company Christmas party, drinking, of course. Some girl who works with me started coming on to me. So I took her home and we had sex. I never wanted to have a one-night stand. I just did it because I was drunk and not thinking. The next morning I looked at her and wanted her out of my place. I made such a mistake. Now every day at work I have to avoid her side of the room. I know she told everyone. I even think that I hurt her; she wanted more from me."

There are times when you may want to alter your sexual guidelines in the heat of the moment. Rather than do that, wait a day or so and think if you should change your guidelines. Please don't get me wrong. I am not trying to tell you that you need to follow strict rules to have sex. In fact, sex should have some degree of freedom or spontaneity. Yet you need to figure out the basic decisions first, or you'll end up too confused later. Also, try not to let your partner pressure you to change your mind. You'd be better off finding someone who is more compatible with you than being with someone who wants you to change.

▼ ▼

If you stick to your sexual guidelines, once you wake up the next morning, you will feel pleased with yourself.

▲ ▲

Deciding Why to Have Sex

Why do people have sex? The reasons are innumerable and include: love, passion, curiosity, reproduction, obligation, and pleasure. When you are deciding whether or not to have sex with someone, examine whether your reasons are good ones for you. What makes sex meaningful is whatever you gain from it, and I don't mean money or a better job. Sometimes it's a feeling of love, satisfaction, increased self-esteem, power, or sometimes it's simply pleasure. Sometimes people have or avoid sex to stay in line with religious or ethical teachings. To help you figure out why you would want to have sex or not, try to figure out what will make sex have meaning for you.

▼ ▼

Decisions on why to have sex can be based on what makes sex meaningful or fulfilling to you.

▲ ▲

Do You Need Love for Sex or Is Lust Enough?

Being close to someone in a sexual way can be a deeply emotional experience. Whether it's intercourse or not, whether it's on the first date or the fiftieth, it still touches you in a way that nothing else can. Part of deciding why to have sex, who to have sex with, and when to have sex may have to do with whether or not you are in love.

What is love, anyway? When people are in love, they express affection, caring, and nurturing. They also open themselves up to get back those same feelings from the person they love. Love, according to twenty-one-year-old Rachel, is "about allowing yourself to be vulnerable." Martin, twenty-six, says, "Loving means giving all you can give to someone you care about." Beth, twenty-seven, describes the love in her relationship: "We are incredibly attracted to each other, but it's much more. We are real friends, which runs much deeper than sex. We are so honest about our feelings, about the things we agree on and the things we disagree on. That is what creates our love."

For some people being in love is the most profound feeling. Love has been expressed in literature, music, films, and art as the wonder of life—the highest form of human companionship. Love has been described as magical, intoxicating, mystical, fascinating, combining body, mind, and soul. In real life, some people do feel that intensity of love. "Loving Sheryl is what keeps me happy about living. This is what life is about," expressed twenty-five-year-old John.

Others feel love in more subtle ways. Twenty-nine-year-old Josh's comments illustrate a common sentiment among people who wish that love would be an overwhelming feeling for them: "I had never told any of my past girlfriends that I loved them, because I didn't think that I felt it. Now, with my new girlfriend, I still wonder, is this all there is? It seems like L-O-V-E should feel like the strongest thing. But I guess I'm in love now. I tell her I love her."

Some people need to feel in love before they have sex; some feel that they cannot fall in love until after they have sex with someone. The old saying is that men give love to get sex and women give sex to get love. While this is not necessarily true, there are some people who get talked into having sex because the partner says "I love you." If you need to be in love to have sex, think about what "love" means to you and to your partner. If one person is thinking, "'Love' means we'll have a monogamous, committed relationship," while the other is thinking, "'Love' means I really enjoy what we have—for now," obviously the first person could get very hurt.

▼ ▼

Sex never guarantees love, commitment, or even phone calls.

▲ ▲

When people have sex thinking that it will lead to a certain kind of relationship, they are kidding themselves. Each sexual encounter should be based on the meaning of that encounter, not on a fantasy about what it could bring in the future. Decisions about when to have sex should not be based on false expectations.

There are people who are capable of being happy in a lust relationship, having sex not with love but with sexual attraction. How do you know when it's just lust? Well, lust is a more desperate feeling. Frances, twenty, explained lust like this: "The moment I saw him, my heart skipped a beat. I knew that I wanted him. I knew that I needed him. I thought that maybe I loved him. We had sex the second time we went out. It was inevitable. There was so much heat between us, this attraction. No words even describe it."

Sometimes people don't want to admit to themselves that they're in lust, not in love. Face it, lust isn't romantic, and it burns out pretty quickly. If your gut tells you that this person is not for you—not someone with whom you'd really want to spend a lot of time for a long time—but you are still trying to fool yourself into thinking that this person is the one for you, then you're probably setting yourself up to get hurt.

▼ ▼

If it's only lust, and you know it, then admit it to yourself and to the other person.

▲ ▲

Once you identify your feelings as lust, you need to decide for yourself if you can you have sex without love. Also, if you want to have sex without a relationship and just for lust, you must make sure that your partner is willing and also lustful. There will be an emotional price to pay if the other person wants a relationship, not just sex, or if the other person is really in love with you. The bottom line is: don't lie to someone else just to get laid—and don't lie to yourself about what's really going on: lust or love.

What Do You Do About Unrequited Love?

When you're sure that you've met someone who is perfect for you, but the person is not interested in you, you must realize one very important fact—this person may have every single quality that you want in a partner, but if he or she doesn't want you, that one quality makes that person entirely wrong for you. If someone rejects you after you ask him or her out two or three times, forget it and move on. Pursuit seldom works, and is often construed as harassment. This also applies if you've been in a relationship with the person for a few days, weeks, or even months, and he or she breaks up with you and you feel dumped.

▼ ▼

You cannot convince someone to like you if he or she is simply not interested in you.

▲ ▲

If you are miserable, accept that you're going to feel miserable for a while, and then work on forgetting what might have been. Play some blues, watch a depressingly romantic movie, mope, but then move on. At first you might have to force yourself to go through the motions of getting on with your life and forgetting about him or her. But soon you will be able to be happy and you will forget your feelings of misery. Believe it or not, you will feel worse the longer you hold on to the fantasy that the other person will suddenly wake up and fall in love with you. Too many people get obsessed when they feel rejected. They end up letting their self-esteem go into the toilet, or doing something dangerous and illegal, like stalking the person who spurned them. Don't let this happen to you. Try to go out and find someone new, or just get into loving yourself. Focus on getting yourself back to happiness with your work, your friends, and your life.

How Soon After People Meet Do They Have Sex?

Just because you feel a magnificent bulge through a guy's pants or see a woman's nipples peeking through her bra does not mean you've got to rip off your clothes and do it. It may not be the right time or place, or right time in your relationship. You can take time to decide at what point in a relationship you want to have sex. Or you can have casual sex. I surveyed 500 people ages 19 to 29 to determine how long they wait after they meet someone until the first time they have sex with that person. Here are the results:

13%	First Date
24%	**Fourth Date to Seventh Date**
19%	**Two Weeks to One Month**
17%	**One Month to Three Months**
16%	Three Months to Six Months
10%	Six Months to One Year
1%	Marriage

It seems that the majority of the people in my survey (the percentages in boldface) reported that they waited to have sex until they knew the person a little, or felt as if they were beginning a relationship, or perhaps felt like they were falling in love. Yet there is still a notable percentage of people who have sex on the first date, many of whom were probably having one-night stands. Do you know if casual sex or a one-night stand is right for you?

Do the Right Fling: Can You Have Casual Sex?

There are both pros and cons to hooking up for one night or having casual sex. For many people, the concept of a one-night stand is better in theory than in reality. In reality, one-night stands may not physically feel as good as sex in a relationship, because often the most intense sex comes from having sex with someone who knows your sexual response. When your partner knows what turns you on, knows how to give you an orgasm, knows what positions you like, talks about sex with you, and is willing to experiment with your sexual fantasies, then sex is often very good. That almost never comes in a one-night stand. Of course, one-night stands seldom have great emotional intensity, either, unless you are getting off on the taboo of having sex with a near stranger. Even so, the next day you may feel guilty, stupid, lonely, or cheap.

Before you have casual sex, you should consider how you would deal with the possible hurt or jealousy if the next day you saw the person with his or her arm around someone else. Also, consider what would happen if you have a one-night stand hoping you will remain anonymous, and you find out later that you two have a mutual friend.

On the more positive side, for some people, one-night stands or casual sex give great pleasure with no emotional regrets. Some people believe that sex in one-night stands is better than sex in committed relationships, because of the newness and the ability to do anything with no strings attached. They say they feel more excitement, more freedom, and more sexual pleasure. Twenty-two-year-old Petra said, "I felt less inhibited when I had a one-night stand. It was like I could do anything, because I didn't care what he thought of me." Jay, twenty-three, explained, "I am more adventurous and less embarrassed when I fuck a stranger. Isn't that funny? If you would have asked me how it is to have sex with a girlfriend, I'd call it 'sex.' It was a reflex when I said 'fuck,' because that's what I feel about it with a stranger."

If you are not sure how you would feel about a one-night stand, casual sex, or sex with a near-stranger, then consider the following:

1. Can you detach yourself emotionally, including the likelihood that you will never hear from him or her again?
2. Will you be able to deal with it if your paths do cross again?
3. Will you be absolutely sure to use condoms?
4. Will you be absolutely sure to use birth control? What would you do if a pregnancy resulted from a one-night stand?

5. Are you are having a one-night stand hoping that it will lead to a relationship? If so, then do a reality check. Having sex the day you meet or on the first date doesn't guarantee a second date, much less a relationship.

Who Should You Have Sex With?

When I've asked twentysomethings "Who should you have sex with?" at first many men and women respond by saying, "Anyone who's willing!" Then they get serious and explain that they have been faced with many tough decisions about who to have sex with. Their decisions involved more than if they were simply attracted enough to the person, or if they loved the person, or if they had a condom handy. Often the choices involved a judgment based on personal ethics.

To help you form your sexual guidelines, the next section of this book explores the following questions:

Should you get involved with: Someone at work, your boss, coworker, employee, a professor? Someone who is a lot older or younger than you? Someone who lives far away from you? Someone who's married or in a serious relationship? Someone who is a friend or a "fuck buddy"? Or someone who is highly compatible with you for a serious monogamous relationship?

If you think through your choices, most likely you will have better sex and relationships. But there are no guarantees that you will necessarily have more successful relationships even if you give them a lot of forethought. If your choice doesn't work out, be able to let go, move on, and find your new adventure in dating. There will be plenty of new people and new adventures out there!

Do You Want to Have Sex with Someone At Work?

It's a feasible and natural outcome of working with a group of people that at some point you may be interested in having sex with one of them. Every day at work you are meeting people who have at least one thing in common with you. Sometimes, your common interest in work, or the sexual tension that is building up between the two of you from seeing each other five days a week is enough to make you consider whether you should have sex with or start a relationship with this person.

Sometimes dating someone at work can have positive outcomes: "Craig and I met at work. We work in different divisions, but we see each other every day for lunch, and we go home together almost every night. Before we met, I used to worry that I'd never have sex again, since I worked such long hours and never got out to date. Now this is the best possible relationship I could have hoped for," said twenty-six-year-old Liz.

In some work environments (especially noncorporate, loosely structured jobs), it's comfortable and appropriate if you are close with your coworkers. Damon, twenty-five, and Regina, twenty-seven, exemplify this type of relationship: "Regina and I are both actors. We met in a show, and have been in love ever since. But for us, we only work together on occasion, so it's not a big issue of 'sex at work.'"

Before you have sex with someone from work, consider how it will affect your reputation. Will people see you as a slut instead of as a potential manager? If, in your office, it's just not appropriate to be making dinner plans when you are supposed to be working on financial plans, then you'll know to stop yourself before you even start the fantasies.

If you cannot decide if you want to pursue a relationship, or if you want to have sex with or go on a date with someone from work, consider if you could handle the possible outcomes if you do have a relationship and then you break up. Life isn't *Melrose Place,* and if your workplace lover breaks up with you, the tension probably won't drive you to alcoholism like it did Alison when she and Billy broke up. In the real world, a failed love affair with a worker will most likely affect the quality of your work. When the relationship ends with a coworker, the person will still be there every day and you'll have to deal with your feelings about the relationship every day at work.

Besides considering a sexual relationship with a coworker, you may be faced with deciding if you want to get involved with a boss or employee. In either case, there will inevitably be some power dynamic between the two of you that could lead to a bad relationship or to a very bad effect on your career. If you have sex with the boss you may be putting your career in jeopardy; he or she can promote or fire you based on the relationship. If you have sex with an employee, if the relationship goes bad and your ex wants revenge, you could unjustly be accused of sexual harassment. The problem of power is also inevitable in similar relationships, such as sex between a student and a professor. It often leads to the student feeling used, and the professor (if he or she is insightful) feeling as if he or she abused his or her power.

If you just want to have sex for sex's sake, then your concerns should be finding partners who will not want an emotional connection and will not influence your life in any other way if you have sex. Emotionless sex should only be tried in nonemotionally-volatile situations. There is enough stress and strain on your career at this time without getting involved with someone at work on top of it. If you don't want to screw up your career, then make careful decisions about screwing around at work.

▼ ▼

It's virtually impossible to have sex with your boss, a coworker, a professor, or an employee and expect that it will be just sex and not affect your job.

▲ ▲

Do You Want to Have a Long-Distance Relationship?

It's fairly common for twentysomethings today to be faced with a decision regarding getting in or staying in a long-distance relationship. Lovers or potential lovers are moving all around the country, going to grad school, getting new jobs, moving away from home, or perhaps moving back home. Unless you are asked (and able) to move with this person, you'll have to decide if you want to have a long-distance relationship.

Your first step in making this decision may be deciding how important this person is to you and what you are looking for out of the relationship. If the person is your long-term college lover who's moving on to a new job, but you both know that you'd love to live in the same place and maybe even marry each other some day, then it may be worth trying to maintain a long-distance relationship, at least for a while. Yet if it's someone whom you've met for two hours (and felt lust toward) in an airport waiting room, then you shouldn't feel invested in maintaining the connection.

▼ ▼

If you are the kind of person who loves having deep intimacy, having sex with one partner almost every day, or going out with your partner whenever you feel like it, then a long-distance relationship may not be for you.

▲ ▲

Long-distance relationships are low on the intimacy scale, since they involve spending very little time together except for the weekend "nookie runs" or the rare week-long visit. Since you must rely on verbal and written communication, if that breaks down, then you have nothing left: "I had thought that having a long-distance relationship would improve our communication, since the only way we had to stay together was to talk on the phone. But he never told me how he was feeling. We never seemed to have anything to say to each other after a while, because our lives were so different. We broke up when I realized that our relationship could have only worked based on hanging out together, not talking," laments twenty-one-year-old Beth.

On the other hand, if you don't mind seeing someone only on occasion, if you trust each other, and if you can maintain good communication, then a long-distance romance may work for you. This was true for twenty-six-year-old Danny: "We had the best time because we were having a long-distance relationship. It gave me freedom to be alone or go out or do whatever I wanted. We both stayed faithful to each other—at least I think she did. We talked on the phone. We'd even have sex over the phone. Sometimes, to make it seem like we weren't so far apart, we'd watch TV together over the phone. Once we rented the same movie and watched it while we were on the phone together, like it was a date."

If you are trying to decide if you should get in or stay in a long-distance relationship, consider how much physical intimacy you like to have, how good you both are at communicating, and how much money you have to spend on phone bills.

Do You Want to Have Sex with Someone Who Is a Lot Older or Younger than You?

Sometimes people meet and are attracted to each other, and the attraction is so strong that the huge age difference between the two of them does not matter at all. Other people go looking expressly for someone who is either a lot older or a lot younger than they are. Depending on their motivation, the relationship and the sex between these people may work well or not work at all.

When the people are looking for the age difference, the

relationship is usually very shallow, just based on sex, as you can see: "I love having sex with men who are like twenty years older than me, because they last longer and I come stronger. They can only do it once a night, but it's so much better than guys my age who can do it all night but each time it only lasts a second, and they don't even know what a clitoris is," said Veronica, twenty-three. Dennis, twenty-nine, also looks for a large age difference between him and his partners: "Sex with younger women is great because they are pure, innocent, and unspoiled. Women I meet who are my age have slept with about thirty men, and I hate that," said Dennis.

If you choose to have sex with someone who is a lot older than you (whether it's a man or a woman) you might find it exciting that they've had a lot of sexual experience. When you have sex with someone younger, you may enjoy feeling more like the teacher, trying to make them feel at ease with sex.

Other people who look for an age difference may not want it solely because of its impact on sex. Judith, twenty-three, for example, says, "I want an older man because they are much more emotionally mature than men my age. We have more to talk about. He doesn't just want to go out drinking, like guys my age."

Jim, twenty-six, experienced a relationship with an older woman who liked his young attitude. "She told me that men her age [forty-three] had more sexist views of relationships. She liked that I wasn't old-fashioned."

▼ ▼

The positive outcomes of intergenerational relationships most often occur when the age difference is not a big issue. When the two people feel like good friends, lovers, and have a lot in common despite the age difference, the relationship can work, just like any other relationship.

▲ ▲

However, if the age difference is the focus, then the relationship may not be successful. Sometimes the older person is just getting off on the fact he or she has power over the younger partner. To the older person, the relationship may be just a novelty or a symptom of a midlife crisis, and not a potentially lasting relationship. If the relationship is more valued by the younger partner, it is that person who may ultimately get hurt.

On the other hand, if the older person is invested in the relationship, he or she may also get hurt because of the age difference. It's common for the younger person to outgrow the older one and want to break up and move on before the older person outgrows him or her.

It may also be difficult to maintain balance in the relationship because of a lot of people's judgment of "May-December" relationships. You may have to deal with teasing from your friends, such as being accused of being a "sugar daddy" or hearing an endless chorus of "sixteen will get you twenty," or "you're robbing the cradle."

Also, most states have laws against "statutory rape" in which a sexual relationship is deemed legally nonconsensual if the younger partner is under a certain age. The age cut-off varies from state to state; usually it is around sixteen or eighteen. So if the younger person is underage (or you are underage), consider the potential legal consequences of the relationship.

To make the decision to be with someone a lot older or younger, consider all of the pros and cons of the potential relationship. Try to let good judgment, not lust or power, guide your choice.

Do You Want to Have Sex with Someone Else's Partner?

Some twentysomethings who have affairs with married people or people who are in committed relationships find these affairs very fulfilling. According to twenty-nine-year-old Joseph, who has had sex with several married women, "Sex with a married woman has greater emotional intensity. She's exciting. She's not the nice, steady reliable girl who begs me for a commitment."

Most people find that if they remain emotionally detached from the relationship, the sex feels good. Often married people are enthusiastic about having sex with their mistress or mister (the term I invented for the male counterpart to a mistress). Some married people will treat you like the most amazing person on earth, showering you with gifts and praise and hot sex. "Our relationship was very good, since he was looking for a woman who wouldn't nag him or argue with him. I helped him overcome the everyday drudgery that his marriage made for him. In exchange we had fun in and out of bed," said Michelle, twenty-seven.

Yet other people who become mistresses or misters do it because they have serious problems with intimate relationships, a strong fear of commitment, low self-esteem, and ultimately are asking to get hurt. The pleasure that they report from the affair usually is an expression of pain that they are covering up: "I felt powerful when I was having an affair with a married man. I thought he must think that I'm an incredibly beautiful woman if he wants me so much that he cheats on her," said twenty-four-year-old Tasha. See what I mean? You can also see the pain in twenty-three-year-old Tiffany's statement: "I had had boyfriends who hurt me by cheating on me. I thought that if I had an affair with a guy who had a steady girlfriend then it would be easier, since I'd already know ahead of time that he was a liar and a cheat. All I knew was how to fall in love with someone who would ultimately hurt and reject me."

If you are trying to get hurt or rejected in any relationship, you will. Don't kid yourself that your lover will leave his or her spouse—that happens rarely. Even if it does, you end up with someone whom you know is capable of cheating. Would you want to be with someone who would cheat on you?

▼ ▼

If you are looking for a healthy relationship with somone with whom you can go out in public, spend holidays, and have a future, then an involved person is not for you.

▲ ▲

Do You Want to Have Sex with a Fuck Buddy?

Some people have emotionally detached sex with a person they don't love and with whom they are not even friends—a "fuck buddy." The two people seldom have much in common except that they get together to have sex. This works for people who can maintain detached physical desire, like twenty-four-year-old Meredith: "There is a man who I have sex with about once every six months, when I'm in between relationships, because he's great in bed. It's animalistic. Neither of us even asks how the other person is or what's new. I make a "late-night booty call." I come over. We have sex. I leave. It's perfect," she said.

On the other hand, twenty-seven-year-old Kevin is an example of someone who had problems with his fuck buddy: "We had casual sex whenever we'd see each other at this night club. We knew nothing about each other. We called each other 'fuck buddies.' Then she started asking if we could date for real. I guess she always felt like she could fall back on me [for a serious relationship] if she never met the right guy. When I found that out I never let her have sex with me again. I don't owe her anything."

As you can see, a complication of having a fuck buddy is if one of the partners starts wanting something more. Another complication can arise if one of the people gets into a relationship with someone else and then has to decide if he or she still wants to have sex with (cheat with) the fuck buddy. If the person does not want to have sex with the fuck buddy anymore, then the rejected buddy needs to face it, move on, and maybe find a new fuck buddy.

Do You Want to Have Sex with a Friend?

Some people like to have sex with a good friend. This is not at all detached like doing it with a fuck buddy. When friends have sex, sometimes the sex is enjoyable because the two people are very comfortable with each other. This is true for twenty-four-year-old Alison who has sex with a friend: "I had felt like we could talk about anything and when we had sex I felt we could do anything."

Some people find that sex with a friend destroys the friendship, like twenty-nine-year-old Suzanne: "Sex with my friend was bad sex, because we both felt too self-conscious. We knew everything about each other except how it felt to have sex with each other. When I found out how it felt to have sex with him, I was too disgusted and embarrassed to ever look at him again." Twenty-five-year-old Mark says, "Having sex with my friend definitely hurt the friendship. We went back and forth from being just friends and from having sex. It eventually ended because we couldn't keep it just friends, but I did not want a relationship."

Another problem of having sex with a friend is that it can negatively affect future relationships for you and your friend. Fred, twenty-eight, complained, "My best friend would not invite me to her wedding because her fiancé found out that during our friendship we had slept together. It hurt me, because it had been so long since we had done it, and at this point we are just friends. Her fiancé just doesn't understand." Amy, twenty-five, had a similar problem: "I had a boyfriend whose best friend was a woman. They would have dinner alone every week and talk on the phone every day. For the first few months of my relationship with him, I didn't mind. I had my own friends, too. Then he finally confessed to me that they had had sex off and on over their eight-year friendship. That's when I decided to dump him. I knew that it was not my place to tell him to stop seeing her for me, but I also knew that I would always feel like he was cheating on me with her."

On the brighter side, other people who have sex with friends find that the relationship blossoms into true love or even marriage. A serious, committed relationship requires a balance of passionate lust *and* intense friendship. Most often when people are dating, the lust develops first, then they wait for the friendship. But when friends have sex, they may already have a strong foundation for a relationship. Max, twenty-nine, and Jan, twenty-five, who were friends for two years before they felt attracted to each other, found that sex transformed their friendship into a wonderful love affair: "When we started fooling around we weren't sure at first if it was the right thing to do, since we didn't want to destroy the friendship. But the sex was great and we got along better than before. We stopped seeing other people, and decided to officially be boyfriend-girlfriend. We love each other, and we want to be together forever!"

Just be careful that if you are making the decision to have sex with a friend or not to have sex with a friend, that you are being rational and intellectual about the choice. Too often people will have sex with a friend hoping that it will turn out like Max and Jan's relationship. But in the end they realize that they were creating a fantasy, and the reality of sex with a friend was not nearly as good.

Are You Looking for a Serious Committed Relationship Before You Have Sex?

As I mentioned earlier, most of the twentysomethings whom I surveyed were looking to have sex in the context of serious relationships. If you are looking for a serious committed relationship, you must know yourself well enough to know what you really want and need in a companion. Most often relationships work best if two people:

▸ have shared values
▸ have about the same level of intelligence
▸ are sexually attracted to each other
▸ like to be touched, kissed, and have sex the same amount and the same ways
▸ feel like friends, laugh together, enjoy talking to each other
▸ have similar or complementary interests
▸ have time to get to know each other
▸ get along with each other's friends and family

Do not put pressure on yourself if you want to be in a serious relationship but you're not finding one. It will happen in time. If you are questioning why you are single, then examine your past relationships and generally the way you relate to people. How long have your relationships lasted? Do they usually end for the same reason? What patterns do you repeat?

If you are having trouble meeting people, then try joining a club, playing a group sport, taking a class, becoming part of a religious group, or starting any sort of group activity that interests you. Meet as many people as possible. If you are in an ordinary place like a supermarket or bookstore and you see a cute stranger, strike up a conversation. Be assertive. If you like someone, tell him or her and ask if you can spend more time together. The worst that can happen is that the person will reject you and you will get embarrassed; the best is that you will have a new person with whom you can be close.

When you are looking for a relationship, be careful that you don't get caught in what I call the "Love Boat Syndrome." That TV show presented the fantasy that it is simple to meet someone to marry. As soon as people boarded the ship, Gopher and Julie introduced them to the future love of their lives. After the first commercial, they'd fall in love on the promenade deck while they were listening to Charo play the guitar. Then, as they left the ship forty-five TV minutes later, they'd flaunt their wedding rings for Vicki and the Captain.

Of course, in real life you cannot find a partner that easily. Good relationships take time. You should treat a potential lover the way you would treat a new friend. When people meet a new friend, they seldom obsess over when he or she is going to call. They aren't nervous the first time they have dinner together. Also, they don't have unrealistic expectations that their new friend will be perfect. Whether they 'fess up to it or not, most people are searching for Mr. or Miss Right. You can't do that! You have to open your eyes to see what the person is really like, flaws and all. You have to be able to like the person, as he or she is, and never try to change him or her. It takes months or years to get to really know someone. In fact, sometimes people are actually turned off at first by the person they end up marrying, and are turned on at first by someone who ends up being a total jerk. You may have to go out with a lot of people before you find that one relationship that you want. Most people today practice "serial monogamy," meaning they are monogamous with one person at a time, then when that relationship ends, they move on to a new one.

▼ ▼

Every relationship will either last forever, or it will end.

▲ ▲

There is no ideal mate, only people who are highly compatible. If you keep looking, you'll find someone who is right for you. As Madonna once said, "The very best thing about being single is that there's always someone else."

How Can You Decide if You Want to Experiment with Different Sexual Practices?

You've been going out with a guy for six months and he admits that he has always wanted to try a three-way. What do you do? Your new lover of three weeks keeps groping you in public, and tells you sex in public would be great. Will you do it? Your lover for the past year keeps hinting about having anal sex. You've always heard that it's painful. Should you try it?

First of all, you should get relevant information about the sexual behavior before you do it. Read in chapter 5 about sexual positions and in chapter 8 about sexual diversity, then you'll know more about the variety from which you can choose. Once you have the technical information, try to tune in to how you would react emotionally to the new sexual experience. For example, if you are a shy, private, or possessive person, then having a threesome with your lover and another person would probably not be for you. Or if you do not like to feel powerless during sex, then trying to be submissive in S/M may upset you.

Think through all of the other consequences involved with sexual experimentation. Some of these include:

▶ Will your partner respect your confidentiality or will he or she tell others of your sexual escapades?
▶ Will you be able to move on without regrets if you end up not liking what you try?
▶ Will your partner agree to stop in the middle if you don't like it and then not pressure you to try again?
▶ Do you understand all of the positive and negative emo-

tional and physical consequences that could come from
the experience?

Answers to those questions will help you decide what to
do, if you keep all of your alternatives in mind:

1. **You could agree to do it.** Make sure you've given serious thought to all of the points that I mention above!
2. **You could give the subject further thought.** In that
   case make sure your partner understands that you
   need time. Also, tell your partner you'll let him or her
   know if you are ready; tell your partner not to ask you
   every day.
3. **You could find an alternative.** For example, if your
   lover wants to take nude Polaroid pictures of you and
   you feel uncomfortable about it, you could tell him or
   her that instead, you'll put on a strip show—that may
   help satisfy the voyeuristic urge. Another example, sex
   in public may feel too risky; you may worry that you'll
   get caught or arrested. To compromise, you could
   agree to find a secluded spot in the middle of nowhere
   and do it there.

You should never ever do anything that makes you uncomfortable, either emotionally, physically, or intellectually.

▼ ▼ ▼ ▼ ▼ ▼ ▼ ▼ ▼ ▼ ▼ ▼ ▼ ▼

If it doesn't feel good, don't do it.

▲ ▲ ▲ ▲ ▲ ▲ ▲ ▲ ▲ ▲ ▲ ▲ ▲ ▲ ▲

To help yourself figure out what you want to do sexually,
go through all of the possible sexual variations that you can
think of and rate how much these acts turn you on, from 0,
Very Turned Off, to 5, Very Turned On. That will help you figure out what sexual behaviors you prefer and what you

might agree to do or ask to try. It will help you figure out how to make a compromise if your turn-on rating is low and your lover wants to try something. For example, if a threesome rates a 2, would engaging in fantasy talk about a third party during sex with your lover rate higher? Would having sex with your lover while you watch a porn video of group sex rate higher? Would having sex on the Internet with your lover and an anonymous third party rate even higher? You can see how the rating system can be helpful for understanding, expressing, and negotiating your feelings and behaviors.

How Can You Decide to be Faithful?

If you have been thinking about having an affair but you and your partner have always been monogamous, you have to sort out your reasons for wanting to cheat. If you made an agreement with your partner that you would not cheat or lie, or have an affair, then what has changed to justify going back on the promise, whether it was explicit or just "understood"? Are you trying to pretend that you don't have to be monogamous because you never actually made a verbal promise that you would be, even though your actions showed that you were committed to an exclusive relationship? Be honest. If you've practically moved into his place, or told her "I love you," or dated for months, it's not fair to assume the other person expects you to be sleeping with other people.

If you are considering sleeping with someone else and not telling your current partner, you need to do some serious thinking. What would an affair do for you? How would it affect your partner if she or he found out? How would it affect your relationship even if you kept the affair secret? Do you want to deal with feeling guilty every time you are with your partner? Do you want to deal with feeling confused every time you are with your mister or mistress? Is it worth the risk of losing your relationship if your partner finds out?

What about STD's? Doesn't your partner have the right to know about the risks you take? How many people would the affair hurt? Would you be hurting your partner or the person with whom you'd be cheating?

People have affairs for many different reasons, some obvious, some not so obvious: for sex, for companionship, to hurt their partner, to decrease intimacy with their partner, to gain power over their partner, to sabotage or end their relationship, or because they honestly feel in love with the other person. Also, once you start having an affair, you've hurt your relationship because you've implanted the seeds of dishonesty. If your partner finds out that you violated the fidelity, she or he may want to forgive you, but may be unable to. Rebuilding trust takes a lot of time and work, and sometimes it just can't happen. Would it be better for you to end one relationship before you start a new one?

▼ ▼

Often when people are contemplating affairs, it means that they are missing something in their relationship. But by having the affair, they are almost always taking so much energy out of their relationship that they are making it even worse.

▲ ▲

If you want to improve or maintain your relationship, then do not have an affair. Instead, work on enjoying your relationship so that it can be as fantastic as you want it to be. Build up the trust and honesty instead of violating it. Instead of cheating, get out of your relationship rut: spice up your sex life; spend a weekend with your partner out of town; be flirtatious; try to entice each other like you did when you first met. Try to keep the energy, the love, and the lust alive and growing in your relationship. Also, if it feels as though it could help, go into therapy with your partner. You may be much happier improving your relationship rather than ruining it by cheating.

If you feel that improving your relationship is the wrong choice for you, then you probably should end it. Much of the time, relationships cannot change, and certainly you cannot change another person. If the relationship is bad, or you two are just not right for each other anymore, you have to admit it and move on. After you end the relationship, you could either go with the potential new lover or just be single. If you know that ending your relationship is really the right thing for you to do, but you just don't have the strength or courage to end it, then you probably need someone, a friend or therapist, to help you sort out why you feel stuck in a (presumably bad) relationship.

What Do You Do if You Regret A Decision

It's unavoidable that sometime everybody will do something he or she regrets. If this happens to you, try to stay in a rational, unemotional state long enough to realize that the negative repercussions may not be as bad as you think. In fact, sometimes, it is regrets about our sexual experiences that help us form our guidelines about sex. Twenty-one-year-old Sue's story explains how her regrets created her new sexual values. Sue was very sexually active her freshman year of college, until one night she realized after letting her date out of her dorm room that at no point had he asked if she was using birth control. Although she was on the pill, her realization that he cared so little about her that he didn't even bother to ask her if she was protected made her feel used by all of the men she'd been with. That is when Sue began regretting having casual sex. She realized from then on she was only going to have sex if it was more meaningful and the men cared about her. She turned her regrets into a learning experience and a new sexual guideline.

If you make a decision that ends up making you feel bad in the end you have to learn to forgive yourself. You will need to get out all of your feelings. Call a friend, cry, scream, write out your feelings about what you did. In some cases, if you are in a close relationship and the sexual regret has to do with something that you did with your partner, you should tell your partner your regrets and discuss your feelings together. In other cases (particularly if the regret has to do with having an affair) you should keep it to yourself, maybe tell your best friend. If you feel isolated and confused, find a therapist to talk to. Try not to obsess over your mistake; try to get back to feeling good about yourself. It's a cliché, but it's also so true: time heals all wounds.

▼▼▼▼▼▼▼▼▼▼▼▼▼▼▼▼▼▼▼▼▼▼▼▼

Forgive yourself, learn from your regrets, and move on.

▲▲▲▲▲▲▲▲▲▲▲▲▲▲▲▲▲▲▲▲▲▲▲▲

CHAPTER 3

Speaking of Sex

Talking It Out

Good sexual relationships invariably involve good communication. Whether you say, "Oooh, it feels good right there," or "Let's use condoms," or "Ouch, you're on my hair," or "I love you," talking can help keep you sexually healthy and happy. Talking gives people a chance to tell partners how they feel about each other. Clear communication helps people to be sure that they want to have sex with each other. Talking before sex helps partners decide if they want to expand their sexual repertoire or work out any sexual difficulties. It also helps them decide what kind of condoms and birth control they want to use.

Communication is necessary to set boundaries in relationships, so a couple can discuss if they are committed to each other or if they are dating other people. When you are not happy or healthy, talking about sex can help you reach the best solutions to your problems. (Besides talking to partners, of course, to stay in good sexual health you'll sometimes want to talk to doctors, gynecologists, urologists, or therapists.) Talking is often the most effective way of initiating sex. Talking during sex gives partners an indication of what feels good and where to move next. Best of all, talking about sex can improve your sex life by keeping you close to your partner and helping you agree with each other on what will make sex mindblowing for you both.

Why Talking About Sex Is Difficult for Some People

If you are going to let another person touch the most intimate parts of your body, then you must be able to talk openly to that special person. Unfortunately, many people never learned to talk about sex. Maybe when they were growing up, their parents told them not to "talk dirty." Maybe they never heard their parents talk about sexuality—some people even thought that their parents never had sex—so they never talked about sex at home. In some cases, parents may have been open about sex, but for whatever reason their children didn't feel comfortable talking to them. It's one thing to ask about where babies come from, but quite another to ask Mommy or Daddy why sometimes it's difficult to have an orgasm.

Certainly, our culture's emphasis on discussions of sexual politics and the lack of or unrealistic discussions about sex in the movies and on TV does not help people learn how to talk about sex. Somewhere between the perfectly choreographed sexuality on MTV and the stilted dialogues on those issues-oriented movies-of-the-week is the reality where it is difficult to talk about our sexual needs in detail without feeling inadequate or hurting our partners' feelings. Unfortunately, because of this lack of good sex education, barriers often get in the way of talking about sex. You may feel:

- ▶ Embarrassment
- ▶ Fear of rejection
- ▶ Anxiety
- ▶ Concern over sexual spontaneity
- ▶ Fear that others know more about sex than you do
- ▶ Desire to maintain confidentially
- ▶ Apprehension about disclosing too much private information
- ▶ Fear of criticism or provoking anger
- ▶ Difficulty acknowledging that you and your partner are actually having a relationship

Keys to Effective Communication

To overcome difficulties of talking about sex, you can learn ways to communicate that will make sex talks feel more comfortable. Talking will benefit you by allowing you to express what you want and need to say to your partner.

No matter what you want to tell your partner—whether it's that you want to have sex right now, or that you are bisexual, or that you want a back massage, or that you are intrigued by transvestism, or that that you want to live together, or anything—there are some basic keys to effective sexual communication that can help in any situation. If you follow these, you will overcome many of the blocks to clear communication:

▶ **Say what you mean.**

If it really bothers you that, for example, your partner never gives you oral sex and you always give your partner oral sex, then don't beat around the bush by saying something like, "I'd like to have more foreplay." Say what you mean: "Please go down on *me* tonight! I know you can be great at it, and I want it so badly. Thank you."

▶ Do not send mixed messages.

The most stereotypical example of this deals with the issue that often leads to date rape. Women need to be aware that flirting is great; women have every right to say no to sex at any point. However, it's not smart for a woman to get into a position where she's alone with a guy she hardly knows, sending him mixed messages about whether or not she's "asking for it." Keep your message clear. If it's "No," act like it.

▶ Be honest.

If you don't want to date someone again, don't say, "I'll call you." If you don't want a committed monogamous relationship, don't say, "I love only you." If you are willing to try anal sex, but are afraid it will hurt, you shouldn't say no to it; nor should you hide your fears and just try it without talking. Be honest. Say, "I want to try anal sex, but I'm afraid it will hurt. Can we stop if it hurts too much?"

▶ Be specific.

If in the middle of having sex, the guy is rubbing the woman's clitoris too hard, she shouldn't say, "Stop," or just wiggle around without saying anything. She should tell him specifically what she wants him to do. She could say, "Oooh, my clit's too sensitive right now. Could you just rub around it a little to the left, instead of directly on it? Oh, yeah! That's fantastic."

▶ Think it out first.

If you just talk without thinking out what you want to say, you may end up saying something that you don't mean or that will hurt your partner's feelings. If you are in the throes of passion, you shouldn't say, "It really annoys me when you touch me that way." Be sensitive and coherent by thinking it out first to come up with a nice way of saying what you mean, like, "Could we try something different this time? How about if you touch me a little gentler?"

▶ State your preferences.

If you like oral sex more than intercourse, tell your partner your sexual preferences. If it's important to you that your partner gets HIV-tested before you have sex, tell him or her. If your first choice for Saturday night is staying in with your partner and having sex, and your second choice is staying in together and watching a video, and your third choice is going out with friends, state your preferences. It's the only way to get what you want, in or out of bed.

▶ Be concise.

Don't go on and on about how your partner is doing. Usually people get the point if you say what you mean concisely.

▶ Don't criticize.

It's never constructive to criticize someone if you want him or her to do something different. Instead of saying "I hate it when you do that. Why are you so bad at knowing how to touch me right?" be nice, start with a positive, and ask for change: "You are really a great kisser. But you know, I'd love it if you'd give me a massage tonight and if you let me tell you how it feels best when you touch me. Then I'll give you a massage. How does that sound, honey?"

▶ Ask for feedback.

Don't assume that your partner likes what you're doing. If your partner doesn't say anything, then ask, "Are you so quiet because you're just enjoying this, or do you want us to try something different right now?"

▶ Talk *with* your partner, not *at* your partner.

Don't interrogate or lecture your partner. Having a conversation about sex means being able to listen and to talk. Make it a real conversation, not a monologue. You may be amazed by what your partner has to say if you listen.

Bringing Up the Subject

Bringing up the subject of sex can be difficult, since it is often a sensitive issue. To make it easier, be sure the time and place is appropriate for the discussion. You should be somewhere where you have privacy and you are both comfortable. Don't bring up an important issue when you are in bed or in a sexual situation. Try to talk about sex in the afternoon, on the living room sofa or some other place that is not too sexual. If you are raising a problem or a very sensitive issue that may upset your partner, it may be better to have the conversation in your partner's place so he or she feels safe on his or her own turf. Ideally, wait for a time when you have plenty of time alone, nowhere important to go soon, and when you both are not too tired. If you have to bring something up when you are already engaging in sex play, then say, "Let's take a break for a minute. Let's talk about [whatever you need to talk about]."

If you are having trouble starting the conversation, then you may want to try referring to a TV show, a book, a song, or some other source as a starting point. For example, if you want to ask your partner if you two can be monogamous, then you may feel more comfortable saying "I saw these people on *Geraldo* who had an arrangement that they can have sex outside of their relationships. Now, I know that life isn't a talk show, and certainly not *Geraldo*, but, in any case, it got me thinking about us. Since we are having sex, I was wondering if you want to be exclusive. We haven't talked about it and I don't want to make any assumptions. Do you only want to have sex with me? Or do you want to keep an open relationship so we can both date other people?"

"Yes," "No," and Everything In Between

Talking about sex can help you get what you want out of sex but not more than you bargained for. Talking is especially important on a date with someone new, when you feel the sexual charge between the two of you but you do not know if you are going to have sex. The jargon of date-rape feminism in the 1980s told us that "no means no," but in the real world expressing how you feel on a date means more than saying "No!" You need to explain your sexual desires and expectations on dates and in a relationship. Whether you are a man or a woman, you need to maintain responsibility for all your actions on dates.

▼ ▼

Sure, sexual tension on a date can be a thrill, but today the whole issue of date rape should be enough to convince you that you can benefit from sending clear messages about sex, talking about your sexual desires and expectations, and setting sexual boundaries before a date.

▲ ▲

Messages about sex can be confused on dates for a number of reasons. Some people think that everyone is doing it, so they expect to be in the sack getting hot and heavy by the end of the evening. Another person might want to have sex with his or her date, but may not want to bring up the subject and explicitly ask, because he or she thinks that sex should be perfectly spontaneous, with no prior discussion. Also, it is common for people to misread nonverbal communication when they don't know each other very well. Usually, if someone likes someone else, the person will flirt and act interested. Then if the other person says, "I don't want to have sex," he or she has created inconsistencies with his or her nonverbal communication.

Twenty-seven-year-old David says, "I am in the situation a lot when I don't know if a woman wants to have sex with me or not. Women always seem to be acting like they want it. My instinct is to kiss her to find out, but I ask her if I can kiss her, instead. If she says yes, then after we are kissing, I ask her if we can have sex."

It is extremely important to remember that you should be assertive on a date. Say what you mean. Too many people will be passive and just take what their partner is offering. Other people will be aggressive and get angry if they don't get their way. The most effective way to communicate about sex is to assert your needs clearly.

If you don't want to have sex with the person on that date, tell him or her. If you may want to in the future, say that. If you don't know what your needs are, or if you are feeling ambiguous, then you need to tell your partner that now is not a good time for you to make a decision. Say, "I'm not ready to talk about this yet. If you want me to go home now, I will, and we can talk about sex in the morning or in a day or two after I've given it some more thought. Otherwise, let's just talk about and do something else now. Because I don't want to do or say anything I'd regret."

▼ ▼ ▼ ▼ ▼ ▼ ▼ ▼ ▼ ▼ ▼ ▼ ▼ ▼ ▼ ▼ ▼ ▼ ▼

Talking about sex will help you both understand each other and have clear expectations.

▲ ▲ ▲ ▲ ▲ ▲ ▲ ▲ ▲ ▲ ▲ ▲ ▲ ▲ ▲ ▲ ▲ ▲ ▲

If you still want to flirt and act sexy on the date, then explain that you are not a tease: acting sexy does not mean that you want to do it. "I tell men that I'm going to act like a slut even though I'm not interested in having sex with them. They get confused at first; then they don't mind because I explained myself," reports Shelly, twenty-one. You are only a tease if you don't explicitly explain that you do not want to do it.

If you want to have sex with the other person but the other person does not want to, tell him or her to let you know when he or she is ready in the future, since you know you want to have sex with that person. If you both want to be sexual together, then decide how far you want to go and what kind of birth control and disease protection you want to use. Discuss anything else on your mind at that point, such as the emotional implications of the sex. If you have sex, does this mean you are a couple?

If your date and you agree on what you want to do sexually, then enjoy yourself and be glad that communication got you what you wanted.

Flirting and How to Read Your Partner's Body Language

Verbal communication is the best way to let someone know that you are interested in him or her, or to let the person know what you'd like to do sexually. Yet sometimes you have to read body language, too.

Body language can indicate whether someone is interested in you or not. If someone is not interested in you they may have "negative body language": sitting with arms crossed, legs tightly shut, and shoulders hunched over, as if tense or angry. Every part of the body will be closed to other people. Unfortunately, some people are not aware that they have this type of body language. Often people who display negative body language are shy or fearful and have trouble making friends or getting dates. Their poses and posture says, "Go away," rather than, "Come talk to me." If you have trouble meeting people, pay attention to the messages that your body is sending.

If you want to assess if someone wants you, pay attention

to his or her body. For example, when someone new is talking to you, get a glimpse of his or her feet. If the person is not interested in you, he or she will point his or her feet away from you, perhaps pointing toward the door as if he or she wants to leave the room. If someone's feet are pointed toward you while you are talking, he or she is probably interested in staying there with you.

If you are uninterested in someone you are talking to, you may start fidgeting and moving your body restlessly. On the other hand, if you are interested in the person you are talking to, you may fidget with your hair or clothes to try to make yourself look more desirable.

If someone is interested in you, he or she will make constant eye contact with you and then move his or her body in your direction. At some point in the midst of flirtation, one person (usually the woman) will casually brush up against the other, inconspicuously making the first move. Of course, smiling is an extremely effective method of communicating, too. With a smile, you can show a stranger that you are interested in meeting him or her. If the person responds with a smile, you know he or she is interested in at least saying "Hi." The next step is getting that verbal communication going.

Opening Lines

Often an honest introduction is the best way to begin communication, but sometimes, clever, memorable lines work well. In the workshops that I conduct at universities around the country one of the activities that the participants always enjoy is sharing opening lines that they have used or heard, such as:

Do you have a quarter I can use? My mother said I should call her when I find my true love.

Would you like to have breakfast with me tomorrow? Should I call you or nudge you?

What's a nice person like you doing in a place like this? (Said with irony, since it's such an old-fashioned line.)

Hey, what's your sign? (Said jokingly, since it's an old line, too.)

Haven't I seen you somewhere before? Oh, I know where. We were lovers in another life. How about doing some past life regression with me?

You look so familiar. Are you a model?

Every person in this place seems to want to meet you. So I came over to find out what's so special about you.

▼ ▼

You don't need to think of a clever opening line to a conversation. You can simply introduce yourself and talk until you find a common area to discuss.

▲ ▲

An easy opening topic is why you are both at the same place. Did the same person invite you? Do you have mutual friends at the party or club? You could discuss why people like going to bars, or why you like browsing in that particular bookstore, or in the produce section, or wherever you are. It's a more specific way of asking, "What's a nice person like you doing in place like this?"

Next, try revealing some things about yourself and eliciting some intimate revelations from your new potential partner. Listen attentively and ask follow-up questions to keep the conversation going. If you two are a good match, then your conversation will probably flow after that.

If you want to get together with the other person again

and the other person doesn't ask for your number, then get his or hers. Don't think that the guy always has to ask the woman. Just find a way to get in touch with each other again, and don't worry about who's asking. Don't be afraid of rejection. Think of it this way: when two people aren't right for each other, there is a good chance one of them will realize it before the other does and end the relationship or potential relationship. Sometimes it will be you who rejects the other person, and sometimes you will get rejected.

Communicating for Initiating Sex

Let's say you've exchanged phone numbers and sultry looks, and maybe a few dates, and now you're at the point where you want to have sex with this person. You need to ask your partner if he or she is turned on by you, in the mood to have sex right then, explicitly consenting, and prepared with contraception and condoms for STD protection. Get specific responses to those questions from your partner. If your partner broaches the subject first, you need to make your response clear. Say "yes," or "later," or "at my place," or whatever.

▼ ▼
Sex in the real world is not like on a soap opera, in the movies, or in a sneaker commercial: you cannot "Just do it."
▲ ▲

Although it can be a sexy fantasy to think that sex should always be spontaneous, the fact is there is just too much to discuss to let it flow like in the movies. Initiating sex with a conversation does not need to interrupt the sexy mood. You can say any variety of things. Here are some samples:

▶ "I want to feel even closer to you."
▶ "I'd love to be inside you right now."

▸ "Let's make love."
▸ "You feel so good. You taste so good. Can we keep going further?"
▸ "You are so sensual. I love your mind, your body. The way you move, the way you touch me. The way we move together so well. Can we have sex?"
▸ "I want to fuck."
▸ "Do you have any rubbers?"

Should You Talk About Your Past Sexual History?

Singles are often told that they should tell every new partner their past sexual history and ask their new partners to tell them their complete sexual history. You can find out if your partner has a sexually transmitted disease, if he has ever gotten anyone pregnant, or if she has been pregnant, how many people he or she has had sex with, what types of sexual activities he or she has participated in, and what was pleasurable or unappealing about the experience. Asking about a new partner's past is supposed to give you indications about how likely it is that the partner will use condoms and birth control, if your partner has HIV or has had an STD, and how likely it is that you two will share common interests in the same sexual behaviors. But will it help?

▼ ▼

No matter what your partner tells you about his or her past, it may have little to do with how he or she will act in the present.

▲ ▲

Your partner might lie or cover up certain aspects of his or her history. Your partner may think you will be turned off if you find out that he or she once had an STD, so you may never know. A study of university students found that more than 50 percent of the students who had been infected with sexually transmitted diseases reported that they had unpro-tected sexual intercourse when they knew they were infected, and nearly a quarter of them did not tell their part-ners. If your partner has an STD, there is no guarantee that he or she will tell you. If your partner once got an STD, it may mean that now your partner will use condoms every sin-gle time in order to protect both of you, but it could also mean he or she will lie and continue to be irresponsible, never using condoms. No matter what your partner tells you, you should use condoms every single time you have sex if you do not want to take the chance that you will get HIV or an STD.

▼ ▼

Condoms are your best protection against someone else's selective memory.

▲ ▲

Similarly, if you do not want to get pregnant or get your partner pregnant, then it is your responsibility to use birth control, no matter what your partner tells you.

If you are a guy and a woman tells you that it is "a safe time of the month" for her, you need to let her know that there is no such thing as a safe time of the month. Tell her that you want to use birth control anyway, just to be sure. Even if she tells you that she is on the pill, or that she has her diaphragm in, or she's using *any* method of birth control, or that she is infertile, you still need to realize that if she gets pregnant it's your responsibility, too. So if you do not want her to get pregnant, use condoms to be sure *you* are pro-tected from pregnancy. If you are a woman, and the guy tries to convince you not to use birth control, don't believe what he says. "I've had guys tell me that they will pull out. I've had guys tell me idiotic things like that they have a low sperm count. It's such bull, " says Beth, twenty-eight. If you don't want to get pregnant, you must use birth control, despite what a lover says in the heat of passion.

It's depressing and frightening to think how often people will lie just to get laid. One study found that over 40 percent of men and women said that if a partner asked how many people they had slept with, they would lie and give a smaller number. Also, people often define "sex" differently, so they might not admit to having sex when in fact they had. A good example of this was in the movie *Clerks*, when Dante is stunned to discover that his girlfriend gave thirty-seven men blowjobs, when he had assumed that she was not very sexually active before meeting him because she had said that she only had sex with three men. All of a sudden his image of her as a near-virgin turned to an image of her as a slut.

For some people it is upsetting to hear about a partner's past. Another example: in *Four Weddings and a Funeral*, when Andie MacDowell's character listed all of the thirty-odd people she had sex with, she shocked her new boyfriend, Hugh Grant's character. Well, if that scene were reenacted in real life, it would probably do one of two things to a relationship: either it would make the man feel closer to her, because he knows what she is really like, and that she enjoys sex; or it could scare him away, making him think that he is just one in a line of men, or that she must have a disease from having had sex with over thirty men. True, in the second scenario, the man is closed-minded if he can't accept her because of her past, but that is a real possibility in a relationship. So consider how your relationship would be affected if you tell all the details of the number of people you've slept with. Similarly, if you are a twentysomething virgin, will that scare away a potential partner? Or will that make the partner want you more, simply for the conquest? You need to get to know someone before you can judge the way he or she will react. Hopefully, you will find someone with whom you can talk—someone who is honest, understanding, caring, and trustworthy.

Besides thinking about how much you should tell a partner, you should think about how much you should ask a partner about his or her past history. For example, if a partner is still friends with an ex or has had sex with his or her best friend, or with a friend of yours, it can be uncomfortable if you learn too much about the sex he or she had with that person, especially if you see that person a lot. It may be easier for you not to know rather than have to think every time you see that person, "I can't believe she gives the rebel yell every time she comes."

▼ ▼

You do not have to tell every partner everything that you've ever done, or ask a partner everything he or she has ever done.

▲ ▲

You need to judge each person and each situation differently. For example, one partner might get really interested, or even turned on, if you tell him or her that you once got into heavy S/M. But someone else might think that S/M is immoral. You have to know your partner before you can tell him or her some things about your sexuality. You need to get a feel for what you can tell, and what things are best to keep to yourself.

If you are trying to decide if you should tell a partner details about your sexual history, or if you are trying to decide if you should ask about his or her history, consider: Does your partner (or you) need to know? Will your partner (or you) lie? How will it affect you (or your partner) to hear stories about having sex with other people? Can you (or your partner) listen without judging or throwing it back in his or her face later?

There are some *good* reasons to hear about your partners' sexual histories. When you know the sexual activities they have tried in the past, and how they felt about them, you can get an idea of what they might want to do with you, or what they might not want to do with you. You do not need to hear names, dates, places, and every gory detail of a new partner's past sex life (unless you can handle hearing and he or she is willing to tell).

What Should You Definitely Talk About Before You Have Sex?

Whether you choose to hear your partner's sexual history or not, there are some things that you should definitely find out from your partner to make sure sex between the two of you will be great:

1. Are there certain sexual activities that your partner is absolutely opposed to engaging in?
2. Are there other sexual activities that your partner is extremely interested in trying with you?
3. What kind of birth control and condoms will you and your partner use?
4. Will your partner agree to using birth control and condoms every time you have sex?
5. Will you and your partner get tested for all STD's and HIV? Even if your partner says he or she doesn't have anything, will your partner still get tested just to make you feel safer?
6. If your sex resulted in an unintended pregnancy, what would your partner want to choose: keeping the child, giving it up for adoption, or having an abortion?
7. What does sex mean emotionally to you and your partner? How will it affect your relationship?

Mindblowing sex will only occur if you two can agree on those issues and feel comfortable communicating about them. If you have fundamental sexual incompatibilities, you can find out by talking about sex, rather than by making a poor choice and regretting it later. Hopefully, you will agree and be compatible, so you can get on to talking about other sexual topics that can enhance sex even more.

Speaking the Same Language

It's important that when you talk about sex to a partner, you are using words that are understood and comfortable for both of you. For example, if you always call a condom a prophylactic, but your partner always calls it a rubber, then in any conversation that you have involving condoms your partner may find your clinical language off-putting. Similarly, if you always refer to female genitalia as "pussy" and your partner uses the word "vagina," then your partner may be offended by your slang. Even if this sounds inconsequential at first, I guarantee that you will have better conversations if you use the same vocabulary, or if you accept the other person's vocabulary.

If the two of you are speaking "different languages," try the following activity with your partner to get your vocabulary to match. Touch your partner's genitals and ask what he or she calls each part. Then say what you usually call each part. Then settle on a shared language. It could get interesting. If the guy says he calls his penis Ralph, then maybe the woman would want to name her body parts, too. I can see it now—"Women who name their breasts, on the next *Donahue*!"

Better Sex Through Better Communication During Sex

Talking during sex can definitely improve your sex life. There is an old story that sex therapists tell that gets this point across well:

A man and a woman did not verbally communicate about sex. They thought that they could communicate by just moving during sex. They found out that they were very wrong. You see, the man liked to have his ear blown into and sucked on during sex. So, to let the woman know, during sex he'd blow into and suck on *her* ear, thinking that she'd reciprocate. Well, the woman hated having her ear blown into and sucked on. But rather than tell him, she would make a point of never going near his ear during sex. Neither partner got what he or she wanted because they never talked about it.

▼ ▼

Unless you are sure that your partner understands what it means when you move around, you need to talk during sex.

▲ ▲

You don't have to carry on an elaborate conversation that interrupts lovemaking. For example, if during intercourse you are on the bottom and you want to be on top, you will get what you want much more easily by saying "Can I get on top?" or "Switch!" (or whatever your partner will understand) instead of huffing and puffing and trying to roll the two of you over. If you want to have sex without talking, you can *try* to roll the two of you over; just be prepared to give up and talk if it doesn't work!

If you know your own sexuality well enough, then you will be able to tell your partner things that will enhance your sex life. For example, if you know that you have the best orgasms from receiving oral sex and you tell your partner, and your partner consents to doing what you like, then you know you will get those great orally-induced orgasms. If you know that you like to have sex every day, then telling a new partner will help you two negotiate how your sex drives match. If you talk about the fact that your partner likes to have sex more or less than you do, then you can negotiate how you will fill the gap—maybe you can watch each other masturbate, or maybe you will agree to have additional sexual partners, or maybe when you talk you will come up with some other creative solution.

▼ ▼

Prior to a sexual experience, you can discuss your sexual needs to make sex more fulfilling.

▲ ▲

Discussing what you like and don't like about your body can also help enhance the sex act. For example, if you hate to have your feet touched because you have always thought that they are sweaty and smelly, and your partner loves touching feet, then this is an aspect of your body image that must be discussed in order to keep you from getting upset during sex (unless you can get over your hangup to please your partner).

It is also great to talk about new variations on sex that you might want to try. Make sure you talk about trying something new before you try it. If you put a blindfold on your partner without asking, you may confuse or upset your partner. Talking about a new sexual variation before you try it can also be an erotic activity. Imagine how erotic it could be to describe to your partner the new sex acts that you'd like to do with him or her. For some fun, if there are some sexual variations that you read about in chapters coming up in this book that you'd like to try, ask your partner to read that section, then discuss it. It'll be a sexy reading and discussion session.

How to Say "I Love You"

Saying "I love you" can be the most difficult sentence to say or it can be the easiest, depending on how seriously you feel it and how secure you feel in your relationship. Twenty-three-year-old Suzanne says, "I always wait until the guy says it before I say it. That's one of my rules." The problem with that rule is that if you wait for the other person to say it, you never know if the other person is waiting for you to say it!

Sometimes it's good to discuss what saying "I love you" means to each of you. To some people, saying "I love you" is not such a big deal. They are usually the ones who say it casually, such as when they hang up the phone, as in, "Gotta go. Love you." Or every night before bed: "G'night. I love you." Others feel that saying "I love you" is much deeper than just a salutation or an expression of like. To them it means a commitment, a connection, trust, a deep respect, and, well, love. Be careful about believing what anyone says when they are in bed with you. When all of the blood rushes away from people's heads and into their genitals, they often say things that they wouldn't normally say. When someone says "I love you" for the first time right after or during sex, often what they mean is, "I loved that sex!"

▼ ▼

Everybody feels love differently. "I love you," means different things to different people at different times.

▲ ▲

When you feel that you love someone, say it. If you want to let the person know more precisely what you mean, you can add a second or third sentence of clarification, like "I love you. You mean so much to me. I feel like you are my best friend, my super lover, and I love having you in my life." Some people (like Suzanne above) are afraid to say it, because they worry about what will happen if the other person doesn't say it back. If you do not feel sure that the other person will say "I love you" back, then you can say it gently, playfully, like, "You are so cute. You know, I just love you." This avoids making a heavy romantic moment, declaring your love for the other person, then feeling let down if the other person doesn't reciprocate. On the other hand, it is really wonderful if you feel safe enough to tell someone that you love him or her by making it a major romantic moment. Perhaps you could say "I love you" for the first time while you two are standing at the top of a hill looking at all of the lights of the city, or walking hand-in-hand in the sunset on the beach. That could be one of the most powerful moments ever.

What to Say When Someone Says "I Love You"

If someone tells you "I love you" and you don't love that person, you could avoid saying "I love you" and instead say, "I really like you," or "I love the way I feel with you." You may be upsetting that person by not saying "I love you," or by saying something that sounds like "Thank you." But upsetting the person is better than lying, then having to deal with the consequences of your lie.

If you love the person, you can say "I love you" right back. "I love you, too" sounds good, but it also sounds as if you couldn't think of anything original to say back, so you're just saying "Oh yeah, ditto."

Often people will try out new responses when someone says, "I love you." Alex, twenty-five, says, "While I'm grinning, I say back to him, 'You better.'" Twenty-year-old Mark says, "I say, 'No, I love *you*.' Then she says, 'I love you more.' Then I say, 'No, I love *you* more.' It gets stupid after a few times, but it's fun."

How about this simple, creative response from the movie *Natural Born Killers*:

MICKEY: I love you, Mallory.
MALLORY: I know you do, baby. And I've loved you since the day we met.

That's certainly a sexier way to say "I love you, too."

CHAPTER 4

Understanding and Loving Your Body

Sexual Plumbing

Sex is more than putting tab A into slot B. If you want to have mindblowing sex, you'll need to understand how your sex organs work and how to get your body to respond the way you want it to. Perhaps in sex education in your high school biology class you were taught about your "sexual plumbing," but you may never have learned how these technical aspects of sex apply to your real life. This chapter covers some of the basics of how you can enhance your sexuality by understanding your sex organs.

In women, the *vulva* refers to all of the external sex organs: the clitoris, the labia, vaginal opening, and the urethra opening. Inside, the parts include the vagina, the cervix, the pubic bone, and the urethra.

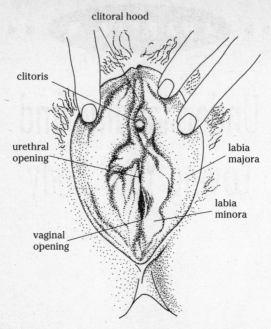

The *clitoris* (pronounced KLIT-er-us—not klit-OR-is) is the most sensitive part of a woman's body. It is like a penis in its sensitivity but while a penis urinates and ejaculates and penetrates, the woman's clitoris has only one function: to give pleasure. Yes, women actually have an organ that is designed only to give them orgasms. (Orgasms may also occur from stimulation of an area on the upper wall of the vagina, called the G-spot.)

The clitoris looks different in every woman. Some women's are hidden under a small piece of skin, called the clitoral hood. Other women's are completely visible. Some are very tiny; others are over an inch long. The external part of the clitoris is actually only a portion of the organ; it extends into the body. When the clitoris is stimulated, blood rushes into the genitals and the clitoris swells and becomes hard and even more sensitive.

The *labia majora* and *labia minora*, commonly called the

lips of the vagina, protect the vagina and help hold lubrication inside it. The labia majora are the outside lips; the labia minora are the inside lips. Sometimes women feel self-concious if they think that their labia are too long or too short. Yet these folds of skin vary in size and shape and look different in each woman. Basically, they fold over, like flower petals, covering the opening of the vagina. (It's a lot nicer to think of them as looking like flowers than something ugly, such as a turkey neck, which is what some women think when they hold a mirror up to their vulva.)

The *vagina* is a tube made of muscular walls that is about three and a half inches long. During arousal, the vaginal walls expand and lubricate to accommodate the size of any penis. The vaginal lubrication, or wetness, is actually sweat that develops on the walls inside the vagina. Since the walls of the vagina are muscular, during intercourse it is possible for a woman to voluntarily make the walls of her vagina contract

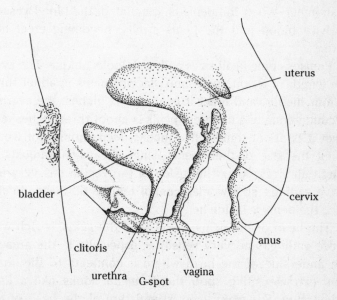

or grip the penis. By contracting the muscular walls inside her, a woman can add to her pleasure during sex. During a woman's orgasm, the walls contract and grip involuntarily. This sensation feels good to both the man inside her and to the woman.

At the back of the vagina is the *cervix*, which is the tiny opening that leads into the uterus. It is important to note that this is the way that sexually transmitted diseases can travel into the female reproductive system and make a woman infertile. Using condoms prevents this problem. The cervix has almost no nerve endings, so it feels almost no sensations. However, some women report that during intercourse if a man is penetrating very deeply they can feel the pressure up against the cervix.

In men, the sex organs that you can see are the penis and the scrotum (the sac that holds the testicles). The *penis* is made up of spongy tissue that is rich in blood vessels. There are no bones in the penis (which is why the term "boner" is a misnomer). When the penis is stimulated, the blood vessels fill with blood and the penis swells, becoming erect and hard.

Penises come in all sizes and each looks unique. The average length of a nonerect (limp, flaccid) penis is about three to four inches, and erect it is about six inches; the average circumference of a nonerect penis is about three inches, and erect it is about four to five inches. Men should not worry about the size of their penis, since the vagina adjusts to match all sizes. Also, the inside of the vagina has very few nerve endings, so a woman cannot tell the difference in size once the penis is inside her.

The head of the penis, also called the *glans*, is rich with nerve endings and very sensitive, especially in the area on the underside of the head where it connects to the shaft. This extra-sensitive spot, the *frenulum,* looks like a little indentation. For many men, stimulation of the head of the

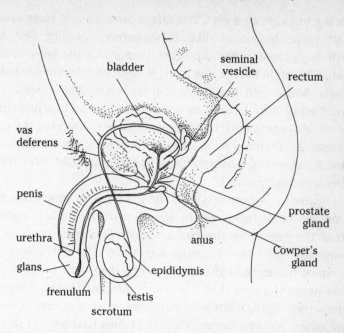

penis will bring them to orgasm. Some men, however, find direct stimulation at the head or the frenulum too intense, and prefer stimulation of the shaft of the penis.

Many men have had their *foreskin* removed through circumcision in infancy for religious or cultural reasons. In those men, the head of the penis is exposed all the time. In uncircumcised men, the foreskin, which is a thin layer of skin, covers the head of the penis when it's limp. When the penis gets hard, the foreskin rolls down to just below the head of the penis. It is a myth that it is dirty not to be circumcised. The head of the penis and the foreskin in an uncircumcised man is as clean as the head of a penis in a circumcised man if he showers on a regular basis. When a man is circumcised, neither his sensation of sex nor his ejaculatory control is affected. Both circumcised and uncircumcised men report the same degree of pleasure from sex.

The *scrotum* is the sac that contains the testes (also known as the testicles or balls). The testes produce and store sperm and male hormones like testosterone. Usually one testicle hangs lower than the other. Usually it's the left one that hangs lower; in left-handed men the right one sometimes hangs lower. Many men like it when their scrotum is caressed or touched or licked. Some men do not like to be touched there at all. Most men have had the experience of knowing the pain caused by getting hit or kicked in the balls, and because of that some men are oversensitive to being handled. Ahh, those precious family jewels!

Inside the scrotum is also the *epididymis*, which is a network of small tubes where sperm matures until is carried from the testes by the *vas deferens*. The epididymis is an important structure to recognize, since it is felt as a small lump at the back of the testes. Some men worry if they feel this lump, thinking that it is testicular cancer. Feel it so you know that it is not a tumor, but if you have a question, see a urologist. The vas deferens are the tubes that are cut during a vasectomy to make a man sterile.

Under the scrotum is a layer of muscle that contracts to raise the testes up toward the body, or expands to lower them. That's how they move up toward the body when it's cold outside (to keep the sperm warm) and down away from the body when it's hot. This muscle also make the testes move during orgasm when the muscles are contracting.

As I mentioned, the testes produce and store *sperm*. From the time a male reaches puberty, he begins producing sperm, and continues to for his entire life. Sperm are microscopic, about $1/500$ of an inch. There are between 120 and 600 million sperm in a single ejaculation. Most of the semen is not made up of sperm. Thirty percent of the fluid is from the *prostate*. The rest, about 70 percent, is made from the fluid in the *seminal vesicles*. Some men produce a bit of fluid from the *Cowper's gland* prior to ejaculation; this is called *precum* or pre-ejaculatory fluid. Sometimes preejaculatory fluid contains sperm (that's why withdrawal is not an effective means of birth control).

The *prostate gland* is a chestnut-size gland located below the bladder and surrounding the urethra. The rectum is directly behind the prostate, so if a finger is inserted into a man's rectum, the prostate gland can be felt. The location of the prostate gland makes it easy for a doctor to examine it by inserting his finger in the rectum, which is important because the gland can become infected or contract cancer. When a man's prostate gland is stimulated by a sexual touch (not a doctor's touch) about an inch and a half inside his anus, the man can feel great pleasure that can enhance his orgasms. He can also feel the pleasurable stimulation of the prostate gland when firm pressure is applied to the outside of his body between the scrotum and anus, the *perineum*.

Your Sexual Response

It is helpful to understand your *sexual response cycle*. In the 1960s, the sex researchers Dr. William Masters and Dr. Virgina Johnson came up with a four-stage cycle describing how people's bodies respond during sex. The stages are: arousal, plateau, orgasm, and resolution. In the 1970s, the cycle was added to by another sex researcher, Dr. Helen Singer Kaplan, to include a phase prior to arousal, desire.

The desire stage means feeling the urge to have sex. The arousal stage means becoming physiologically and psychologically ready to have sex. The plateau stage is the state of extended arousal and pleasure during sex. Orgasm is the sexual release. Resolution is the stage that the man goes through at the end of the cycle to wait until he can get another erection. Women can repeat the cycle immediately.

Many times people move in succession from desire, to arousal, to plateau, to orgasm, and then to resolution. You may need to adapt this general concept of sexual response to fit each sexual encounter. For example, during plateau if a woman is on top, with a man's erect penis inside her vagina, then she gets off, withdraws his penis from her vagina, lies down next to him and just gently strokes his body, there is a chance that his erection may go down a bit and his arousal may wane. Yet then if she kisses her way all down his body, then starts to suck on his penis, he will probably become hard again and they can resume intercourse. You can see how they'd be going from plateau to arousal, then back again. If you understand the basic cycle of sexual response, you will know how your body will respond. But you should also understand that it does not have to be a rigid prescription for how sex should go. You can move up and down, hovering on the brink of orgasm.

Orgasms

You saw in the last section that orgasm is just one part of the sexual response cycle. However, orgasms do need some special attention in our discussion of sexual technique, since there are some special things you can learn about orgasms that can enhance your sex life.

Why is an orgasm so special? An orgasm (or climax or coming) is an intense physical sensation followed by the deep relaxation of "resolution." The release of sexual tension is triggered by the response of the nervous system to a combination of physical and psychological experiences. During orgasm, heartrate, breathing, muscle contractions of the genitals as well as other body parts, and pelvic thrusting occur. Sometimes an orgasm may feel like a little flutter in your genitals. Other times, it feels so strong that your toes curl, your eyes roll back in your head, and you'd swear that you'd do anything just to feel that feeling again. The difference in intensity of orgasms mostly has to do with the individual circumstances of each sexual or masturbatory encounter.

In a woman, orgasm usually occurs from the stimulation of the *clitoris*. Rubbing the clitoris causes the tremendous concentration of nerve endings in the clitoris to produce the orgasm.

Some women also get sexual pleasure that contributes to orgasm from stimulation of another area, called the *G-spot*. While there is some controversy among sexologists about whether or not stimulation of the the G-spot actually causes orgasm, there are some facts about the G-spot that can help demystify it. The G-spot is an actual area in the vagina. It is simply the name for an area on the upper wall of the vagina about one-third of the way inside the vagina where there is a concentration of nerve endings. This area is called the G-spot after the sex researcher Ernst Grafenberg, who first found the area significant. If you put a finger or two inside your vagina, or your partner's vagina, with the fleshy part of the finger facing up, like you are motioning in a "come here" motion, then you may be able to feel a slightly raised or harder area on the upper wall of the vagina that is the G-spot. For women who do get pleasure from the G-spot, they will find that they have orgasms more easily when it is stimulated. During intercourse, women who feel the G-spot stimulation may prefer positions in which the penis is pushing against the upper wall of the vagina, such as when he is thrusting from behind, like "doggy style."

Some women report that they ejaculate a fluid when the G-spot is stimulated to the point that they have an orgasm. Female ejaculation is not completely understood by sex researchers. They report that the fluid is not urine and is not just a lot of vaginal lubrication. Female ejaculation doesn't occur very often, even if a woman feels sensation in her G-spot. But if it does happen, enjoy it.

With all of this talk of the G-spot, I must make it clear that most women have orgasms from their clitoris, not from G-spot stimulation. If you're a woman and are not sure if you've ever felt sensation from your G-spot, then try finding it, and experiment with touching it while you masturbate. But if you don't feel anything, then don't worry or get frustrated—just enjoy your clitoris!

In men, orgasms are not the same as ejaculation. The orgasm is the muscular contractions; the ejaculation is the emission of semen. Each ejaculation is about a teaspoon of semen. The amount that is ejaculated is decreased if the man already has ejaculated several times that day or the day before. Each man ejaculates with different force each time he comes, and it takes about five to eight contractions for the semen to come out. Sometimes, during the first two to four contractions, the semen can shoot out of the penis forcefully and fly about two feet from the tip of the penis. Then, during the rest of the ejaculation, the semen comes out with less force. Sometimes, even in the first of the contractions, the ejaculation does not have much force—the semen may just kind of dribble out. The force usually depends on when the man last ejaculated. The longer he goes in between ejaculations, the more forceful they will be. Because orgasm and ejaculation are separate, the pleasure is the same whether he ejaculates far or not.

In a man, after an orgasm and ejaculation, the penis resumes the state that it was in before he became aroused. Then his body goes though a refractory period during which the man cannot have another orgasm or ejaculation. Even if the man's penis gets hard during this time, the erection will subside. This period of time varies greatly from man to man and is based on the age of the man. In young men, this period of time is relatively short, usually between 15 minutes and a few hours. As men age, it can become longer, several hours to a day.

Orgasm often becomes a major issue during intercourse.

Because a man often needs some time to get hard again or come again after he has just had an orgasm, it is common for him to want the woman to have an orgasm before he does, so intercourse can end with his orgasm.

Often a man will expect that a woman should have an orgasm each time they have sex. Yet for many women, it is difficult to have an orgasm during intercourse. The reason is that the motion a woman needs for an orgasm is a circular motion; the motion a man needs for an orgasm is a back-and-forth motion. Yet during intercourse, while the man is being satisfied by the back-and-forth motion of thrusting, the woman is only getting her clitoris stimulated if she is rubbing her clitoris up against the man's pelvis (unless she is using her hand or a vibrator). Therefore, it may require a little more effort for the woman to have an orgasm during inter-course.

Then there's the whole issue of simultaneous orgasm. It's a different experience to have orgasms in turn or to have them at the same time. If both people come at the same time, they may feel a great connectedness, but they miss experiencing, seeing, and hearing the other person's orgasm, because usually a person is so into his or her own orgasm. However, if people come in turn—first the woman has an orgasm—then the man does, then they can both be free to experience the other person's orgasm. So both ways have their pluses and minuses.

Next is the issue of multiple orgasm. Men do not usually have multiple orgasms, although there is a current trend in sex education to try to teach men to have them. Commonly, men need to get hard again before they have a second orgasm, so they have to wait until after that refractory period before they have another one.

Women can have true multiple orgasms, coming again just seconds after having an orgasm. Some women like continued stimulation after their first orgasm. This causes them to keep coming, feeling orgasms roll over them like a flowing stream, one orgasm after another. Women who have only one orgasm at a time are often the ones who find that their clitoris is too sensitive to be touched after the first one.

Both men and women need to know the easiest way to have an orgasm. Through masturbation you can learn what type of pressure and intensity makes you come. When you are having intercourse, you can experiment to find out in what sexual positions you have orgasms. You'll learn how and when you'll have an orgasm. Once you gain a greater understanding of your own orgasms then you'll be able to teach a partner how to help you have a great orgasm.

Accepting Your Body

Men and women who do not feel good about their bodies are often sexually inhibited and feel uncomfortable getting close to another person. Poor body image ruins sex or even a non-sexual date when a women thinks she's too fat to be touched. If a man is worried about his penis size, he is often too distracted to have a good time and to give his partner a good time. If they both are worried about their bodies, they may not be able to have fun and relax.

The body shouldn't be such a big deal. It's simply the vessel that carries us through life. However, as most of us know, body image is inextricably linked to sexual pleasure. Living in a culture where Cindy Crawford and Tom Cruise are the ideals, it is difficult to ignore our bodies' flaws and our partner's body's flaws. Short, fat, thin, or tall, bodies will only give us pleasure if we can accept them. You need to learn to feel so good about your body that you are no longer distracted by it.

Thigh Anxiety: Women's Body Image Problems

According to a recent study, 70 percent of women under thirty years old do not enjoy sex as much as they could because they do not like their bodies. This sad statistic is partially a result of the pressure that our culture puts on women to have perfect bodies. Women are shown a stream of gorgeous models and are told that they should be thin, tall, and muscular, with large breasts, a tiny waist, big eyes, flawless skin, a little nose, straight white teeth, and a perfect haircut. Some women worry about every little aspect of their body. Have you ever seen how close some women get to the mirror when they are examining themselves? It's as if they are looking to change any tiny "imperfection."

One of women's greatest concerns are their breasts. Women may worry if their breasts aren't symmetrical, or if they are large, or too small, or they sag, or have stretch marks, or they have inverted nipples, or hair on them. Many women don't stop to realize that the beauty of breasts is their diversity and the natural way they feel. Most men love to touch and see and enjoy a woman's breasts, no matter what she thinks of them. If a man compares a real woman's breasts to the image in his mind of "perfect" breasts that is based on a picture in his stash of porn of Miss September's air-brushed implants, then he is not interested in the beauty or pleasure that a real woman can give.

Another great concern for women is being overweight. Too many women think that they have to be thin to please a man. This can create a great paradox, since a man usually asks a woman out to dinner. While she is waiting for that big date she'll try to knock off a few pounds by crash dieting. At dinner, the woman feels self-conscious about eating more than a salad in front of the man, because she doesn't want him to think that she is going to get fat. Also, if she wants to have sex after dinner, she won't want to eat because it will make her feel fat and she won't want him to touch her. Of course, she also has a lousy time on the date because she's so distracted by her hunger!

The truth is that many men do not want thin women, and any man who has the tiniest bit of sensitivity certainly does not want a woman to starve herself for him. Twenty-nine-year-old Tim says, "If I go on a date with a woman and she doesn't eat like a normal person, then I lose interest in her. I want a woman who can eat, not some toothpick." But despite men's voices and opinions, many women continue to think they are too fat.

Jackie, twenty, worried so much about her weight that she forgot to enjoy sex: "I always would roll over so the guy couldn't see my ass. It's fat and bumpy. I thought that if a guy saw it he'd go into shock." How could Jackie be enjoying sex if she was always trying to get into positions so the guy wouldn't see her from behind? What if that guy liked big bottoms?

People often forget that everyone has different preferences in the kind of bodies they'd like to have sex with. The best example of this is exactly what was going on with Jackie. There are many guys who like large asses in women. Jackie's problem is that she keeps thinking about Kate Moss, rather than thinking of the Sir Mix-A-Lot song "Baby's Got Back" or the Spinal Tap song "Big Bottom." If she just felt good about herself and realized that the guy should be damn glad to be in bed with her, then she wouldn't think about her inhibitions.

Certain people are more attracted to certain bodies. Yet many times, it does not matter what your body looks like.

▼ ▼

When you fall in love, you fall in love with the person, not the form.

▲ ▲

Does Size Matter: Men's Body Image Problems

Some of men's complaints about their bodies are that their pecs or biceps or shoulders are not big enough, they don't have a washboard stomach, they have skinny "chicken" legs, they have too much body hair (hair on their back, for example), or they don't have enough hair on their head. Men also worry that they are too fat or too thin.

However, of all of the men whom I have talked to about sex, they have the most trouble accepting the size of their penis. They think that penis size is the most important factor of their body image. In fact, in a recent research study when men were asked which is more important to them, their height or their penis size, 62 percent of the men said that they'd rather be 5'2" with a 7" penis compared with 36 percent who would rather be 6'3" with a 3" penis. Most men think that their penis should be long, fat, and straight.

Where women compare their breasts to the media image of breasts, men mostly compare their penises to what they see in the locker room. The fact that men see other men's penises in the locker room is both a good thing and a bad thing. It's bad because they almost never see erections in the locker room. Penises look different when they are hard. A small, soft penis may get to be much larger when it's erect than a large, soft penis gets when it's erect. So a man can go through life thinking that his penis is small, when really it's the same size or larger than the one he spied on.

Maybe men could get over their hangup over penis size if they realize that penis size is not important for a woman's sexual pleasure. Since a woman's most sensitive spot is her clitoris, she does not even need penetration for pleasure. An aroused woman can't notice how big a penis is when she's being penetrated since the vagina itself has very few nerve endings and adjusts to the size of the penis. Creativity, sensuality, and eroticism are much more important than size. As the old saying goes, "It not the size of the ship; it's the motion of the ocean."

Also, but to a lesser extent, men worry about the shape of their penis. If their erection bends to the side or bends toward their stomach, they wonder if that's normal. It is normal; it's also a perfect example of how every penis is different. Some men find that they get a very positive reaction to a penis that is not straight. Twenty-four-year-old Jeff says, "Girls tell me they like it, because it hits their G-spot." No matter what your penis looks like, what matters is how it feels to you and to your partner.

Some men who are circumcised worry that sex would be different if they were uncircumcised. Or vice versa. Yet circumcision has no known effect on sexual pleasure. Women report different reactions to circumcision. Compare these opinions: "I have never seen an uncircumcised penis, and I don't think I ever want to. It seems gross," said Pam, twenty-three. "I like uncircumcised penises much more, because there is more to play with," said Susan, twenty-nine. It's all a matter of individual preference.

▼ ▼ ▼ ▼ ▼ ▼ ▼ ▼ ▼ ▼ ▼ ▼ ▼ ▼ ▼ ▼ ▼ ▼ ▼

You never really know what someone else will think of your body, so the most important thing is for you to love your own body.

▲ ▲ ▲ ▲ ▲ ▲ ▲ ▲ ▲ ▲ ▲ ▲ ▲ ▲ ▲ ▲ ▲ ▲ ▲ ▲

Improving the Way You Feel About Your Body

To reduce your inhibitions about your body there are many things that you can do alone or with a partner. First you should look at your body, and learn to feel comfortable with the way you look naked.

Take off your clothes. Look at your nude body in a full-length mirror. Notice all the things you do not like. Then notice all the things you do like. Focus on the good things. Stay naked for an entire day alone. Feel what it is like to be naked. Take every opportunity to look at your body and to touch your body. Also, take a hand mirror and make a close examination of your genitals. You should be able to identify all the parts of your sex organs, explained earlier in this chapter. The more you know your body, the more comfortable you will feel when someone else sees it.

Sometimes the oddest thing about getting sexual with a new partner is that you two are naked together. Being naked with another person can be a wonderfully freeing feeling if you both feel comfortable with your bodies. To get rid of some of your hangups, it may help to expose them. When you have a partner, try looking at your nude bodies together in a full-length mirror. Tell your partner the things that you do not like about your body. Ask your partner not to say anything like, "Oh, but I love the way your legs look." Just have your partner hear how you feel about yourself. Then say all the things that you like about yourself. Then listen to your partner tell you what he or she likes and doesn't like about his or her body. This exercise will bring you two closer together. It creates honesty and can lead to freedom being naked together.

Letting Go: Enjoying and Accepting Your Body During Sex

It can be difficult to relax and let go during sex if it is the first time you are having sex with a new person. It's easy to start worrying about a million things during sex. You'll probably find that you'll enjoy sex more if you think a little less while you are doing it. This may be easier said than done. Yet if you try to let go of your worries, anxieties, and expectations, you'll enjoy your experience and be in the moment.

The way to let go during sex is to be able to enjoy what your body is doing. You need to accept the things that your body is doing, even if you don't like them. That even means accepting things such as if you or your partner passes gas during sex, or if you hear the sound of air in the vagina during intercourse making a farting sound, or if one of you pees a little during sex. Reading it here may make you embarrassed or uncomfortable, but mindblowing sex means you can laugh at yourself or ignore things like these.

Also, letting go means getting over the fear and anxiety of being looked at during sex. If you are worried about your body or worried what you look like during sex, or confused over what part of your body to move next, then you will become a spectator at your own sexual experience, rather than a participant.

Relax during sex. Focus on your breathing. Let the good feelings wash over you. Focus on the way your lover looks, feels, smells, sounds, and tastes. Let whatever happens happen. Let the freedom and the connection of sex blow your mind. Get into it—feel the pleasure!

▼ ▼

Mindblowing sex is when you are totally in the moment.

▲ ▲

CHAPTER 5

All the Right Moves

Sexual Positions and Sexual Techniques

Getting Into Position

Remember when we were kids and sex was scored according to four bases, the four "F's"? First base: Frenching. Second base: Feeling. Third base: Fingering. Fourth base: Fucking. As adults, we don't necessarily pass through those stages at each sexual encounter. Yet in fact, many people follow cultural patterns of sexual behavior like the ones we scored by years ago. These untaught, unwritten, instinctive patterns are called "sexual scripts."

The most traditional sexual script in our culture, when you meet someone with whom you have a mutual attraction, goes something like this: (1) brushing up against each other; (2) touching non-sex-specific body parts (arms, legs, face);

(3) holding hands; (4) closed-mouth kissing; (5) open-mouth kissing (French kissing, tongue kissing); (6) fondling sex-specific body parts through clothes (breast, crotch); (7) fondling each other's nude bodies; (8) fondling genitals; (9) kissing each other's nude bodies; (10) kissing, licking, sucking genitals; (11) intercourse; (12) increased sexual variation.

Does that pattern sound familiar to you? If it does, I'm sure you can imagine how odd it would seem if you went from holding hands to intercourse without ever kissing or touching! Sexual scripts are somewhat different for each individual, yet most people in our culture share that traditional pattern.

Sexual scripts have changed over the generations. In our parents' generation, oral sex did not precede intercourse. Back then, most people thought of oral sex as a more intimate act saved for after intercourse or later in marriage. Today, many twentysomethings say that intercourse is more intimate because of the connections that it has to love and the risks it has for disease. Therefore, the script changed over the years, making it more common for people to have oral sex before intercourse.

Understanding the pattern of how sexual intimacy increases is extremely helpful in sexual decision making. Twenty-five-year-old Nicole says, "If I don't like the way a man kisses, I'd never want to have intercourse with him because kissing is important to me. So I know to stop there, and not lead him on anymore." Of course, people do not have intercourse with everyone they kiss; they do not follow the sexual script through to completion. In fact, many people have a great time doing everything but intercourse.

Everything But

There are so many totally erotic things that people do without actually having intercourse. These activities are sometimes called foreplay, but I don't like that word because it implies that it comes before intercourse, when in fact intercourse may not occur at all. In the sex education field there is a trend to use the words "outercourse" or "noninsertive sex" instead of foreplay. Those words aren't good, either, because when people are being sexual, even if they are not having intercourse, they may be putting their fingers inside each other's genitals, or their genitals inside each other's mouths. So I prefer to call this way of being sexual, "totally erotic activities that people enjoy without having intercourse." I know it's longer than saying some snappy phrase, but it expresses what's really going on when people do "everything but."

Instead of intercourse, or as a prelude, people can hold each other, massage or rub each other, and kiss in ways that are immensely sensual. Looking into someone's eyes and just kissing can carry as much emotional-sexual connection as intercourse. Playing with each other's genitals is very erotic and very intimate, whether it is masturbating your partner to orgasm or just touching for a little while.

Touch Me, I Want to Be Flirty

From stroking someone's hair to stroking their genitals, touch is one of the most important aspects of sex. When people touch they are communicating without using words. When you first meet someone, if you touch his or her arm you are subtly saying, "I want you." When you walk down the street holding someone's hand, just knowing they are there holding you can fill you with a feeling of love and affection. Touch calms. It brings people close together. Touch also excites. When you experiment with touching— how hard or soft you and your partner like to be touched and where you like to be touched—you'll expand your potential for closeness, pleasure, tenderness, and excitement. In chapter 7 on using your senses to enhance sex, there are exercises that you can do to explore the eroticism of touch.

Sometimes touching leads to sex. Twenty-year-old Tania says, "In college, if you ask someone for a backrub, you might as well be saying, 'I want to have sex with you.' It's the only kind of foreplay I ever have." Other times, touching is great without sex. Twenty-seven-year-old Sharon says that "a great massage is better than a great orgasm and less trouble than having sex. I know I'm lazy, but I'd rather get it than give anything." Whether you are giving or receiving, it's great to know how to touch to please your partner, or to tell your partner how to please you. A touch may or may not be sexual, depending on how much clothes you each have on and how you feel about each other.

Pucker Up

Has anyone ever told you that you are a great kisser? Have you ever really felt attracted to someone, then as soon as you started making out you never wanted to see the person again? When kissing is a perfect fit, it's fantastic, but unfortunately, it can range from too wet, sloppy, intrusive (with too much tongue) to too impersonal, too dry, too soft (with not enough tongue). If you and your partner are compatible kissers, it may not even occur to you that you have something really special. But once someone sucks on your lip when you only like to kiss on the lips (rather than have them sucked) you'll realize what a drag it is to be incompatible kissers!

If you don't like the way someone kisses when you first start kissing, it is possible to change the style of kissing by telling and showing him or her the way you like to kiss. If your partner is open to experimenting, then just say, "Relax your mouth and I'll show you the way I like kissing." If your partner is responsive to the change, in a matter of seconds you should feel his or her tongue adapt to your style, mingling with your tongue or not moving at all, depending on your preference.

Some people will not intentionally change their kissing styles because they are so used to the way they kiss. If you or your partner are set in your way of kissing and even experimentation won't lead to change, then chances are that if you stay together, eventually you will both adapt your styles slightly so you are at least comfortable together. If you really hate kissing someone and that person won't adapt, you may realize that compatibility in kissing may be as important to you as compatibility in sex—or in any other area—and you may go looking for another partner. But let's hope you'll start your next relationship by saying, "Has anyone ever told you that you are a great kisser?"

You Let Me Touch Yours, I'll Let You Touch Mine!

When two people are getting sexual, they begin to touch and explore each other's genitals, maybe to the point of orgasms. Mutual masturbation can mean touching each other's genitals simultaneously, or both people masturbating themselves while they watch each other.

For some people, having their genitals touched by the other person is more intimate than intercourse because they grew up with a taboo against masturbation. (You can read more about how to enjoy masturbation in chapter 8.) Once you are comfortable with your own masturbation, you can enjoy having someone else masturbate you or masturbate yourself while someone else watches. You can then experiment with seeing the other person's orgasm and learning how you can give them an orgasm.

Lick Me Good Like You Should

While for many people oral sex precedes intercourse, it is an incredibly intimate experience. More than with any sexual position, when you receive oral sex you are exposing the smells, tastes, and sight of your genitals to another person. Unless you are great at yoga, you will never be able to see, smell, and taste yourself the way someone else can.

Because it's virtually impossible to feel the sensations of oral sex without actually having someone else do it to you, many people really loving getting oral sex. Giving oral sex is immensely pleasurable to people who are turned on by the eroticism, the creativity, and even the control of getting someone off with their mouth. Other people are not as enthusiastic about giving oral sex, and may not do it at all, or may only do it in return for receiving it.

Sometimes, giving oral sex for the first time is a difficult experience. Roger, twenty-seven, described it this way: "The first time I ate a woman, it was stupid. I didn't know what I was doing. I just put my head down there and sucked on it. And asked if I was doing it right. She said, 'I don't know. What do you think?' I was fifteen and she was fourteen. Now when I go down on a woman, I'm like a wild animal—rolling in my prey—getting the scent all over me for what I am about to devour."

Jane, twenty-four, described it like this: "I thought I should try to put his whole dick in my mouth, down my throat. I almost puked all over him, I gagged so much."

Those quotes explain what I mean when I say that sex is a skill, not just an instinct.

For a man to become better at performing oral sex on a woman, he needs to understand how her body responds to his touch.

If a woman has the best orgasms from clitoral stimulation, the man can please her by finding her clitoris and stimulating it with his tongue. If she likes the feeling of penetration during oral sex, he can put his tongue or his fingers inside her vagina. Most of all, he can experiment with different types of licking and kissing around her vulva. (He should never blow into the vagina. Doctors report that blowing into the vagina can lead to the possibility that air bubbles could be picked up by blood vessels and cause a blockage, or embolism, that could be fatal, especially if the woman is pregnant.)

Also, remember that the vagina is actually not a dirty place. The vagina is a self-cleaning organ, and in fact has fewer germs than your mouth. Every vagina has its own unique scent and taste, which are usually mild since the vagina keeps itself so clean. There are many men who love the taste of a woman. For a man who does not like the natural mild odor, he and the woman should know that if she showers just before sex there shouldn't be much of a smell or taste at all. Women should never douche—not only is it unnecessary, it's actually very bad since it upsets the natural balance in the vagina by washing away the good bacteria with the bad. No matter what your gender, or your partner's gender, if the smell or taste of your partner is not appealing to you, just say, "Hey, let's shower together before we do it."

When receiving oral sex, you should let your partner know what feels good and what doesn't. It's usually best just to say what you like. Sometimes it works to try to guide your partner's head where you want it, or to move yourself around to a better position, but sometimes this just confuses the other person. Also, you need to relax to enjoy the feeling. Try not to be embarrassed or feel shy about having someone seeing and tasting and smelling you. Your partner wouldn't be doing it if he or she didn't get pleasure from going down on you.

While some women report that they feel self-conscious when a man performs oral sex on them, almost *all* men report that they love getting blowjobs. What's the best way to get a man off with your mouth? Some men will only come from oral sex if you suck on the head of his penis. Other men like only "deep throating," when the partner's throat relaxes completely so the whole penis can fit inside it. Some men like it when their partner's mouth moves up and down rapidly on the penis imitating the motion of intercourse. Incidentally, even though it is called a "blowjob," blowing on a man's penis will not do much for either of you. Many men like a combination of stimulation, like sucking the head, then licking the shaft as if it's a lollipop. To perform oral sex on a man, you should be aware of the most sensitive parts on that man's penis. All penises are not alike. It's all a matter of a man's penis's sensitivity. Speaking of sensitivity, most men do not like the feeling of teeth raking on their penis, so be careful to use your lips to shield your teeth from coming in contact with it. Be aware that you do not have to let the man ejaculate in your mouth. If you don't want him to come in your mouth, and you talk about this before you go down on him, you should ask him to say, "I'm about to come" (or something like that) to give you enough warning before the explosion.

Some people like the taste of semen. I've heard people try to explain the taste by comparing it to the taste of a variety of foods and drinks, ranging from Fritos to Diet Peach Snapple to a Coconut Frozen Fruit Bar. One woman said that she'd never taste it because to her it smells like Clorox bleach. Just in case you were wondering, semen has about 40 calories per ejaculation, and it's mostly made up of proteins and sugars.

Of course, a strong argument against tasting semen is that if someone has the HIV virus that causes AIDS, it will be present in his semen and could be transmitted to you through swallowing or a cut in your mouth.

When receiving a blowjob, the man should encourage his partner to do what he likes the most, by talking and even gently guiding or holding the partner's head. I do not mean that he should grab his partner's head by the hair and force his partner to "face-fuck" him. Encouragement, rather than force, will keep someone interested in continuing. Also, let your partner know right away if you feel teeth scrape you. That way your partner will become aware of how to keep them out of the way. Communicate about ejaculation, and ask if your partner wants you to pull out before you come.

Many couples enjoy "69," having oral sex on each other simultaneously. If you haven't figured it out already, it's called 69 because if two people are lying side by side or one on top of the other while they are going down on each other, their entwined bodies are inverted like the number 69. Besides 69, for more variation during oral sex, you can experiment with getting into different positions, such as lying on top of the each other or kneeling. You can also experiment with giving oral sex to your lover in exotic locations or at unexpected times. For a delightful surprise, you can awaken your lover in the morning by performing oral sex on him or her.

The Ins and Outs of Sex

When it comes to intercourse, the possible variations of positions are innumerable. Here are some of the basics:

MAN ON TOP

Also known as the male-superior position or missionary position, this has many variations because it allows the man complete freedom of movement. In the most traditional image of the position, the man would be lying with his legs between the woman's thighs and lowering and raising his pelvis to thrust. The woman can put a pillow under her butt, thus tilting her pelvis and allowing for deeper penetration. She can also raise and lower her hips to meet his thrusts.

This may trigger his orgasm faster, and may even help her have an orgasm, if she can simultaneously rub her clitoris on his pelvis. Also, the woman can vary her leg position. She can lie flat, or bend her knees, or lift her legs up high. The farther apart or the higher she raises them, the deeper the man can penetrate. If she is flexible, she can rest her feet on his shoulders. She can use her hands to rub or hold his butt or his entire body. He usually has to use his arms to support himself, so he cannot touch her; however, he is free to kiss or lick her on the face, neck, or, if he can reach, her chest. If he keeps his eyes open, he can choose to look at her or bend his neck down to watch his penis go in and out of her vagina.

This position is the most common sexual position, but it does not work well for some people. It is not good if the man is very overweight. If he suffers from premature ejaculation, it could be a bad position because it is the one in which many men come the most quickly (although this position could also help the premature ejaculator take longer to come if he thrusts very slowly and feels in control of his thrusting). Man on top is also the position in which conception most easily occurs, because of the angle that the penis is aimed in the vagina and the depth of penetration if the woman's legs are raised.

The man-on-top position can evoke a variety of emo-tional-psychological responses. Sometimes it can feel like a very intimate position because it's face-to-face and the two people can rest their entire bodies on each other. Other times it can be a very aggressive position, when the man is thrusting hard. Elissa, twenty-three, expressed this best when she recounted her thoughts on her sexual experiences with this position with two different men: "There was this one guy who I only had sex with once. He climbed on top of me. First he asked me if I could put my legs up over my head or on his shoulders. But when I couldn't reach, he said, 'Well keep them up high. Get ready. I'm going to fuck you hard now.' I still can't get those words out of my head, because it was so disgusting. I just laid there, trying to hold my legs up in the air, as he banged away at my body. He wasn't looking at me. His arms were stretched all the way out, his body at an angle. He just pounded away until he came. I couldn't wait for him to get off. With another guy, who I went out with for a few months, we would mostly have sex with him on top, but it was really good, not at all like that other guy. When he'd get on top, the position was different. He'd look into my eyes. He'd put his arms down near mine, rest his chest on my breast, and his thighs on top of mine. Then he'd like glide in and out of me. We'd kiss. We'd move together. I felt completely in love with him, during sex. When he was on top of me it felt intense—like I was inside of him—like we were one."

WOMAN ON TOP

This position allows the woman more freedom to move her body. She can also be in charge of how much of the penis she allows inside her, and at what pace. This position is one of the most effective ways for a woman to have an orgasm from her clitoris, since she can easily rub her clitoris against the man's pelvis to have a clitoral orgasm. She can also provide the type of friction she desires to have an orgasm in her vagina by moving—lowering and raising—herself on the partner's penis. In woman on top, the clitoris can be stimulated by hand, and either partner can caress the other. Also, in this position the man can move his head up to suck on the woman's nipples while he is inside her.

Visually this position can be a turn-on. Many men like looking at the woman's body when she is on top. Twenty-six-year-old Robert said, "I get so damn hot when her breasts are bouncing up and down when she's riding my cock."

One way for a woman to be on top, and often the most comfortable way for her and the man, is to have her legs outside of his legs, slightly bent at the knees (almost kneeling or sitting). She can support herself by extending her arms, putting her hands on either side of his head. Then she can lean toward the man and move her pelvis, thrusting at an angle. (Occasionally, during vigorous thrusting, the penis could slip out of the vagina, and one partner will have to put it back in. Sometimes, this can be frustrating. Also, if the woman is moving up and down on his penis very rapidly from a squatting position and the penis starts to slip out, she must be careful not to lower back down on the penis or she could hurt the man by bending his penis.)

Also, she can be on her knees (positioned on either side of his thighs), raising and lowering her entire body on his penis. In this position, her arms are free to fondle his body or her own body. For full body contact, she can lie completely on top of the man. For a different sensation, she can lie with her legs between his legs, or she can face away from him, sitting on his penis.

This position is good for men who are trying to get more control when they ejaculate, because it often slows down ejaculation. The man can hold and move the woman's hips to indicate to her the pace at which he'd like her to move. This position is also good if the man is tall and the woman is short.

Psychologically, this position contradicts traditional gender roles, because the woman is more in control than the man, which makes some people uncomfortable while turning others on.

SIDE BY SIDE

This position often begins when the couple is in the man-on-top or woman-on-top position and they roll over onto their sides. Sometimes the penis stays inside the vagina; other times it has to be put back in. The couple lies face-to-face, so this position allows for full body contact, eye contact, and equal freedom of movement for both partners. They may both have their legs closed, or she may lie with her legs apart on either side of his legs, drawing up her knees for deeper penetration. Or she can lie with her top (right) leg over his top (left) leg and her bottom (left) leg between his legs. (This is one of those positions where you'll wish that for a little while you could remove one of your arms or legs!) If he moves his thigh against her vulva, it may help her have an orgasm.

SITTING

Sitting face-to-face the man can put his penis inside the woman's vagina. To vary the depth of penetration either of them or both of them can lean back on their hands or wrap their legs tighter around the other person. Since face-to-face positions are very intimate, people enjoy this position if they want to see each other.

REAR ENTRY

Here the man faces the woman's back and enters her vagina from behind. She could be on her hands and knees in the variation of this position that is often called "doggy style." Many men enjoy "taking a woman from behind," because it allows for deep penetration and vigorous thrusting. The woman, too, may like that feeling of having deep penetration. Also, it allows either the woman or man to set the rhythm and intensity of the thrusting. While it does not allow for any eye contact, it gives the man the visual stimulation of watching the woman's ass move against his pelvis, or watching his penis move in and out of her vagina. It also allows the man complete freedom with his hands to fondle the woman's ass, breasts, back, legs, stomach, or to stimulate her clitoris.

Another variation is for the woman to lie flat on her stomach, with her legs together or apart. In this position, she could arch her back, raise her butt in the air, or place a pillow under her pelvis to allow for deeper penetration. In any of the positions where the woman is lying on her stomach, she can easily slide her arm under her body and stimulate her clitoris with her hand. Psychologically, some people enjoy this position, because it can make the man feel very dominant and it can give the woman the chance to feel vulnerable, to relax, or to fantasize. Others do not like it because it makes the woman feel helpless and the man feel overpowering.

For more variation, the woman can bend over the edge of a bed or table, and the man enters her from behind. Also, rear entry can be done when the couple is lying side-by-side in "spoon position." In this position, the woman can have her knees slightly raised to vary the depth of penetration. Twenty-three-year-old Zoë says, "Side-by-side sex from behind is great, because it's gentle sex. I like it when he's inside me and he kisses my neck from behind. I also like doing it that way because I can reach around and play with his ass. I like to feel his ass muscles clench as he moves inside me."

STANDING

This position works well for partners who are roughly the same height. If they're not the same height, the man can hold the woman up, or one of them can stand on a book or step. The couple can stand next to each other, face-to-face, and put the penis in the vagina. This does not allow for deep penetration, but they can both reach each other's genitals easily and hold each other. From this position, the man can lift up one of her legs and stimulate her clitoris with his hand. In other standing positions, the woman can wrap both her legs around the man's waist and hold on to him around the neck. Meanwhile he can hold her up off the ground by either holding her under her ass, under her knees, or around her back.

The standing position is often used for spontaneous sex,

as twenty-nine-year-old Tony found out: "One of the wildest times I had sex was totally unexpected. I was in the kitchen with a woman I was dating. She was leaning up against the counter when I was cooking dinner for us. I went over to her and we started kissing. Then the next thing I knew, we took off our jeans, and we did it right there standing up in the kitchen."

There are lots of other positions that are variations of the ones I mentioned. Experiment to find positions you like. You can come up with so many variations simply by moving your bodies into any positions your bodies will go.

Anal Sex

While oral sex and doggy-style are well accepted these days, anal stimulation is still a big taboo for many people. Interestingly, practically every week on my radio show, callers ask me questions about anal sex. It seems that lots of people are trying it and enjoying it.

Both men and woman may have some reluctance to experiment with anal stimulation because they were always taught that the anus is dirty and not meant to give pleasure. However, the reality is that the anus is rich with nerve endings that can feel really good when they are stimulated. Men can experience additional stimulation from the prostate gland, which can be stimulated by reaching about an inch and a half inside the anus. The prostate gland can also feel stimulation if it is pressed through the skin of the perineum, the area between the scrotum and the anus. Most men report that stimulation of the prostate gives them great pleasure and fantastic orgasms. Twenty-six-year-old Bill said, "The orgasm is deeper and longer when I put my finger in my ass and rub." Men sometimes have a psychological problem dealing with anal stimulation: they may be afraid that if they like the feeling then it means they are gay. But if they realize how good it can feel, they can get over their psychological barrier.

It's fairly common for people to enjoy anal stimulation manually. That means that either the man or woman may reach around and gently put his or her finger into the anus of the other partner, often during intercourse. Many people also enjoy oral-anal stimulation, which is sometimes called rimming. Betty, twenty-six, says, "I love getting rimmed. It's a delicious pleasure. I like feeling it so much, that I never mind giving it." It is healthier to make sure the anus is clean, so you do not pick up bacterial infections from rimming. Before oral-anal contact, take a shower or gently wipe with warm water and mild soap or use a latex barrier during oral-anal contact.

There are lots of men who really want to try having anal intercourse with a woman for variety. I have often been asked, "Why is anal intercourse such a thrill to some men?" So I have been posing this question to men. Sometimes I hear that men truly like the way it feels. Sometimes the men tell me that women love the way it feels. Then I've gotten a number of comments like this one, from twenty-four-year-old Duane: "When I was inside her ass it felt different, but not necessarily better. It's tighter, but not a lot tighter. It's the psychological part that made me come. Also, when I had anal sex, it was like I could check it off. You know, after the first time I was in a woman's ass, I thought, there, now I've done it."

If you have anal sex you must *always* make sure that the man is wearing a condom, and always use plenty of lubrication inside the anus and on the outside of the condom.

The first time a couple tries anal sex it can be very painful for the partner who is receiving. To make the first time easier, prior to the experience, the recipient should get used to feeling a finger or fingers in the anus. Then the first time they try anal sex, if the recipient tries sitting down on the penis it may go inside easier, since the recipient is controlling the penetration. Overall, as with any sexual practice, you should only do anal sex if you both want to.

▼ ▼
People are the most compatible sexually when they both like the same types of sex and the same amount of sex.
▲ ▲

You've Got the Moves; I've Got the Motion

Part of what determines a couple's sexual compatibility is how their bodies move together during sex. It's the rhythm and the tempo. You learn about this from feeling your body moving against a partner. I was discussing this concept of the rhythm and tempo of sex with Mary, a twenty-three-year-old whom I interviewed, and she told me a funny story about how this idea was first relayed to her.

"When I was fifteen, my first boyfriend told me that I was good in bed. All we did was kissing and petting, so I was really confused about what he meant. I asked a friend and she said 'good in bed' means that you move around a lot. From then on, when I would have sex I would move around kind of wiggling. Until finally, when I was having sex with one guy, he held my body still and said, 'I am never going to come if you keep moving around like that. Hold still!' It took me a while to realize that sometimes 'good in bed' means being completely still; sometimes it means moving in rhythm with your partner."

Knowing how much to move or how much to thrust requires being comfortable with the other person. It usually takes a while for a new couple to feel comfortable having sex together, because everyone's sexual style is different. Unless there is an instant lustful connection between two people, when two people first start having sex they have to settle into each other and figure out how sexually compatible they are.

That's part of the reason why it's important to talk with your partner about sex. You can talk before, during, or after sex. Find out what feels good to your partner. Tell your partner what you like. During sex, try to learn how your partner's body responds to your touch, how your partner has orgasms the most easily, and how your partner likes to have sex. You'll probably find that the more you talk about sex and the more the two of you have sex, the more you'll fit together sexually.

As your sexual relationship develops with someone, either of you can control the tempo of sex by moving or thrusting faster or slower. If the other person likes that pace, he or she will follow. If one partner doesn't like the pace he or she should speak up and ask to control the tempo for a while. Compatibility means fitting together, moving the way you both like. If you don't seem to be compatible at first, don't be afraid to try adjusting the way you move together, even if it feels awkward at first.

Getting It On from Dusk to Dawn

There is no way to tell how long sex should last. Some people like to have sex as quickly as possible, just to have an orgasm. These people could get very frustrated if they don't come and end sex in under four minutes. Plenty of times, people just want a quickie because they don't have a lot of time, but they still want to have sex.

There are other people who want marathon lovemaking sessions. For them, mindblowing sex lasts for two hours or more. Sometimes sex lasts a long time when it includes lots of non-intercourse sex play. Other times, a couple might try to manage intercourse so the man stays hard and both partners hold off on having an orgasm by stopping and starting.

For example, they might just hold still each time either of them feels like they are going to come, until they are finally ready for their orgasms. Sometimes, as I discussed earlier, people can have multiple orgasms, or the man can get another erection quickly, which allows a couple to have intercourse again.

Most of the time, sex falls somewhere in between the marathon and the quickie. On average, the pre-intercourse sex play may last ten to fifteen minutes and the intercourse about ten to fifteen minutes. If you are unhappy with how long sex usually takes, talk to your partner about it. Maybe you can have longer sessions on Saturday mornings when neither of you has to rush off to work, or in the early evening before one or both of you is too tired for more than a quickie. If you are looking for more quickies, ask your partner to indulge you at least some of the time. Compatibility means finding a middle ground that makes you happy.

Taking Charge

Sometimes even the most liberated women and men do not want to initiate sex, because they fear rejection. If couples have good communication with each other, then initiation will feel natural. There are some couples who function best when only one partner initiates sex. Yet often relationships work best when both partners feel free to initiate it whenever they want sex. If it seems that you are the only person who is initiating sex, and you want your partner to initiate more often, then ask your partner why he or she doesn't initiate sex. Open up the lines of communication. If you want to have sex, ask your partner outright. If you prefer a more subtle approach, such as a suggestive glance or a sexual touch, just be absolutely sure that both you and your partner will understand the message.

Enough Is Enough

It is difficult to say how often people have sex because frequency of intercourse varies tremendously from one relationship to the next. It varies according to whether or not the couple is married, how long they have been together, if they have children, how much leisure time they have, and how old they are.

Also, I am always reluctant to answer this question with statistics, because I am afraid that people who have sex more than the "average" will worry that they are too interested in sex, and people who do it less than the "average" will worry that they should be doing it more. As long as you and your partner are happy with how often you have sex, don't concern yourself with the statistics. Remember, these are only averages, and who wants to be average, anyway?!

From a compilation of statistics from several recent research studies, I have come up with these average figures:

for 18–24-year-olds: 3.25 times a week
for 25–34-year-olds: 2.55 times a week
for 35–44-year-olds: 2 times a week
for 45 years and older: 1 time a week

Of course, if you do not have a partner and are having sex zero times a week, you should try to feel good knowing that you can masturbate as many times a week as you like.

Sometimes people who have sex a lot (much more than the "averages") worry that they have a sexual problem, such as a so-called sexual addiction. Sometimes people who almost never have sex worry that they have a sexual problem. The truth is that you cannot have sex too much, unless you are having sex so much that it interferes with every other aspect of your life, or it is leaving you completely physically sore every day. Also, if you are *happy* abstaining or not having sex often, then there is nothing wrong with you, either. You must make up your own sexual "averages." There is no amount of sex that is normal or abnormal; it's all individual.

When Sex Isn't Like a Box of Chocolates

Sexual boredom happens frequently when couples have fallen into regular patterns of having sex. It even happens to young couples. Boredom is *not* an indication that it's time to find a new lover; it's only an indication that it's time for you two to spice up your sex life. Fortunately, with a little imagination, a little new information, a little sense of adventure, and a lot of communication, you and your partner can add a large amount of variety to your sex life. If you get bored, here's your assignment: Privately, both you and your partner should make lists of thirty new, exciting ways that you might want to have sex. Use your imagination to think up what kinds of sex you'd love to try. Try to think of a new position, or a new location, or a new time of day. Try anything that seems sexy and fun. If you can't think of anything new, then read on; this book is filled with hot, sexy tips. Pay attention to everything in this book, ranging from how to give a great massage to how to practice sadomasochism. When both you and you partner have made up your lists, then compare lists. Decide what you'd both be willing to try. Then go for it! Have mindblowing sex.

CHAPTER 6

Mindblowing Sex *with* Condoms?!?

What Are You Whining About?!

"It's like taking a shower in a raincoat."

"It's like smelling a rose when you have a clothespin on your nose."

"I don't have to worry about AIDS. I'm clean, and the people I sleep with just aren't the type who get it."

Gripe and whine and make all the excuses you want, but the fact is there are really only two reasons why people don't use condoms: ignorance and the quest for greater sexual fulfillment. If you don't know all the facts about how HIV and other STD's are transmitted, I'll spell it out for you so you can see for yourself how vital and simple condoms are to use. Then I'll explain lots of fun things to do with condoms. That's right—*fun*. Even though condoms have been thought of as barriers to good sex, the reality is that they're truly only barriers to diseases.

▼ ▼

Condoms do not have to get in the way of sexual fulfillment. In fact, there are dozens, perhaps hundreds, of ways that condoms can be used to actually enhance sex, making it more erotic.

▲ ▲

If you want to have mindblowing sex, you need to stop for a second and think about how the realities of sexually transmitted diseases fit into that concept. If you are worried about getting a disease, you'll be distracted, inhibited, detached, and unhappy during sex. And if you do get a disease from sex, then you will have some major problems to deal with. Fear, embarrassment, and uncomfortable doctor visits do not have to be part of your sex life. Mindblowing sex doesn't just mean how sex feels while you are doing it. It's also how sex feels and what you are thinking afterward.

▼ ▼

If you're worried, or if you get sick, then it was really bad sex, no matter how it felt in the moment of orgasm!

▲ ▲

Mindblowing sex with condoms means more than just feeling secure that you won't get a disease. It also means being so adept at using condoms that you can transform them into sex toys. There are simple ways to make condoms feel more comfortable on the penis. Also, there are hot games you can play with them that can really be amazing. I'll get into all that later. First, the facts about HIV transmission.

The Fact of the Risks

In the 1960s people said, "Let's wait to have sex until we're stoned." In the 1970s they said, "Let's wait to have sex until we're at an orgy." In the 1980s they said, "Let's wait to have sex until the party's over and the coke is all gone." Today we have to say, "Let's wait to have sex until we have some condoms."

The extreme freedom and promiscuity of the 1960s, 1970s, and 1980s is not feasible anymore. We still have a lot of freedom and opportunity to have sex since we are young and unmarried, yet we also must confront the added responsibility of watching out for our sexual health. Today STD's are no longer mere inconveniences; they are life-threatening. Everybody needs to know the risks of how HIV, the virus that causes AIDS, is transmitted.

▼ ▼ ▼ ▼ ▼ ▼ ▼ ▼ ▼ ▼ ▼ ▼ ▼ ▼ ▼ ▼ ▼ ▼ ▼

When people are HIV-positive, you cannot tell by looking at them.

▲ ▲

People with HIV do not look or act any differently from when they did not have it. HIV is a virus that affects people's bodies inside by breaking down their immune system so much that eventually (in a matter of months or even years) they start getting rare diseases, which are collectively labeled as AIDS. People living with HIV often do not know that they have been infected. It takes up to six months after a person contracts HIV for it to show up in a blood test, but as soon as someone becomes HIV infected, he or she can pass it on to other people knowingly or unknowingly. (Read chapter 10 for more about getting tested for HIV, symptoms of AIDS, and how the disease progresses.)

▼ ▼
**The HIV virus is present in three body fluids
that are involved in sex: blood, semen, and vaginal secretions.
The highest concentration of HIV is in blood, the second
highest concentration is in semen, and the lowest
concentration is in vaginal secretions.**
▲ ▲

In order to get HIV from someone who has it, the virus must get into your bloodstream. That means blood, semen, or vaginal secretions must get into your bloodstream. You can *not* get the virus by having sex if there is no exchange of these body fluids. You can *not* get HIV from saliva, sweat, tears, snot, urine, a mosquito, a tick, donating blood, swimming in a pool, sharing food or drinks, holding hands, touching, fondling, hugging. (There are other ways that you can get HIV that do not include sex, like sharing needles during intravenous drug use, including steroid use. Also, during birth HIV can be transmitted to the newborn from the mother, or the baby can get it from its mother's breast milk.)

People always ask me specifics about "does this or that behavior transmit HIV?" Well, here's the bottom line. If you always remember the following then you will always be able to answer those questions for yourself.

▼ ▼
**If you do not know someone's HIV status, or if you do know if
someone is HIV-positive, never let that person's blood, semen,
or vaginal secretions into your body.**
▲ ▲

If blood, semen, or vaginal secretions from someone else gets into your body, then the HIV virus can get into your bloodstream. The inlets to your bloodstream consist of small tears that normally occur during sex. You do not have to be having rough sex. Every time you have intercourse, small tears occur on the penis or in the vagina. If you're having anal sex, the lining of the anus will always tear. Also, it's common to have inlets to your bloodstream in your mouth, such as canker sores, open gums, or small cuts, especially since many people brush their teeth before sex. Cuts on your hands or your cuticles can also allow HIV to enter your bloodstream if you use your hands to touch your partner's body fluids. Be aware of any points of vulnerability on your body before you get sexual with someone.

Not all kinds of sex carry the same risk for transmission. You can determine that certain types of sex are more likely to transmit the virus because the concentration of the HIV virus is higher in blood than in semen and in semen than in vaginal secretions. You can never say that there is absolutely no risk of transmission, but you can figure that some kinds of sex carry a lower risk. Most of the time it's easy to figure out when blood, semen, or vaginal secretions could come in contact with an opening into your bloodstream, but sometimes there are gray areas. You need to decide for yourself if you are willing to take small risks, or no risks at all.

How Do You Protect Yourself?

All you have to do to protect yourself is:

1. Pay attention to where your body fluids and the other person's body fluids are going.
2. Use latex barrier protection. Condoms provide a barrier during intercourse to prevent the exchange of body fluids. When used consistently and properly, condoms are about 98 percent effective for preventing the spread

of HIV. If you want protection when you perform oral sex on a woman you can use a dental dam (or some kinds of Saran Wrap), and if you have cuts on your hands or finger or cuticles, you can wear rubber gloves.

HIV Transmission Quiz

The following quiz will do more than help you see where to apply the basics of avoiding HIV transmission to situations of real-life sex, it will help you see where your personal risk assessment and your sexual guidelines will need to come into play.

1. Can you get HIV from deep tongue-kissing?

No. You can't. And why not? Well, what are the chances that from kissing blood, semen, or vaginal secretions will get into your bloodstream? (Remember, HIV can only be sexually transmitted from blood, semen, or vaginal secretions.) Unless the other person bleeds into your mouth and you have a cut in your mouth, you are safe. You can't get HIV from kissing. Make out to your heart's content!

2. Can a woman get HIV during vaginal intercourse if the man pulls out before he ejaculates?

Yes. This still carries a big risk. Even if a man pulls out before he comes, there will still be semen in the vagina because of the small amount of semen that is expelled before he ejaculates (precum). Anyway, how can you be sure that he will always pull out in time? Frankly, if you are asking this question you are grasping at straws: still trying to enjoy sex without having to worry about AIDS. If everyone could understand that condoms don't have to reduce pleasure all that much, then they'd stop trying to find out how to avoid using them.

3. Can a man get HIV from having unprotected vaginal intercourse with a woman?

Yes. He can if her vaginal secretions get into a tiny cut or tear on his penis. The small cuts on the penis almost always occur during vaginal intercourse, but are seldom seen since they are very small. Also, if the woman is menstruating, then the risk is greater, since blood carries a much higher concentration of HIV. Use condoms.

4. How about if someone performs oral sex on a man?

Possibly. This is an area where you have to assess your risks. Yes, it is *possible* to get HIV from giving a blowjob. If you perform oral sex on a man, you are taking the risk that the semen could get into cuts in your mouth or gums. So if you want to avoid all risk of getting HIV you would put a condom on the penis before letting it into your mouth. If you're willing to take some risk, you could try giving oral sex without getting the head of the penis, or any precum or cum, into your mouth. That would probably work best if you suck on and lick the shaft and use your hand on the head of the penis. If you are going to take a bigger risk, you could give a blowjob but not let the man ejaculate in your mouth. In that case, your risk would be if the precum got into a cut in your mouth. It's your decision. If you do want to be totally protected, use a condom and never let a man come in your mouth.

5. What about performing oral sex on a woman?

Possibly. Performing oral sex on a woman carries a little lower risk of HIV transmission than performing oral sex on a man, since the concentration of HIV in the vaginal secretions is lower than in semen. In order to get HIV from having oral sex on a woman, the woman's vaginal secretions would have to get into a cut in your mouth or gums. If you want to avoid all risk, you should not let vaginal secretions in your mouth.

If the woman is menstruating, then there is a much greater risk, since blood carries a much higher concentration of the HIV virus. To avoid any risk use a piece of latex called a dental dam, or a piece of plastic like Saran Wrap.

6. Can the receiver of oral sex get HIV from the giver?

No. This risk is *extremely* minimal, if any. If blood from the giver's mouth gets into a tiny tear or cut in the vagina or penis of the receiver, then it's possible. Or if the giver has his own semen in his mouth or her own vaginal secretions in her mouth and it somehow gets into a tiny tear in the receiver's vagina or penis, then theoretically it's possible. Even if it is virtually impossible for the receiver to get HIV from the giver, the receiver still should use protection to make sure that the giver is not taking any risks. If you are the receiver you may care about the giver's health.

7. Can you get HIV from masturbating a partner, either fingering a woman or giving a man a hand job?

Possibly. If you have a cut finger, or a torn cuticle, or a hang nail, then you have an opening to your bloodstream. If you stick that finger inside someone's vagina then there is the risk of getting vaginal secretions in your bloodstream. If a man's cum or precum gets into the cut, then it can get into your bloodstream. If you stick that finger in someone's anus, then there is the risk that the fragile lining of the anus may tear and even that tiny cut could get blood into the cut on your finger. To protect yourself, you can wear a latex glove, or if you are just using one finger, you can cut one finger off a latex glove and use that. Also, in drugstores or sex stores you may be able to find "finger cots," tiny condoms that fit on one finger.

8. Why is it easiest to get HIV from anal sex?

Anal sex is the easiest way of transmitting HIV from sex because the anal lining tears very, very easily during anal sex. When a penis (without a condom on it) is in the anus, the semen or the precum has an immediate path into the bloodstream.

9. Is it easier for women than for men to get HIV through vaginal intercourse?

Yes. Women are more susceptible to getting STD's and HIV through intercourse than men, because women have an "open system." The cervix can be an open path into the uterus, so the bacteria or viruses can get right into the bloodstream through blood vessels. Also, it is more common for the vaginal lining than penile lining to tear during sex. That's why during intercourse women need to be especially conscious of not getting semen in their vaginas.

Other Important Reasons to Practice Safer Sex

While AIDS is the most serious sexually transmitted disease, there are also other diseases to watch out for. Using condoms can reduce the risks of getting chlamydia, herpes, gonorrhea, and syphilis. It may help reduce the risk of transmitting genital warts if they are inside the vagina or on the penis. And, of course, condoms also greatly reduce the risk of having an unintended pregnancy. In other words, there are a lot of reasons to use condoms. Believe the risks. How many more "regular people" have to get pregnant unintentionally, contract sexually transmitted diseases, or *die* before you admit it can happen to you?

Why Is It So Important to Use Condoms Every Time?

You may think that you know your partner. You may think that the person looks fine. These partners may have told you they're healthy; or they're a virgin or near-virgin; or their last relationship was long-lasting and monogamous; or they got tested; or their last partner tested negative and they never cheat; or they know they are "clean." What if they tell you their complete sexual histories? Does that matter?

▼ ▼

Many people lie or cover up their true sexual history in order to have sex without a condom.

▲ ▲

A recent study of college students found that over 40 percent of men and women said that if a partner asked how many people they'd slept with, they'd say that they actually had sex with fewer people than they did. Also, 36 percent of the men and 21 percent of the women reported being sexually unfaithful to their current or previous partners. Another study found that more than half of the students who had sexually transmitted diseases reported that they had had unprotected intercourse when they knew they were infected, and nearly a quarter of them did not tell their partners. Isn't it human nature that when you want something, you try to make it sound as appealing as possible? Have you ever lied, covered up, omitted, or conveniently forgotten a couple of ex-lovers here and there, when you were telling a new partner your sexual history?

Picture this scenario. Diane has been going out with Brad for five weeks. They haven't had sex yet, but they know they want to soon. Diane asks Brad what he thinks about using condoms. This is what he says: "I've only slept with my three steady ex-girlfriends. I tested negative after the second one.

Cover your tree or get HIV

Then, the third one was practically a virgin; she had only had sex with one guy before me, so I knew she didn't have AIDS. She never cheated on me, and I never cheated on her. I know

I don't have anything. So you and I really don't have to use condoms."

Sounds good, right? Wrong. It just sounds more appealing than saying the real truth. Based on the history that he just told, here's the real truth for Brad: "I'm not 100 percent sure, you never know, do you?"

▼ ▼

If you knew that the person you were having sex with is HIV-positive then you would either abstain from sex or use condoms (and every other precaution) every time you had sex. Then if you do not know for sure if someone is HIV-negative or -positive, then you should take those same precautions.

▲ ▲

Just because someone says they've been safe, or says they don't have it, you will never really know for sure. When people have the HIV virus, you cannot tell by the way they look or act or what they tell you about their background. Don't you dare think that only gay people, or bisexual people, or drug users get HIV. It has spread completely into the straight population. Also, you cannot tell if someone is more at risk to have HIV based on whether they say they are gay or straight. Sometimes men have sex with men and still call themselves straight. You might think that if a guy's not effeminate he couldn't be gay, but that's simply not true. Sometimes people who shoot up and share needles don't look like the stereotypical image of a junkie. Most important, the virus can't tell if someone is gay or straight, white or black, a high school dropout or an Ivy League grad. Any one of your potential sex partners could have HIV.

Therefore, it does not matter who you are having sex

with. If you do not know a person's HIV status for sure, wouldn't it be safest to treat that person the same as some-

Don't be silly protect your willy

one who has it? If you do not know someone's status, assume he or she has the virus and take the necessary precautions. You are taking unnecessary risks if you get blood, semen, or vaginal secretions in your bloodstream by having unprotected vaginal-penile intercourse, or oral sex or anal sex.

Many people have become jaded about the AIDS scare. You've heard a thousand times that you should use condoms, but maybe you can't see why you should, because you still think that a nice person like you couldn't get it. Sure, you've heard about Magic Johnson, Easy-E, Arthur Ashe, Ryan White, Alison Gertz, and Pedro Zamora, but maybe you still don't know anyone *personally* who has it. You may read that the risk of heterosexual transmission is slim, but the reality is that AIDS is an actual threat. It could affect you, your friends, and your families. Don't just think, "OK, yeah, yeah, I'll use condoms." Practice safer sex every time you have sex. If you are going to take some risks, do not take the risk of vaginal intercourse or anal sex without condoms. Why have to worry about the risks? If you are responsible then you can have mindblowing sex, during which AIDS never crosses your mind. Now on to the more fun topics.

Buying Condoms

Every one of our fathers probably remembers when he was about fourteen years old buying one condom "just in case." He put it in his wallet and never got the chance to use it, but it was cool to have that permanent ring embossed in the leather of his wallet. What was once a mark of innocence and adventure is now a mark of maturity. Today, men and women are buying condoms not to keep in wallets because it's cool looking, but to use them. (Besides, a wallet is not a good place to store a condom for any length of time.)

A lot of people have anxiety about buying condoms. You know, it's that fear of having the guy at the checkout shout into the PA, "Hey, we need a price check on the condoms." The truth is that the person behind the counter doesn't care. To get over the embarrassment of buying condoms, you need to keep in mind that all it means when you buy a condom is that you are a responsible

> **The right selection: protect your erection**

person who likes to have sex. In my opinion, there are plenty of more embarrassing things to buy, like a ton of junk food, or a tube of Preparation H, or the *National Enquirer*. Anyway, what does embarrassment matter when AIDS is so serious?

One of the best pointers I can give you about buying condoms is that you should always buy more condoms than you think you will need. They're cheap so you can keep plenty on hand. Since you cannot reuse them, you always need new ones. The more you have, the more sex you can have, and the more you have the easier it will be to throw them away if you unroll one improperly, or for some other reason have trouble putting it on. Also, you will never have to interrupt sex to run out in the cold to the drugstore at 3 A.M. if you just used your last condom.

Storing Condoms

You should store condoms in a place where the package will not get wet, and where it is not cooler than 50 degrees or hotter than 90 degrees. That means you should never store them in a car or glove compartment, and only put them in your wallet or purse when you are carrying them for a couple of hours.

If you want to have mindblowing sex with condoms, then try not to let them interrupt the spontaneity of sex any more than is absolutely necessary. That's why it's great to keep them where you will need them. For most people, a logical place to keep them is on the night table next to the bed, or in a small box under the bed. Sometimes, just before sex, you can slip one or two under the pillow or under the mattress within easy reach. If you like to have sex in lots of different places, then you can keep condoms in every room of the house. You can slip some under the sofa if you like to do it on the floor. As long as you don't get them too close to the stove, you can keep them in a cabinet in the kitchen, for when you really start cooking. If you very carefully put them in a Ziploc bag, then inside a sealed soap dish, you can even keep them in the shower. (Just remember to throw them away if you don't use them in a day or so, because the bathroom can get hot and humid.) It's also a good idea to keep them near the front door of the house, so you remember to take them with you if you have sex around town. If you always remember to bring them with you, then you can have condom-sex spontaneously anywhere! Remember that if you put them in your wallet or purse, put in new one every day or so, since it may be hot in there.

> **Don't be a fool; protect your jewel**

Most condoms have an expiration date stamped on the package. Don't be cheap. Throw them away after this date. If a condom contains spermicide, it may only be good for about a year. If it does not contain spermicide, it should last about three to five years.

How to Choose Condoms

When you go into any drugstore, you'll find almost as many varieties of condoms as varieties of hair products. Part of the thrill of using condoms is that you can experiment or change brands to add variety to sex. You could even say to a lover some night, "Hey, let's buy ten kinds of condoms and try them all tonight and see if we can feel the difference." If you are in between sexual partners and you just want to investigate condoms for the fun of it and for future use, you can have a great time buying a whole bunch of kinds and opening the packages and comparing them. You can buy the Magnum or Maxx condoms for larger size penises and hold one up to a regular size one to find out for yourself what the big deal is. Or you could buy those ribbed or studded condoms, and test it on yourself to see if you can tell the difference.

What's also great about all of this condom variety is that you can try all different kinds until you find one that you like best. If you set out on your quest for your perfect condoms, I expect that you will find your #1 favorite kind. Don't just stick with using the first brand you ever used in your life because it's the only one you've ever used. If you try some other kinds, you may find that there is one out there that feels more comfortable to

> **Cover your snake if you're on the make**

you. When I hear people complaining to me that condoms don't feel good, often it's because they are using one that is the wrong size or thickness for them.

▼ ▼

Finding the condom that is right for you is a big step toward having mindblowing sex with condoms.

▲ ▲

All condoms are not created equal. To choose the best condoms for *you,* you need to evaluate their differences and try them on your own body. Here are the differences:

Packaging: Even before you begin to explore the difference in condoms, you need to take a look at the packaging to determine whether a condom will be the most appropriate one for you. Condoms generally come in square or rectangular foil or plastic packages and are packaged inside a small, thin cardboard box. The most effective condoms are those that have not been exposed to air or to light. When they are packaged in a box, this initially protects them from light and air. But once you get them home and take them out of the box (or if you buy them individually), the packaging must protect them. Plastic packages that are clear, allowing you to see the condom inside, also allow in light that could damage the condom. The package should be completely sealed so that air doesn't affect the condom. You'll find that some packages are not sealed well, like the Gold Circle metal condom packages that look like the package for chocolate coins. These are great for playing dreidel at Hanukkah, but you'll notice how easily the condom can slip out of the package. It might have been exposed to air, so that's not good to use for sex. (Incidentally this same company does make a round *plastic* package that seals in the condoms fine.) Therefore, my recommendation is to get the most effective type of packaging: foil or opaque plastic, sealed in a box.

Receptacle tip: When a man ejaculates into a condom, the semen needs someplace to go. That's why most condoms have a "receptacle tip," a tiny nipple-shaped end on the condom. (When you roll on a condom, you must make sure that all of the air is out of the end of the condom, so the semen can go there. More on this later.) If a condom does not have this receptacle tip, you must leave ¼ inch of room at the end of the condom as you roll it on the penis. My feeling is, if you have to leave room at the end of the condom because it doesn't have a receptacle tip, then why bother getting any kind other than receptacle tip condoms? It just saves time and effort. If you find a condom that you love, except that it doesn't have the receptacle tip, then perhaps you should use it and leave room at the tip. Otherwise, I recommend getting the ones with the tip already there.

Thickness: Sometimes the claims about a condom's thickness or thinness are exaggerated, since they are all fairly similar in this category; yet I still recommend that you try the variety to feel the differences. If you want condoms to feel as unobtrusive as possible, then try the condoms labeled "thin" or "extra sensitive." Buy the thicker "extra strength" condoms if you like to have very rough sex, or if you have a problem with premature ejaculation, or you often find that condoms break when you use them, or if you have a sexually transmitted disease.

Size: For some people this is a difficult issue to address honestly. Many men (and more than a few women) are obsessed with penis size. To find condoms that work for you, you have to be realistic. If you can be honest with yourself about the size of your penis then you will have an easier time wearing condoms. So once you assess your (or your partner's) penis size, you can pick the best fit. Some people like tight-fitting condoms, other people like looser-fitting condoms. For larger size penises, you might like the larger size condoms, such as Magnum, Trojen-Enz Large, and Maxx. Most of these are longer and larger around the

> **No cover wang, no get bang**

head of the penis than average condoms. There is a new variety of condoms called Pleasure Plus that has a baggy sack of latex at the head of the condom, so it provides a very loose fit around the head of the penis. Men who have large penises often like the looser feel that these condoms have at the head; yet sometimes couples find that the excess latex is just inconvenient. For men with penises that are smaller or who like a tight fitting condom, they might want to try Snugger. Also, all brands of Japanese condoms are made slightly smaller (no joke!). If a man has a problem with condoms slipping off during sex, the tighter ones are good to use. Also, if a man wants to stay harder longer, tighter condoms may help. Or he could try wearing two tight condoms at once, a.k.a. "double-bagging it." (It's like using a cockring, only not quite as kinky—or kinkier, depending how you look at it.)

Color: If you like sex to be as natural as it can be, then you'll like the clear, transparent condoms. If you'd like a little wild, goofy variety, then you'd like assorted colored condoms. You can buy them in red, green, blue, and yellow. You could be festive and use red for Valentine's Day, green for St. Patrick's Day, blue for the Fourth of July, and yellow for—well, maybe if there's a war. Be creative. There are also black condoms, although they are more difficult to find than your primary color condoms. If you like sex to seem clinical, then buy the ones that are opaque white (to me they look like kitchen garbage bags).

Texture: There are condoms that have slightly raised bumps, called studded condoms, or slightly raised lines, called ribbed condoms. Most of the time the packages for these condoms say something like, "For Her Pleasure." They make it sound like teensy tiny raised ribs on a condom will give a woman a better orgasm. The truth is that most woman cannot feel the ribs or bumps on the latex, since women do not have many nerve endings in the inner two-thirds of their vagina. Also, since most women have orgasms from their clitoris, the texture of the condom would have no effect anyway. Some men report that if they turn the ribbed condoms inside out then they can feel the raised lines on their penis. If a guy tries this, he must be *very* careful that the condom doesn't slip off during sex, since condoms are not designed to be worn inside out. I don't recommend turning condoms inside out for men. You may want to try textured condoms just out of curiosity.

Taste and smell: There are a few brands of specially flavored condoms, like mint flavored, that are made primarily for use in oral sex and are also FDA approved for HIV and pregnancy protection during intercourse. Most regular condoms have at least some mild flavor or scent, even if it's just a hint of latex. If you just use the condom for intercourse and not for oral sex, then the taste or smell usually won't matter much. If you use it for oral sex, then it matters more. Lubricated condoms taste like the particular lubricant. Sometimes the lubricants (especially nonoxynol-9 spermicide) can make your tongue feel fuzzy, which is quite a distraction during sex, and often makes kissing taste disgusting. Unlubricated condoms are covered in a slight bit of powder; some people also dislike their taste. It's best to experiment to see which have almost no odor or taste, or an odor or taste that appeals. Or you can wipe off whatever powder or lubricant you don't like and add a flavor you do like. I'll tell you more about this in the later sections "Lube Your Tube" and "Tastier Safer Sex."

Lubrication/spermicide: Many condoms come with a small bit of lubrication on the outside. The lubricant that helps kill sperm and also helps kill the HIV virus is called nonoxynol-9. There are other lubricants, such as SK 70, that help kill sperm but are not effective against viruses. I recommend that if you are going to buy a lubricated condom, you might as well get the type of lubricant that will help kill HIV—the nonoxynol-9 spermicidal lubricant.

A few words about novelty condoms: There are many types of condoms that are just meant to be joke gifts and are not to be used for sex. Glow-in-the-dark condoms, which were made popular after a funny scene with them in the 1989 movie *Skin Deep,* are not FDA approved and are not meant for sex. Some of the glow-in-the-dark condoms contain phosphorescent dyes that can be harmful. Condoms that have writing on the latex are not FDA approved. Some flavored condoms, like chocolate flavored, are not FDA approved but may be OK for oral sex. Basically if you're unsure of whether a novelty condom is effective, read the label. According to the law, if a condom is not FDA approved, the statement "For novelty use only" must be printed on the label. Also, use "condom sense": if someone gives you a fortune cookie and inside is a condom, don't trust it for real protection.

A few words about lambskin condoms: Do not use these condoms for disease protection. The FDA has only approved lambskin condoms for protection against pregnancy. FDA studies have found that there are tiny pores in lambskin condoms that the HIV virus can pass through. Lambskin condoms are made from the intestinal lining of a lamb. Some people like using lambskin condoms more than latex, saying that they feel more natural and less like using a condom. Other people dislike lambskin condoms because they think that the condoms smell like rancid lamb chops, are sticky, and don't stretch much. In any case, you should not be using them if the reason you're using condoms is to prevent transmitting disease.

Lube Your Tube

Any kind of water-based lubricant can be used on condoms. You cannot use any oil-based lubricant with a condom, since in about a minute it will destroy the condom. If you want to see this for yourself, blow up a condom like a balloon, then rub some baby oil on it. In a minute or so, it will explode! Some of the oil-based lubricants that you must *never* use with condoms are: baby oil, mineral oil, suntan lotion, petroleum jelly (like Vaseline), cold cream, any variety of hand lotion, vegetable oil, shortening (like Crisco), and butter. Sorry, if you're using a condom you cannot reenact the butter scene from *Last Tango in Paris*!

Using lubricants with condoms is important. If you put a small drop of lubricant inside the condom, it makes the condom more comfortable for the man. Putting lubricant on the outside of the condom decreases the chance that the condom could break. This helps even if your partner is well lubricated.

Also, it is important to keep a supply of nonoxynol-9 spermicidal foam or lubricant, because if the condom breaks, this spermicide should be put inside the vagina (or anus).

One terrific water-based lubricant is saliva. It's sexy, it's free, and between the two of you there is usually a plentiful supply. There are lots of water-based lubricants that you can buy that are made for sex. Some

If you go into heat, package your meat

have spermicide and some do not. There are some that are on the sticky side, like KY Jelly and Gynol II. There are others that are not quite as sticky, like ForePlay, PrePair, and Elbow Grease. Then there are some that are designed to feel slick and slippery: Astroglide, Probe, and Wet. I usually recommend Astroglide, since many women report that it feels the most like natural vaginal lubrication, and many men report that it lasts the longest without evaporating or getting too gooey. However, you really need to try several brands to find out what you like best. There are many, many brands. You can find the greatest variety at adult/sex stores or direct mail catalogues, but some drugstores have a good selection, too.

Condom Communication

Now that you have them and you have decided that you are committed to using them, when and how should you bring up the topic of condoms to a new lover? What should you say? Ideally the best time to talk about condoms is as soon as you decide you will be having sex with someone. Don't wait until your clothes are off to talk about it. It's best to talk about it when it's a seemingly "nonsexual time," such as in the afternoon, while sitting on the sofa, or driving in a car. The best times are when you have privacy and time and are not fooling around or about to have sex.

You may want to start with an opening line like one of these:

> "I'm a little nervous about bringing this up, but do you have any condoms or should we buy some before we go back to your place?"

> "I was in the drugstore today and I couldn't believe how many brands of condoms they had. What kind of condoms do you use?"

> "I don't want to have sex right this second, but I know we're getting to that point and I want to make sure you know I always use condoms."

If you don't get around to talking about condoms until the heat of the moment, the best thing to say is often, very simply, "Let's use condoms." That expression works really well, because you are making it sound like something you are doing together. (That's also why you should carry them with you.)

If you don't use condoms from the beginning of a relationship it may be difficult to ask your partner to use them because then your partner may suspect you are cheating. In this case, just explain that you regret not using them before and you want to change now. If your partner resists, take a firm stand. Say something like, "Look, it was a mistake not to use them last time, but I just can't enjoy sex when I'm worried about AIDS or pregnancy. It's not a big deal. I'll make the condoms feel good for you. Let's use them, okay?"

When you make the decision to use condoms, stick to it. Don't cave in to lines like, "Just this once we won't. Once can't hurt." Or when a penis is right outside a vagina (when it is very easy for it to slide in), one frequently used line is, "Let's just put it in for a second."

Don't go for it! Do not let yourself be susceptible to the other lines that people will use when they don't want to use condoms. If someone tells you that he or she loves you, so you don't need to use condoms, remind yourself and your partner that the difference between AIDS and love is that AIDS lasts forever. Tell your lover that to you, love also means respect and part of that is respecting that condoms make you feel more comfortable during sex. If a man says that he'll lose his erection if you use condoms, then tell him that it's OK if he loses his erection because you'll help him get it back up. If the woman says she's on the pill so she doesn't have to use condoms, remind her that pills don't prevent her from getting diseases

> **If you're not going to sack it, go home and whack it**

that you might not even know that you have. It's really sad when you are trying to convince a partner to use condoms with you and they get offended and say things like, "I'm not diseased! I can't believe that you could even think that I have AIDS. Don't you trust me?" Or they may think that it means that you have a disease if you want to use them. First explain your reasons for wanting to use condoms: it makes you feel safer and therefore sexually freer, and so on. Then tell them all the fun things that you can do with condoms, which I will get into more in this chapter.

▼ ▼

Be positive and enticing if you have to convince a lover to use condoms.

▲ ▲

If you can't convince your partner to use condoms, you could get confrontational, by saying something like, "Why are you being such a jerk! I thought you cared how I felt. I thought you cared about helping me enjoy sex." No matter what, be strong about your choice to use condoms and stick with it. If you want more advice on this topic, read the later section "What if My Partner Still Doesn't Want to Use Condoms?"

How to Use a Condom

So, now that you know how to choose condoms and how to ask a partner to use them, I think it's time I review how to put them on. One pointer: If you are drunk or on drugs, it's much more difficult to put a condom on properly and sometimes difficult to stick to your decision to use them. Try not to mix too much alcohol or drugs with condoms. (But if you are tanked and intent on having sex, try your best to concentrate on putting it on properly.)

To become proficient at condom use, men should practice when they masturbate. Practice on fruits, vegetables, or dildos if you are a woman. If you practice a lot, you may even get to be so familiar with the proper way to put on a condom that you could do it in the dark!

1. The first step in using a condom is opening the package with your hands. Be careful not to use your fingernails, and never use your teeth, which can tear the latex. Do not unroll the condom yet.
2. Once you take it out of the package, you need to see which way the rim of the condom is rolled. You can see

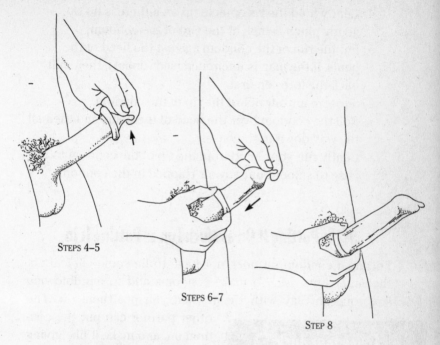

Steps 4–5

Steps 6–7

Step 8

which way the rim will roll by gently moving it a tiny bit with your fingers. Be sure not to unroll it; just move it enough to see where it would roll. Hold the condom so it will roll down. This is very important, because if you try to unroll the condom on the penis and it doesn't go, because it is inside out, then you will probably get semen from the precum on the end of the condom—the end that is supposed to be on the outside. Since this defeats the whole purpose of the condom, you'll have to toss it and unwrap a new one.

3. Next put a small drop of water-based lubricant inside the condom, near the tip, but not clogging the receptacle end. This is going to make the condom feel better, more sensitive against the penis. If you've only tried dry condoms, you'll realize that there's a big difference in sensation when you use a little lubricant.

4. Gently hold the receptacle tip or, if there is no tip, gently pinch ¼ inch at the end of the condom.
5. Put the rim of the condom against the head of the penis. If the man is uncircumcised (uncut), then pull back the foreskin first.
6. Squeeze any air out of the tip of the condom.
7. Roll the condom over the head of the penis and then all the way down to the base.
8. Gently run your hand from the tip of the condom to the base to smooth out any air trapped in the condom.

Make Putting It On as Much Fun as Putting It In

Putting a condom on does not have to be some clinical act that interrupts sex. To make condoms add to mindblowing sex you can play with them when you put them on. The other partner can put the condom on, and make it like giving a hand job. The other partner can also put the condom on using the mouth. Here's how: Place the condom in your mouth, holding the tip with your lips. Use your lips to gently squeeze the air out of the end of the condom. Then, without letting your teeth touch the condom, and keeping your mouth in an "O" shape, use your lips to push the condom over the head of the penis and all the way down the shaft. Be very careful not to tear the condom with your teeth. Practice on a banana and you'll perfect this technique in no time.

> Cover your duck before you fuck

How to Take the Condom Off

Soon after the man ejaculates, when the penis is still hard, hold the base of the condom while pulling out the penis with the condom on it. Take the condom off carefully so the semen does not spill out. Then throw the condom away. If you knot the semen-filled condom before you throw it away it won't leak or smell in the trash. You could also wrap it in a tissue before you toss it, to be extra discreet. Don't flush it down the toilet because it's bad for plumbing. And don't let the dog get a hold of it because the dog may choke on it.

If you and your partner are going to be touching each other any more after this, then make sure to wash your hands.

How to Prevent Condom Breakage

When used properly, condoms will rarely break. Don't believe me? Try stretching a condom to see how much abuse it can take. You'll find that they are so strong that you can stretch them over your entire arm, or even over your head!

If condoms break during sex, then you are doing something wrong. Here's how to prevent breakage:

- ▶ Do not unroll the condom before you roll it on the penis. If you unroll it first, then try to pull and stretch the condom over the penis, it may break.
- ▶ Add water-based (never *oil*-based) lubricant to the outside of the condom before sex. If the condom gets too dry the friction could cause it to tear.
- ▶ Be careful that your fingernails don't rip the condom while you are putting it on.
- ▶ Make sure you squeeze out the air when you are putting the condom on.
- ▶ Check to make sure that the condom is not breaking during sex by feeling it or by pulling out and looking at it.
- ▶ Change the condom if it's an extra long session of sex. Too much friction during marathon sex can dry it out and wear it out.

▸ Store the condoms properly in a dry place between 50 degrees and 90 degrees Fahrenheit.

▸ Change brands if your condoms often break.

What if the Condom Breaks During Sex?

If a condom breaks and you notice it during intercourse, but before ejaculation, pull out, dry off a little, and put on a new condom. You can add some nonoxynol-9 spermicide inside the vagina (or anus). If the condom breaks *after* ejaculation, first of all, *do not douche.* Douching in the vagina (or anus) after a man ejaculates inside will tear the lining and will cause the semen to be pushed further inside, making disease transmission or pregnancy more likely. What you can do is apply nonoxynol-9 spermicide foam inside and around the vagina (or anus). The partner who ejaculated should gently wash his penis with soap and water and urinate to clear the urethra of any microorganisms. This could help him from contracting anything that may have gotten on his penis when the condom broke.

Safer Oral Sex on a Woman

As I discussed earlier, generally the risk of getting HIV from having oral sex on a woman is not a tremendous risk. However, if the woman is menstruating, there is a bigger risk. If you want to have totally safe oral sex on a woman, you should use a piece of latex called a dental dam. A dental dam is a six-inch square of latex used by dentists to protect the gums and face during oral surgery. The biggest problem with dental dams isn't using them properly, it's finding them! I always need to bring some along to show people in my sex education lectures, because so few people have ever seen them. I've never seen them at drugstores, although I have sometimes seen them at adult/sex stores or health centers. I always buy them at a dental supply store, and my dentist is always willing to give them to me. However, for people who are not sex educators, it's a little embarrassing to ask your dentist for a sexual device, and who's got the time to track down a dental supply store in your neighborhood?

What can you use as an alternative to a dental dam? First, you can adapt a rolled condom by cutting from the outer edge to the center tip. This will give you a small sheet of latex; use an extra large condom for a slightly larger sheet. You can hold this sheet of latex over the vulva, or even better, you can attach the cut condom to a small embroidery hoop, which you can find at any crafts store.

Does that mean that if you want total protection during oral sex on a women you have to go to a crafts store or a dental supply store? No, you could also go to a supermarket. You can use plastic wrap, like Saran Wrap, to make the piece as big as you want. It's easy to get, cheap, and plentiful. The problem is that it still is not known if HIV can penetrate some kinds of plastic. Most reports state that plastic wrap is thick enough so that the HIV virus cannot get through. However, there is still some debate over whether microwavable plastic wrap is better for oral sex, or whether you should not use microwavable plastic because it may have tiny pores in it that the virus can pass through. It seems logical just to avoid the microwavable kind, because no one seems to know for sure. Also, you could take one piece of plastic wrap, put spermicide on it, then cover it with a second piece of plastic to be extra, extra safe.

Tastier Safer Sex

I know what you're thinking, who wants to taste latex during sex? Well, you don't have to. If you are going to have oral sex on a man who has a condom on, it helps to add non-oil-based "condom-ents" after you've rolled the condom on the erect penis. Smear on some honey and try to suck it off the condom; it's sticky, but bee-licious. Drizzle on some chocolate syrup and snarf down your sexual fudgsicle. Spread some Smuckers grape on the condom, and you'll enjoy a penis and jelly suckwich. You could spray whipped cream all over the condom, put a cherry on top, and lap away your cream-dream penis sundae. It'll look so good he'll wish he could eat it himself.

If you're gonna bean her, cover your weiner

You could also try to use food for oral sex on top of the plastic or latex barrier if you perform oral sex on a woman; however, because people usually have a hard enough time getting the latex or plastic to stay down against her vulva, I do not recommend this. If you use the embroidery hoop technique, perhaps you can find a way to make that ice-cream sundae on the hoop. Experiment and be creative.

Some More Funny Ways to Use Condoms

To add to the fun of using condoms, you can make up games or role plays. These things may sound too silly or juvenile for you, yet you never know if the silliness of them could make a truly unique, funny, memorable experience. Just for fun, you can pretend that you are a condom salesperson and your lover is buying condoms; then you seduce each other. You can play doctor and pretend

If you think she's spunky, cover your monkey

that you have to examine the penis, then put a condom on it and have sex. You can pretend that you are a French maid, dusting and cleaning, and putting on the condom, then having sex. You can tie up your partner (with his consent, of course), then put his penis in bondage by putting a condom on it. Or you can pretend that you are a sex educator and are instructing your lover on how to use a condom.

Reality: The Condoms for Women

Reality, the new condom for women, is designed to line the inside of a woman's vagina to provide a barrier protection inside so semen cannot get inside the vagina and vaginal secretions do not come in contact with the penis. If a woman uses Reality the man does not have to wear a condom. Research on the condom for women has found that sperm, the HIV virus, and all other known STD's cannot pass through the condom for women. Therefore, if used properly, it is fairly effective in preventing pregnancy and the spread of STD's, including AIDS. However, the Centers for Disease Control has not yet said whether the condom for women is as effective as the regular male, latex condom for preventing HIV transmission.

Reality is available in most drugstores. The condom for women is a loose-fitting plastic (polyurethane) sheath that is about three inches wide and five inches long with two flexible plastic rings, one at each end. One ring lies inside at the closed end of the sheath and serves as an insertion mechanism and internal anchor. The other ring forms the external edge of the sheath and remains outside the vagina after insertion. Reality is inserted inside a woman's vagina just prior to sex. She inserts it as she would insert a diaphragm; once placed inside the vagina, the inside ring holds the sheath behind the pubic bone. The plastic sheath covers the cervix, and then spreads out against the walls of the vagina. The plastic actually adheres to the walls of the vagina, so it does not move around when the man inserts his penis. The outer ring protects the labia and external vulva, so that the base of the penis is not in contact during intercourse. This provides broader coverage than the regular male condom, helping to prevent the spread of STD's that can occur on the outside of the vulva or on the base of the penis, such as genital warts and herpes.

There are both advantages and disadvantages to using the condom for women. The plastic of the condom for women is stronger and thicker than the latex of the male condom. It reportedly does not decrease a woman's sensitivity during sex, since the vagina has very few nerves inside. Also, the plastic is resistant to oils, so the couple can use a broader range of lubricants. Because the outer ring hangs outside the vagina, some people find that it causes self-consciousness or discomfort. Yet other women find that it gives them extra pleasure, since the outer ring may rub against the clitoris during intercourse. The main advantage is that the condom for women gives couples an alternative to using regular condoms.

> **Guard your box before he knocks**

What if My Partner Still Doesn't Want to Use Condoms?

If your partner does not want to use condoms, first try the communication techniques that I discussed earlier, such as trying to persuade your partner by saying it will make you feel safer and freer during sex, or enticing your partner by saying something sexy like you can put the condom on him using your mouth. Then, if your partner still won't use condoms, you have to decide if you are going to compromise your values and risk your health or your life. You're an adult, and by now you understand the consequences of your actions.

If *you* are committed to using condoms, but nothing will convince your partner to use them with you, you have five choices:

1. You may decide not to have intercourse and just engage in other kinds of safer sex like touching, mutual masturbation, or safer oral sex.

2. You could get your partner to agree to letting you use the female condom instead. If used properly, it provides good protection.

3. You could get tested for HIV and convince your partner to get tested; then use condoms together for six months; then get tested again, and if you are both negative the second time, *and you are 110 percent positive that you can trust him*, then you could decide to stop using condoms. I probably shouldn't make this sound like so much of an option, but if you really want to take the risk of having sex without condoms, it's your choice.

4. You could risk getting HIV or another STD by having sex without condoms and without having your partner and yourself get tested for HIV. Remember, I'm still advising you never to have sex without condoms. However, it's not my life, it's yours. If you choose to have sex without condoms, I think you are making a poor choice.

As a sex educator, I must be responsible by telling you that if you choose not to use condoms for vaginal intercourse, you may be able to *slightly* reduce the risk of becoming HIV infected by using nonoxynol-9 spermicide with a diaphragm or cervical cap. Using spermicide alone is not a true method (and a very poor method) of HIV prevention, but I am going to let you in on it, only because if you were planning on using nothing, this is better than nothing. *This is not a method that is approved by the Centers for Disease Control, and this is not a method that I endorse for HIV prevention.* If your partner is HIV-positive, and this is your only protection, then you are at great risk for becoming infected with HIV.

The studies that were done on nonoxynol-9 were only done in laboratories. While in the test tubes nonoxynol-9 killed the HIV virus, it probably does not work as well in the vagina. Either the HIV could get into the bloodstream before it hits the spermicide, or there may not be enough spermicide if the man ejaculates a lot. You are taking a big risk that you could contract HIV if you only use spermicide and do not use condoms. Yet in theory the spermicide may help kill the virus, and if you use a diaphragm or cervical cap it may help protect the most fragile parts of your reproductive organs located beyond the cervix.

If you were planning on taking the stupid risk of having sex without condoms, this is what you can do for at least a tiny bit of protection. Insert either a diaphragm or a cervical cap inside your vagina. Then insert two applications of additional nonoxynol-9 spermicide foam just prior to vaginal penetration. Also, if the man withdraws before he comes, this can cut down on some risks. Before you consider having sex without condoms, consider your next choice.

5. Dump your partner. If your partner will not use condoms and you want to, you could break up and never have sex with him or her. A very important thing to keep in mind if you are ever in a relationship where you partner does not want to use condoms is that *you deserve better*. Now, I know I'm getting preachy, but I feel really strongly about people being able to respect each other's values. You must realize that if you want to use condoms and your partner refuses to use condoms it means only one thing: your partner is not compatible with you. Your values do not match. Your partner does not care if you feel uncomfortable fighting or begging to use condoms. He or she does not care if you'll feel angry or scared after sex if you give in. He or she is not respecting your very real fear of contracting AIDS. In fact, he or she probably doesn't care much about himself or herself if he or

she is taking the risk of sex without condoms. I think that it's a terrible choice to choose to be with people who don't care about you or about themselves. You deserve better. You can and will find partners who will respect your values and who are willing to use condoms every time.

Can a Committed Couple Ever Stop Using Condoms?

In our parents' generation, when someone said that they were saving themselves for marriage it meant only one thing—they were going to stay virgins until marriage. Today "saving yourself for marriage" might mean waiting until you are married or engaged to stop using condoms! But is it OK to stop using condoms if you have a steady relationship? I'm not talking about a situation in which one of you objects to condoms; I'm talking about if you both want to stop using them in a mutually monogamous relationship.

The reality is that even if both you and your partner test negative for HIV, your partner may cheat on you and contract an STD or HIV from another person, so you should always use condoms. Yet the reality of sex in the real world for real people is also that many people don't want to "save themselves for marriage." Despite the risk that a partner would cheat, they still want to stop using condoms as soon as possible.

If you and your partner both insist on not using condoms, here's how to properly deal with getting tested. You and your partner can go to an HIV testing center and get tested for HIV. Even if you both test negative at that point, you must still use condoms for six more months, because the virus has a window period of up to six months from your last possible exposure until it is visible in the test. What this means is that if you are exposed to HIV today, an HIV test may not register it for up to six months. If you and your partner both retest negative after six months, then this means that you two cannot pass HIV to each other, because you do not have it. If you are both *absolutely sure* that you can trust that neither of you will cheat on each other, then you can stop using condoms.

▼ ▼ ▼ ▼ ▼ ▼ ▼ ▼ ▼ ▼ ▼ ▼ ▼ ▼ ▼ ▼ ▼ ▼ ▼

You both need to be disease free, monogamous, and of unquestionable integrity in order to stop using condoms.

▲ ▲ ▲ ▲ ▲ ▲ ▲ ▲ ▲ ▲ ▲ ▲ ▲ ▲ ▲ ▲ ▲ ▲ ▲

If one of you cheats, the whole process of getting tested and using condoms for six months and getting retested should be repeated to be sure you are still uninfected. Read chapter 10 for details on how to get tested and what the test results mean.

For Mindblowing Sex, Don't Avoid Condoms—Enjoy Them

AIDS is a fact of life. Condoms are a fact of life. Most people who don't want to use condoms simply don't know how to enjoy them. That's another fact of life. Don't try to find a way to avoid using condoms. Enjoy not taking unnecessary risks with your life. Experiment with condoms, and learn

Love me, love my condom

to have fun with them. The better you feel about condoms the better they will work for you. Once you discover how to have mindblowing sex with condoms, then you can move on to experimenting with even more variety and more pleasure and more freedom in your sex life.

CHAPTER 7

Coming to Your Senses
Using All Five Senses to Enhance Sex

Tune In, Turn On

Seen the latest Victoria's Secret catalogue? Was it a turn-on? Have you ever walked past a stranger who was wearing your favorite perfume and thought, "How could I get her attention?" Or have you ever gotten aroused by hearing a song that reminded you of a past lover?

Too often people think that orgasm is the whole point of sex so they just do a lot of rubbing and thrusting. Don't get me wrong—orgasm is great. In fact, orgasm *is* a very good point, but it is not *the* point. If you learn to stimulate and be aware of all five senses, then your pleasure will be greatly enriched. This chapter discusses methods to tap in to your mind and all five of your senses and provides examples of erotic stimuli for each sense. Sex can totally blow your mind if you use all of your senses.

Look Out!

Too many people keep their eyes clamped shut during sex. Sometimes darkness or closed eyes can make sex exciting because it can heighten all your other senses, yet often blocking out sight during sex detracts from the full sexual experience. To get the full experience of sex, try opening your eyes sometime and watching the action. Steve, twenty-nine, explains why he likes to have sex with the lights on and his eyes open: "It's more personal, more intriguing, and more vulnerable, because you can't hide your emotions and expressions. It's more honest." Twenty-five-year-old Cathy says, "I feel more connected when I can look in the guy's eyes. It makes me more into sex when I can see what's happening and see his expressions."

Mary, twenty-six, has a different explanation for her preference for having sex with her eyes open and the lights on: "I like a guy to see my great tits when we're doing it." Mary would probably be compatible with John, twenty-four, who says, "I like to see a woman's ass slap against me when I take her from behind. It's never as good in the dark. I come much harder when I see myself going into her, or when I see her tits or ass."

If you get really turned on by looking at each other during sex, and you are sure you can trust each other, you can take this a step further and photograph yourselves. If you want to turn each other on when you are not together, try taking Polaroid photographs of each other. (Use instant, not regular pictures, so the person in the developing store doesn't get to sneak a peak.) You can have fun with this, pretending one of you is modeling for *Playboy* or *Playgirl*, while the other is snapping away and encouraging more erotic poses. Also, if you both agree, you can try videotaping your sexual experience, but you may be disappointed with what you see when you watch the videotape. Twenty-eight-year-old Andy said,

"Me and an old girlfriend of mine videotaped when we had sex. It was horrible. Our bodies looked gross. Since we put the camera on a tripod, it shot one angle of us up from behind. It looked nothing like we thought it would—nothing like real sex movies, where the camera moves around and gets the good angles."

When you videotape or photograph a sexual experience, be sure that you can trust your partner enough to let you decide what to do with the end results. You can erase the tape afterward or destroy the photos, if you don't want to take the risk of having them around. If you keep them, you are risking that someday somebody, maybe even your next lover or the other person's new lover, might come across your performance. On the odd chance that you are ever planning to be famous, you would also have to worry that it may end up on—*Shoom*—*A Current Affair,* like the Tonya Harding video of her stripping out of her wedding dress, or that it would be sold underground and be shown ad nauseam on cable, like the infamous Rob Lowe sex video. In any case, make sure that you and your partner agree on the fate of your video or photos before you shoot them.

Besides preserving the visual experience of sex, you can enhance the visual arousal of the actual sex by putting variation into what you see during sex. Try playing with the lighting. Try doing it in bright daylight or with a bright lamp on. Put a colored light bulb in the lamp for an exciting change. Light a candle or several candles—candlelight softens lines and bulges, so everything looks sexy while you are cloaked in the soothing light.

You can also add to the visual experience by putting variety in the things you wear before or during sex. Why not rebel against this generation where everybody shops at the Gap and go for some sexy tried-and-trued visual stimulation? If you are a woman, you can pick any of the thousands of types of lingerie, from trampy corsets and garter belts and stockings to pantyhose or thigh highs to "fuck me" high heels to romantic little silk nighties to vampy clingy lycra, rubber, or leather clothes that reveal your shape but not your skin to sequin pasties with tassels to a simple sexy new bra and matching panties. You can experiment with different cuts and colors of bras and underwear. Try a push-up bra (such as the overpublicized Wonderbra) to give yourself some sexy cleavage. Try a bra that is one size too small and check out that cleavage! (True, it's not exactly comfortable, but if it gets your partner hot, you'll be taking it off in a short time anyway.) You can vary your underwear styles and colors, from a plain, boxy white cotton undie to a high-cut bikini panty that has a peek-through lace window, or a G-string (even if *you* don't like your ass, he would probably love to see it). Day-to-day, if you have one steady lover, it can be a great erotic thrill to wear a different color bra and matching panties every time you see each other undress.

If you want to get more ideas on what kind of sexy underwear to wear, you can browse in a department store lingerie section or in any lingerie store. Also, you can check out the slutty-looking outfits in magazines like *Penthouse* or *Hustler*, or look at a variety of sexy and romantic lingerie in the Victoria's Secret catalogue (you can buy from any store, and just use the magazines or catalogues for ideas).

If you are a guy, and are still only wearing white briefs or cotton boxers that have your college emblem on them, then it's time to add some seriously sexy underwear to your wardrobe. Try silk boxers, colored briefs, mesh briefs, or high-cut briefs that have a sexy feel, tight fit, show off your butt, and make your bulge stand out. Check out the Calvin Klein underwear packages, or magazines like *Playgirl* or *Honcho* or the International Male catalogue for more ideas. You could look distinguished in your new silk boxers, or like a funky Marky-Mark stud in your new sexy briefs.

Often men don't find sexy underwear comfortable, especially if they are accustomed to the style they've been wearing for years. Kramer (Michael Richards) on *Seinfeld* explained this well when he said, "I wore boxers for about a month, but I couldn't stick with it. I need the secure packaging of Jockeys. My boys need a house!" Yet men should remember: you do not need to wear sexy underwear every minute; you can just wear them for sexy visual variety when you want to turn on your lover.

You can get more into the idea of clothes affecting the look of sex by putting on a sexy strip show for your lover. Strip by wearing a usual outfit on the outside, and then tantalizingly revealing the sexy outfit under that, then taking it all off. Before you start, put on some sexy music that you can move to. Seat your lover down to watch your show. Move your body to the beat. Tease and turn on your lover. Drop a shoulder strap, then pull it back up. Unbutton your shirt, but leave it on a little longer. Pull off your pants, and reveal your sexy underwear, but then zip back up again, until you finally start taking it all off. Touch your lover a little during your strip, but don't let your lover touch you. Once you strip all your clothes off, you can undress your lover and then ultimately have hot contact skin-to-skin. For more on how to strip check out some classic movie strip scenes, like Kim Basinger stripping to "You Can Leave Your Hat On" in *9½ Weeks* or Jamie Lee Curtis stripping for Arnold Schwarzenegger in *True Lies* or the "schoolgirl" strip club scenes from *Exotica*.

For another erotic twist, you could have sex wearing a mask. You could wear any type of Halloween mask, from Bart Simpson to O. J. Simpson. Or you could wear a mask made from feathers or leather. It's an interesting way to change what your partner sees during sex. You can try having sex wearing any type of costume, perhaps the classic French maid's costume, nurse's costume, or Superman costume.

For another sensory variation, try having sex when you

both keep your clothes on, only unzipping where you need to in order to have the vulva and penis exposed. Or take off all your clothes, but have your lover keep all of his or her clothing on.

Consider enhancing the space where you have sex. You can redecorate your bedroom to make the visual experience more powerful. Make the bedroom an exiting place to have sex. Add romance with a vase of fresh flowers, candles, big pillows, champagne glasses, or anything that makes you feel sexy. Strategically placed mirrors are amazing in the bedroom! If you are with a steady lover, it may add to the intimacy to display some of the memorabilia from your relationship: photos of yourself as a couple, the first thing your lover ever gave you, the first piece of sexy lingerie you ever wore for your lover, matches from the first place you ever had dinner together. Get rid of ugliness in the bedroom that could detract from the erotic experience. Don't dump the pile of dirty laundry on the chair. Take down pictures of friends or family so they aren't staring at you when you are having wild, mad sex. Get that TV out of the bedroom, or at least keep the tube turned off, unless you find it erotic to have Beavis and Butthead watching you naked.

Of course, the bedroom isn't the only place where people are pulsating in passion. If you completely change the setting of sex, then you can add to the visual experience. The setting for sex can actually add to all five of the senses, yet it especially adds to the visual experience, since you are seeing new surroundings. You can have sex in every room of the house. Or experiment with the excitement or fear of getting caught by doing it in a public place.

So what are some of the most exotic locations? Your place or mine? Or, as the Beatles asked, "Why don't we do it in the road?" Where would you do it if you could do it anywhere? To give you some ideas, here's a list of some exotic locations where people I interviewed had sex:

in the tiny bathroom of an airplane somewhere over the
Midwest

in a satellite dish at a neighbor's house in New Jersey

in the handicapped stall in a bathroom in a Chinese
restaurant in Boston

in his kid cousin's treehouse in Atlanta

in the Grand Canyon on a hiking trail during winter

in the shower at his place before work

in the stacks of a library at Stanford University

at the 13th hole of a golf course in Ft. Lauderdale

in a taxi stuck in traffic in Midtown in New York City

in her parents' bed in Connecticut

on the desk in his office in a building in Chicago

on the beach in California during the day

on a crew boat on the Charles River in Cambridge

in the kitchen waiting for our families to come over for
Thanksgiving

on a bench in Central Park in New York City at 3 A.M.

on Amtrak from Philadelphia to Washington, D.C.

in the desert near Phoenix at midnight

in the woods off Route 27 in Montauk

behind the monkey house at the San Diego Zoo

on the ground during a Lollapalooza concert

in an S/M club in New York City

in the limo before the senior prom

in a swimming pool at Club Med in Jamaica

on top of the bar after closing in a San Francisco club

in a parking garage in Baltimore

oral sex on the Métro in Paris

oral sex in the seat of an airplane under the little airline
blanket

oral sex in a movie theater during *Forrest Gump*

oral sex in the Small World ride at Disney World

Reach Out and Touch Someone

During sex people notice touch more than the other senses. Touch gets people aroused; touch relays affection; touch makes people have orgasms. The pleasure of touching and being touched is what keeps couples connected, from the first time they brush up against each other when they meet, to the way they move together during sex.

When people turn each other on, they love touching each other's body, just for the feeling. This is why people shouldn't be self-conscious about how they look. How fat or thin you are or how big or small your sex organs are does not matter at all when you are touching and being touched by someone who just loves the way you feel. When people are turned on and are running their hands along each other's bodies, they aren't usually thinking, "Eeeuw, there's fat here. Ugh, it's sweaty over there." Usually they are thinking, "Ah! This feels so-o-o good." It's simply the body-to-body, skin-to-skin contact that's arousing.

You can make sex more varied by touching in new ways. During intercourse, you can vary touch through changing positions. Sex feels different when the penis is thrusting in the vagina at different angles, varying the depth of penetration. It also feel different based on which body parts are touching during sex. For example, if you are having sex with the man on top, lying flat down on the woman, he can feel her breasts on his chest; versus, if you are having sex in "doggy style," then he feels her butt against his thighs.

Some more interesting ways to stimulate your partner through touch is to experiment with temperature during sex. Try fooling around under the covers on a hot day and let the sweat drip all over you and your lover. Have sex in a hot tub. Try doing it in the snow. Play with ice cubes. Try mixing hot and cold during oral sex by keeping a cup of warm water and a cup of ice water near you and alternately swishing your mouth with each before you go down on your lover.

It's amazing that so many people have the expectation that touch should always only be gentle and loving. If you are one of these people, start experimenting to find other kinds of touches that feel good. Try harder touches. Try scratching each other. Try tickling. Try brushing your partner's hair. Try using extra lubricant. Try spanking your partner. Try oiling up your entire body and rubbing it against your partner's. Try not shaving and feel what it's like to scratch your partner's skin. Try using a feather or a piece of fur to stroke your lover's body. Try anything you can think of!

As I discussed in an earlier section, making love in exotic locations also adds to the touch. See how touch is affected by exotic locations:

Doing it in the woods can allow you to feel the breeze, the sticks on your back, the branches pulling at your hair, the mosquitoes biting you, the warmth of the sun through the branches. Doing it in the shower lets you feel the temperature and pressure of the water, plus it makes everything slippery and sleek. Doing it the kitchen you can feel the stickiness of the kitchen floor or counter, you feel what it's like to do it on a hard surface rather than on a bed. Doing it in a car you feel the sensation of confinement, the cold of the glass window against your arm, the plastic seat stuck to your bottom.

Besides touching *during* sex, you can give pleasure just from touching alone, especially by giving a massage. People can give a massage either just because it feels good or to turn a lover on and to initiate sex. Try it!

HOW TO GIVE A GREAT BACKRUB

This is a basic ten-minute backrub. You can vary the time for a longer or shorter backrub. Make sure your partner is lying on a comfortable, flat, firm surface, like a bed or a carpeted floor.

Step 1

With the flat of your hands, using gentle, solid, even pressure, press your palms down on either side of the spine (about two inches from either side of the spine—never press on the spine); move down from the shoulders toward the lower back. Then, rub from the shoulders to the lower back in one long stroke. Repeat that long stroke twice. All of this should take about one minute.

Step 2

Knead your partner's shoulders. Then massage up the back. Beginning at the lower back, using the heels of your hands, push up and out from center of the back toward the sides, moving up the back. Then knead the shoulders some more. This should take about three minutes.

Step 3

For the next three minutes, focus on the parts of your partner's back that are sore or seem especially tight and unpliable because the muscles are tense. Usually this means rubbing your thumbs in a circular motion on pressure points like the lower back, the neck, the shoulders, and behind the shoulder blades.

Step 4

Repeat step two for about two minutes. Add any creative touching that feels good to your partner. Try tapping your fingers, or drumming them like you are impatient. Try running your fingertips up and down. Try making the pressure firmer, by straightening your fingers and elbows, or lighter by not pressing so much.

Step 5

To relax the person and to gently let him or her know that you are ending the backrub, use your fingertips to gently stoke their back in long, feathery strokes for about one minute. At this point, to finish off, sometimes it's fun to use your fingertips to draw squiggles on their back or to write words. If you feel like talking you can ask the person to guess what you're writing. But if the person is too relaxed to talk— the usual case— then just keep your words to yourself.

Onomatopoeia

If you've ever heard your noisy neighbors screaming "I'm coming, I'm coming," you've probably though about how you sound during sex. Silent sex could be a turn-on for some people, because they don't have to worry about being heard. Yet making noise during sex is often the most natural way to express your feelings.

Bob, twenty-eight, says, "I love to hear a woman scream during sex. It's such a turn-on, probably because it makes me think that I'm doing something that feels good to her. It's positive reinforcement if she makes a lot of noise." Twenty-two-year-old Bill says, " I like a woman to make low deep moans, like a cat in heat."

On the other hand, twenty-six-year-old John says, "I only want her to make noise if it's real. All that crap about getting a woman to scream is about a guy feeling macho. Whenever I've heard a woman make sounds during sex, I can tell if she sounds phony, like she's trying to get a part in a porno. She should only scream when she has to."

Saying sexy things can also be a turn-on during sex, adding to the arousal if you or your partner say what you are doing, or want to do. General communication, like "a little more to the left" or "let me get on top" can enhance sex because you are getting to do what you want to do. Try to make this kind of sex talk a little erotic, so it doesn't sound like you're directing traffic, such as, "Oh, baby, stick it in," instead of, "I'd like you to put your penis in my vagina now."

Making noise during sex is not necessarily a preference, sometimes it is an uncontrollable reflex. Many people scream, or moan, or groan, or talk during sex because it comes out of their mouths with them having little awareness of all the noise they are making. Sometimes making noise during sex can be liberating, and can make sex feel freer. If you are normally quiet because you are inhibited, then try to go with the natural urge to make noise. Experiment with making sounds, or talking dirty. You might like the way it feels to express yourself through sounds during sex. You can even try experimenting with making noise while you are masturbating. The idea is to open your mouth and just let out whatever is there. If it feels phony or weird, then you don't have to do it. But when something feels good, let out the natural sounds. Many people find that making noise enhances the feeling of pleasure. If you are trying too hard to be quiet, especially when you are having an orgasm, you can shut off too much of your experience and maybe even decrease the power of the orgasm.

If you find that you really get turned on by sound during sex, then try having phone sex with your lover. That way you are taking the excitement of sound to another level: you are not having the physical touch of sex, instead you are just having the sounds of it.

If you normally make a lot of noise during sex, you may want to go to the other extreme and experiment with being silent during sex. Sometimes blocking out the sound can make sex more erotic since you are ignoring one of your senses.

The sounds our bodies make during sex aren't just vocal. From the squishy sound of a penis thrusting into a vagina to farting, we cannot control all of the sounds our bodies make. Part of enjoying sound during sex means looking forward to hearing the natural responses of our bodies. If you hear natural sounds you should feel glad that you are healthy and doing what comes naturally. Don't be embarrassed; it's just your body, and people's bodies make noises (sometimes gross noises) whenever they give up control, like during sex.

If you want to mask those natural sounds, or if you want to add to the mood, you can play music. Sometimes people choose to play songs that remind them of a romantic moment in their relationship. When I asked people what songs they think are romantic, I realized how much times have changed. In our parents' generation, "their song" may have been something like "Only You" by the Platters. In our generation, a couple's song may well be "I Want to Fuck You Like an Animal" by Nine Inch Nails.

Musical choices for sex vary, based on the partners' taste in music. If you like classical music, you may like to have sex to a classic favorite such as Ravel's *Bolero*. If you're a Deadhead, the only way to go might be listening to Jerry Garcia's jamming. However, you may want to try to vary the music for a new sensation. Maybe heavy metal will make you more aggressive in bed, while soul, jazz, or Patti Smith might make you more sensual. It can feel good to move your body to the music. Many people like the pounding sexual beat of music during sex because it gives them a rhythm to move their bodies to.

Scratch and Sniff

Smell can influence sex by adding to the mood. It is also common to associate smell with a lover or a sexual experience. Twenty-six-year-old Lisa only remembers the feel of sex and the look of sex with her first lover because of her memory of the smell: "He used to wear Obsession. I'd nuzzle my head in his neck during sex. I'd drink in that smell. It's been nine years since we had sex, but every time I smell Obsession it comes back to me. I can almost feel his hands on my body and my face nuzzled up against his neck." Dan, twenty-nine, had a similar smell association with a past lover: "When I was in college, my girlfriend was a fine arts major. She always smelled like oil paints. When we broke up I was glad that sex wouldn't smell like paint anymore. But now if I have the opportunity to smell oil paint I always do. Once I went into an art supply store and opened up a tube of oil paint. I got an instant erection." If you want to have an impact like that on a lover you can try being consistent with what you smell like. You may be able to imprint that smell on your lover's sexual response, like what happened to Lisa and Dan.

If you want to vary the smells each time you have sex, you'll notice how powerful smell can be to set the mood. Try using a different perfume. Try putting a female perfume on the man for a different sensation. Try using a different odor of deodorant and see if your lover is in tune enough with smell to notice. Try using incense. Make love outside in a rose garden or on a lawn with freshly cut grass. Make love in a musty area. Make love after you've cooked a big meal and the whole place smells like food. Make love in dirty clothes when you've just gotten back from the gym. Make love outside in the rain. Make love on the beach and smell the ocean. Overall, no matter what smell it is, keep your nose in tune with smelling during sex. Keep your mind open to the possibility that the smell is influencing your sexual experience.

As with sound, there is a certain amount of smell associated with sex that is natural. Obviously, if the natural smells of the body are too strong, then there are simple remedies to change those smells during sex, like showering and using deodorant. Yet rather than trying not to smell them, you can realize that these natural smells are healthy. By realizing the uniqueness of each person's smells, you can enhance sex. Instead of trying to shut out the smells of sex, think about whether they only turn you off, because you *think* they should turn you off. I'm not saying that you should stop showering. Yet if you open your mind, and your nose, you may realize that your lover's smell arouses you.

Mmm Good!

If you always associate the taste of sex with soap and deodorant and toothpaste, then sex probably isn't blowing your mind. Why should sex always taste like peppermint and Old Spice? Some people are afraid to kiss unless they have just brushed their teeth. Isn't that inhibited and boring? The natural tastes of your body and your lover's body can enhance lovemaking if you are open to enjoying the experience. Everyone tastes different, from the inside to the outside. If you want to experience the full sensation of taste during sex, then stop using anti-taste products to mask taste during sex. Taste all of your lover. Go ahead and lick your lover's armpit, suck your lover's toes, lick your lover's entire body. Does tasting your partner make you feel closer and hornier? If you like that, then experiment with adding variety to your taste buds during sex.

You can have erotic experiences with food. I discussed in chapter 6 how you can use food on a condom to enhance oral sex. Try some of those ideas. Then try using any food that seems erotic to you.

Here's an incredibly erotic, exciting tasty game you can try: Tie your lover's hands behind his or her back, and blindfold your lover. Put one drop of honey somewhere on your *own* body. Don't tell your lover where the honey is. Then tell your lover to find that one tiny drop of honey. The catch is that since your lover is bound and blindfolded, your lover must only use his or her tongue and mouth to find it!

Erotic food experiences do not even have to involve the sex organs. Licking food off your lover's stomach or toes or lips can be as sensual—or more sensual—than licking it off their penis or vulva. Try any of the following suggestions, or just play with whatever food you happen to have on hand:

Hold a mouthful of champagne in your mouth, then pass it to your lover's mouth with a kiss.

Feed each other grapes, or strawberries, or raspberries.

Spray whipped cream all over each other and lick it off.

Try licking marshmallow fluff off your lover.

Drizzle chocolate syrup anywhere on your lover and lick it off.

Put honey on your lover and lick it off.

Make an ice-cream sundae on your lover's body, complete with ice cream, chocolate syrup, whipped cream, and a cherry on top, then eat it.

Put a peeled banana inside the vagina, eat it out, and give new meaning to the term *banana split.*

Browse in cookbooks and supermarkets to come up with more exotic ideas.

Varying Sensations by Working a Buzz

Many people try to vary the feelings of sex by using drugs and alcohol. (By the way, I must say that I am not endorsing drug use. I'm only reporting the realities of sex in the real world.) Drugs can affect all of the senses involved in sex. While some people find that drugs and alcohol enhance sex and make it more pleasurable, using drugs and alcohol also impair judgment during sex. Most women who are victims of date rape had been drinking with their dates. Many times people forgo using birth control or safer sex because they are under the influence. Often people have regrets about the sexual decisions they make when they are on drugs or alcohol. If you drink or do drugs, you must be aware of the risks that you are taking.

Now, on to explanations of how these substances affect certain people's sex lives.

Alcohol lowers sexual inhibitions and may make people more likely to have sex because they feel less in control of the things that they are thinking and doing. Twenty-year-old

Jack says, "I call alcohol 'liquid panty remover.' It's always easier to get a girl to have sex with me if she's drunk." Sharon, a twenty-two-year-old, enjoys sex with alcohol: "I love going to a bar and getting trashed and then having sex. It's great sex. Drinking makes me totally free." On a more negative note, one of the problems of alcohol is that it decreases sensations. It can make it more difficult for men to get erections, and men or women may not have orgasms as easily when they have had even a couple of drinks. Since the senses are decreased, the experience is much more one of disorientation during sex.

Marijuana, like alcohol, can break down the defenses and destroy inhibitions. Some people find that marijuana turns them on. It makes them aroused faster and it makes them have more intense orgasms. For example, Jill, twenty-six, reports that "pot makes every part of my body tingly. I want to be touched everywhere. I get very horny on pot." Whereas, twenty-three-year-old Henry finds that marijuana shuts him down. "Pot makes me zone out. I'll just stare at the wall when I'm stoned. If a naked woman came over to me and sat on my lap, I'd still keep staring at that wall."

Psychedelics such as mushrooms and LSD reportedly do not increase sexual desire, but they often give people a unique type of sexual experience in which they think new thoughts about sex. Joan, a twenty-three-year-old, said, "When I had sex on LSD, I was much more aware of the biological process of sex. I could see my cells mixing with his. I could see the heat of our bodies. At that moment, I thought that the meaning of sex was about the merging of two bodies' cells to create a new source of energy. It seemed to make sense at the time. My thoughts were very clear at that moment. I had figured out the meaning of sex! Looking back on it now, it was a great experience, but I cannot make sense of anything that I *thought* I had figured out."

For some people, some drugs may have the effect of an

aphrodisiac. According to Karen, twenty-six, on Ecstasy "everything is velvety and you feel like you could love and fuck everything." This was a similar report to the feeling that twenty-nine-year-old Jason had on Quaaludes: "I was so excited about having sex. I was in love with her and with sex and with the world. I wanted to have sex forever."

On cocaine, Joe, twenty-six, reports that the sensation "is a uniformed heightening of awareness during sex to the point where ordinary movements and sensations can be experienced as though it was the first time. I wanted to go all night." Some people find that cocaine makes them too self-absorbed so they don't want to have sex. That happened to twenty-eight-year-old Michael: "When I was coked up I thought I was too good for the girl I was with, so I didn't let her touch me." Other negative reports about coke are that it prevents orgasms or ejaculation by numbing the system. The comedian Robin Williams once said about cocaine, "What a wonderful drug, it makes you paranoid and impotent."

Amyl nitrate, also called poppers, is inhaled most often for the sole purpose of enhancing sex. It is said that this drug makes orgasms more intense by increasing blood flow. Jason, twenty-three, said, "The time I used poppers, my muscles were relaxed and it felt great when I came. The feeling of the drug didn't last long, though." The drug has many negative side effects of dizziness, headaches, and fainting. Also, since the drug was popular in the gay subculture during the 1970s and 1980s, there was a theory that it lowered the body's resistance to HIV; however, there is no evidence that this drug leads to transmission of HIV, especially if safer sex is being practiced.

The most negative reports about the effects of drugs on sex are from people who use heroin or morphine. These drugs lower sexual interest, since users and addicts are often more interested in getting a hit than getting an orgasm.

If you do drugs, your experience of sex on the drug will

probably be a very individual experience. Whether it dulls or excites your senses, it will at the least give you a new sensation. Drugs will vary the sensations, but don't forget that they also make it more difficult to stick to your sexual guidelines and practice safer sex. Consider the sexual risks of doing it under the influence.

CHAPTER 8

The Wide World of Sex

Understanding Sexual Diversity and Accepting Your Erotic Potential

What Has Influenced Your Ideas about Sexual Diversity?

Have you ever thought of doing it the way Madonna did in *Sex*? Or dressing up like Ru Paul? Or would you prefer to abstain from sex before marriage like Donna on *Beverly Hills 90210*?

For many people, the characters from television and movies are the primary source of education about alternative sexual behaviors. Even before most of us reached puberty, we had seen every kind of sexuality from the "ordinary" to the "bizarre" illustrated in the media. Everyone who has ever watched a television talk show has had a cross-dresser in the living room! The media has heightened awareness about the wide range of sexual styles, yet instead of liberating sexuality, the depictions of sexual diversity end up repressing individual sexuality by showing negative, distorted, sensationalized images. Mostly we hear about sex as something weird or bad, unless it is part of heterosexual, monogamous relationships. What is seldom shown is the natural, beautiful eroticism in the tremendously broad range of sexuality.

Do You Judge People Because You Believe Myths about Sexual Diversity?

What do you think about people whose sexuality is different from your own? Sometimes it's not easy to accept others until you understand them. I remember the first time I met people who had sexualities that were different from those I had encountered. Although I had studied sex and knew a lot about these behaviors, the very first time I actually met people who enjoyed abstinence, people who practiced S/M, transvestites, prostitutes, and others with out-of-the-ordinary sexualities, I thought they were somehow bizarre. Probably I thought those things because of the years and years that our culture spent pounding it into my mind that alternative sexual behaviors must be deviant.

After I spent some time around these people and saw the realities of their sexual behaviors, I realized that these people weren't weird. The reality of their sexuality was different from what I had been learning about, but their sexuality wasn't bizarre or strange—just diverse. Sexuality, like any aspect of personality, is unique.

We all feel differently about how important our sexual behavior is in our lives and in the way we define ourselves. For example, if a man has sex with other men, he may not see himself as gay or bisexual. Another man who has sex with men might completely identify himself as gay. Sexual preferences do not necessarily define who people are, yet sexuality is a very important aspect of who they are. If you can accept people for their differences—for what makes each person unique—then you are on your way to accepting others whose sexual behaviors may seem odd to you at first.

Sexual diversity is something everyone needs to understand in order to be prepared to accept a reality of life. Accepting the complexities of sexuality will help you to be more accepting of others and more accepting of yourself.

Can You Be Free to Practice Any Type of Sex You Choose?

Besides just accepting them and understanding different types of sexuality, I want you to accept that aspects of these different sexualities could be part of you. Everybody has the capacity to be sexually any way they want. By learning about all these different types of sexualities you can understand why you like or don't like them. If you want to expand your sexual repertoire, first you need to truly understand that you are free to do absolutely anything sexually.

Some sex researchers say that we are the way we are sexually because this is the way we were born, the way we were destined to be. Others say that in our childhood incidents occurred that alone formed our sexuality. Also, our personal experiences and what we see, in our lives and in the media, influence our sexuality throughout our lives. It is unrealistic to deny these influences on our sexuality, yet certainly now, as adults, we can choose how we want to behave. We need to be able to get past the powerful messages we get from others, whether they are our friends or our favorite musicians, to discover what is right for us. Also, we need to realize that sexuality develops as we grow, and over time our sexual interests may change.

As adults, we have the ability to make decisions and choices, even to decide not to have sex at all. Sexuality is highly individualized. When we learn what is out there for us, then we have the freedom to be turned on by anything. Because of the ways that the media represents sexual diversity—that is, the full range of sexual expressions—most people aren't aware of their erotic potential. In order to explore your erotic potential, try to keep an open mind and forget about what you've learned from talk shows, soaps, or movies. Any judgments that you have already made about particular sexual behaviors are probably based more in fantasy than in fact. The fact is, once you understand the realities of all different sexual behaviors, you can make a decision about whether or not you want to practice them. To help you enhance your erotic potential—your capacity to enjoy or choose not to practice any sexual expression or lifestyle— you need to learn more about the many sexual behaviors open to you.

▼ ▼

As humans, we are capable of having sex more frequently and more creatively than any other living species.

▲ ▲

You have to base your own sexual choices on eroticism, creativity, and excitement along with consent and responsibility. I don't endorse any one particular type of sexual behavior; rather, I want you to learn the positive, realistic, accurate, unsensationalized aspects of sexual behaviors and practices, including abstinence, traditional relationships, group sex, masturbation, sex toys, fantasy, phone sex, computer sex, stripping, prostitution, tantric sex, foot preferences, transvestism, and S/M so that you can understand others' sexual choices, experiment if you like, and make more rewarding decisions about your own sexuality. Though some of these behaviors may seem bizarre to you, for people who enjoy these behaviors, everything that I will discuss is pleasurable, consensual, erotic, sensual, healthy, and even loving.

Traditional Sexual Behavior

What do you think of the term "traditional sex"? Maybe you think of the stereotypical example:

Heterosexual. Missionary position. Man on top. Woman on bottom. Boom boom boom. He has an orgasm. It's over. They go to sleep. Or maybe they watch Letterman's Top Ten before they doze off. Sex is only at night. Only in the dark. Only once a week. The same night every time.

Well, if that's what you think, then stop. The truth is that there are a lot of *positive* qualities that make up traditional sexual behavior. Intimacy, commitment, trust, companionship, security, familiarity, and social acceptability are some of the most positive qualities of good traditional relationships. Traditional relationships begin with a man and a woman dating. The commitment becomes greater and the two people agree to date and have sex only with each other. Then if the commitment and the relationship continues, the two people get married (sometimes after living together) and have children. Some people still think sex before marriage is wrong; most others think that it is okay if you're in a committed relationship.

Good relationships come when you treat each other with respect and affection, you enjoy the amount of time that you spend together, you enjoy the things that you do together, and you enjoy the sex. Twenty-three-year-old Adam said, "It's the most comfortable situation to have sex with a long-term lover, because you know what the other person likes and they know what you like." Kim, twenty-six, who's been married for four years, said, "With my husband, sex is the best in the world because we know how to make each other come and I can predict which way he will move."

▼ ▼

Although it may seem ordinary and mundane, traditional sex does not have to be boring or repetitive.

▲ ▲

Traditional sex is not limited to the missionary position. It can include penis-vagina intercourse in any position, oral sex, anal sex, touching, kissing, and more. If you think monogamy can't work because eventually the passion has to die, you're very wrong. Twenty-eight-year-old Joshua said, "I love being married, because it's safe to ask my wife if she wants to experiment. She's usually into it. I act out her fantasies for her, too. We never get bored!" Take a look at all of the great ideas in this book for keeping your sex life fun and exciting. Many of them work wonderfully in monogamous traditional relationships.

Even though this section is about "traditional sex," I have to point out that the definition of "traditional" has now expanded to include committed relationships of gays and lesbians and heterosexual relationships that are not committed exclusive relationships. It's not accurate anymore to call living together or having sex outside of marriage "premarital sex," since marriage is no longer the goal for many people, and most people have sex before marriage. Traditional relationships change with the times. Twentysomethings today are creating new sexual traditions based on what we find pleasurable and fulfilling.

Accepting Your Sexual Orientation

Being gay or straight is not a simple black-and-white issue. Sexual orientation is a gray area according to most sex researchers. Back in the 1940s, Dr. Alfred Kinsey developed a six-point scale that rates people from 0, exclusively heterosexual, to 6, exclusively homosexual. That means that some-one who only has sex with the opposite gender but feels a strong attraction to the same gender might be a 1. Someone who has had a little sexual activity with the same gender but is primarily straight is a 2. Someone who is bisexual is a 3. Someone who has a little sex with and is attracted to the opposite gender, but mostly has sex with the same gender is a 4. Someone who is gay but may be attracted to the opposite gender is a 5. What Kinsey found was that 75 percent of the population is exclusively heterosexual, 2 to 10 percent of the population is exclusively homosexual, and about 20 percent of the population is bisexual, or falls from 1 to 5 on the scale.

Even within each division of gays, lesbians, and bisexuals, there is variation among the ways that people express them-selves sexually. For example, there are many types of bisexu-als. Some people who are bi feel totally free to go out with, or have sex with, either gender anytime. They are often called 50:50 bisexuals, because they have an equal preference for men and for women.

Other bisexuals have a preference for one gender but are accepting of sex with another gender. Some bisexuals are "sequential" bisexuals, which means that they only have one lover at a time, sometimes a man, sometimes a woman. Yet other people who are bisexual are "cyclic" bisexuals. They go through cycles where, for months or years, they might only be attracted to men, having no sexual attraction at all to women. Then, at some point, their desire switches to a desire for women. There are also incidences of "situational" bisexuality, when people are segregated by gender for a long period of time and they begin to feel attracted to their own gender; this happens often in prison or in the military. Also, there is the "transitory" bisexual, who passes through a bisexual phase on the way to becoming exclusively homosex-ual or heterosexual.

No one exactly knows why people are gay, straight, lesbian, or bisexual. It is widely believed that sexual orientation is just part of who you are, it's not changeable. People often report that their sexual feelings are instinctual or stem from intense internal desire. However, not everyone agrees that sexual orientation is determined before you are born. Some bisexual women say the reason they are bisexual is because their emotional needs cannot be met by men. There are also reports of women who became lesbians for political, radical-feminist, anti-male reasons. Similarly, some research on bisexual men reports that men are bi because they desire creativity and variety in their sex life. Some people believe that you can choose to be with anyone you want, regardless of gender, and it's not based on some internal orientation.

▼ ▼

Regardless of why you feel attracted to your gender or the opposite gender, you will usually be the most fulfilled when your sexual identity matches your sexual orientation.

▲ ▲

Sexual identity is how you view yourself. It's your self-label, your self-identification; it's subjective. It's whether you say you are gay, straight, or bisexual.

Unfortunately, some people lie about or deny or are unsure of their sexual orientation, so they construct a different sexual identity for themselves. Gene, twenty-six, explains the evolution of his sexual identity: "When I started college I was sure that I was gay. I always looked at men like I wanted them. But I kept denying it, because I did not want to be thought of as a fag. I was in a fraternity, so it was tough. I dated a women openly, took her to all the formals, would have her spend the night, so the brothers would think I was straight. Then I would sneak out to gay bars and pick up men and have sex with them. If anyone ever asked or suspected, I would say, of course I'm straight. I identified myself as straight. Sometimes I had even convinced myself that I was straight. I knew in my heart I was gay. Eventually, I knew that it was wrong for me to call myself straight when I was gay—I was having sex with men!—and I came out."

No matter how hard you try to create an image, if you hide too much of your private self, people may wonder if you are being honest. Even if you try to defend yourself, you still may look like a poseur. How many people really believed that Michael Jackson and Lisa Marie Presley were happily married lovers just because they kissed on the MTV Music Awards? Did it make any difference when Cindy Crawford and Richard Gere took out a full page ad in the *Times* of London publicly declaring that they were heterosexual and in love?

Although it won't always be easy, in the long run you will probably be happier and live more peacefully if you are honest with yourself and with other people in your life. If other people make assumptions about you, you'll be more equipped to ignore them if you are truly honest and happy with yourself.

Part of the reason why people make assumptions that someone is gay or straight is because they have a stereotypical image of what gay behavior is, but not all gay men are "swishy," and not all lesbians are "butch." Some gay men are very masculine, while some gay women are quite feminine. There is some social stigma attached to any type of gayness, lesbianism, or bisexuality, because most people are heterosexual, and many straight people can't conceive of why anyone would want to have sex with someone of the same gender. (Plus the taboo against homosexuality has been firmly rooted in history because in many religions it is considered a sin.)

To some degree, bisexuality and "lipstick lesbianism" have become trendy, in the media as well as in certain social circles. Straight men are often turned on by thinking of two women having sex. (Although, at the same time, many straight men also think that all lesbians need is a "good man" to change them. While lesbianism is viewed more positively than it was in the past, male homosexuality is still, for the most part, taboo, possibly because of the misconception that gay male sex leads to AIDS. Even gays and lesbians are not always completely accepting of other people's orientations. Sometimes they view bisexuals with suspicion or hostility because they think a person is only bisexual for social convenience, dating the opposite sex to fit in with straights and the same sex to fit in with homosexuals or to be chic.

Despite the stigma and discrimination, today more than ever support for gays, lesbians, and bisexuals is growing. It used to be that gays, lesbians, and bisexuals were invisible; we never heard about them or saw them. Today, more gays and lesbians are coming out to their families, friends, and even the general public. Many famous people are expressing their sexual orientation openly, showing that people of all sexual orientations are everywhere. Famous men who have come out as gay or bisexual include Elton John, Harvey Fierstein, entertainment mogul David Geffen, Andy Bell of the group Erasure, and diver Greg Louganis. Some famous women including k.d. lang, Melissa Etheridge, Martina Navratilova, and Amanda Bearse (who plays Marcy on *Married with Children*) have come out as lesbians. David Bowie, Madonna, and Sandra Bernhard have all said that they have had sex with both men and women.

This new openness has affected movies and television, too. It was only a few years ago that every couple on television was straight, and a typical television commercial showed a man picking up a woman for a date and noticing her gleaming white teeth, polished by the advertised toothpaste. Today, there are recurrent characters who are gay, lesbian, and bisexual on hit TV shows including *Melrose Place* and *Roseanne,* and at least one groundbreaking commercial for IKEA showed a gay male couple shopping for furniture for their home.

Acceptance of homosexuality and bisexuality has also led to more and more cities adopting "domestic partnership" laws that help couples of any sexual orientation obtain some of the rights of married couples. Also, some churches openly support gay and lesbian members.

If you feel you are gay, lesbian, or bisexual, it is easier than ever to accept yourself and even come out, but that's not saying it's easy! For one thing, even if you can accept who you are that doesn't mean people around you will. If you think that you are gay, lesbian, or bisexual, before you come out you may find it helpful to talk with someone in a support group. Check your local phone book for one in your area. You should not need to deny your orientation, like Gene, mentioned earlier. If you think (or know) that you may be gay, lesbian, or bisexual give a call to a support group, go to a bar or event for people of varying sexual orientations, and try to make friends or find lovers in the subculture to feel your sense of belonging. You do not need to change your political and social views based on your sexual orientation. You may, however, feel more comfortable spending time with others who are of the same orientation as you. In order to enjoy your sex life, it is important that you accept your sexual orientation and be proud of your sexual identity. Then you can have mindblowing sex with the person of your choice.

Abstinence

When most people try to think of reasons why someone would choose to abstain from sex, usually they come up with the negative reasons: fear of AIDS, fear of pregnancy, inability to find a partner, religious taboos, insecurity about sexual ability, poor body image, lack of desire. But there are, in fact, many positive reasons why people choose to abstain from sex.

▼ ▼

Some people who choose abstinence find more enjoyment spending time doing things other than having sex.

▲ ▲

They often feel relieved that they do not need to think about who they will have as a sexual partner—they're not pressured to find the next orgasm. Some people would prefer abstaining until they have the relationship in which they can have both love and sex. Others who choose abstinence believe that they can save their sexual energy and transform it into energy for work, school, or creativity. Sharon, a twenty-six-year-old ballerina, said, "I put my creative energy into dance—that's my sexual expression." They may abstain for religious or spiritual reasons to enhance spirituality.

Abstinence as a way of life, or as a temporary sexual state, is often treated as disrespectfully as are other behaviors that are seen on the fringes of traditional. There is a lot of pressure in our culture to have sex. That's why it's important for abstinent people to understand why they are abstaining and to feel good about their decision.

Love the One You're With: Masturbation

What are people doing if they want to have orgasm or sexual pleasure but don't want a partner? Masturbating!

Almost everybody masturbates. The statistic is that 99 percent of men masturbate; the joke is that 1 percent lie. Statistics show that a slightly lower percentage of women masturbate, between 65 percent and 85 percent.

Growing up, many people were given negative messages about masturbation. When we were babies, many of our parents slapped our hands when we touched ourselves. Instead, parents should be telling their children that masturbation is natural and normal but should be done in private. Through the teen years, fears about masturbation are perpetuated through the retelling of jokes and myths, such as that masturbation causes poor vision, loss of memory, and hair to grow on your palms. Even our government has perpetuated the taboo about talking openly about masturbation. President Clinton seemingly slapped the hand of every American and reinforced the masturbation taboo when he fired Surgeon General Dr. Joycelyn Elders for her brief mention of the fact that masturbation is normal and could be discussed in sex education classes as an alternative to intercourse.

▼ ▼ ▼ ▼ ▼ ▼ ▼ ▼ ▼ ▼ ▼ ▼ ▼ ▼ ▼ ▼ ▼ ▼ ▼ ▼
Masturbation *is* normal, safe, and feels so good.
▲ ▲ ▲ ▲ ▲ ▲ ▲ ▲ ▲ ▲ ▲ ▲ ▲ ▲ ▲ ▲ ▲ ▲ ▲ ▲

Now all we have to do is get masturbation out of the closet—or out from under the covers, I suppose.

The truth is that masturbation has many health benefits: it helps release stress and tension. It increases your understanding of your own body, and it teaches you the best way to personally achieve orgasms, which is extremely helpful to know when you have sex with a partner. Masturbation is a therapeutic technique for teaching women who have never had an orgasm how they can have one and for helping men who are trying to learn how to take more time before they ejaculate. Masturbation also is an alternative to intercourse.

You cannot masturbate too much, unless it gets in the way of your life. As long as you are not obsessed with masturbating, to the point that you no longer go to work or school, have no friends, or never leave the house, then it is healthy to masturbate as often as you like. Enjoy it and don't feel guilty or anxious about it. Some people masturbate every day; some people three times a day; some once a year;

some once a month. The point is that each time you masturbate, you should have a good time.

Perhaps the most positive reason for masturbating is that
it gives you great pleasure. You can be in charge of your own
orgasm and have an orgasm any time you want, any way you
want. After all, who knows better than you what feels good
for your body?

Explaining how people masturbate is not simple, because
everybody masturbates slightly differently. In masturbation
both men and women experiment with different rhythms and
pressure to bring themselves to orgasm. Men may use their
hands to stroke the shaft of their penis in a back-and-forth
motion. They may concentrate on rubbing the head of the
penis and the glans (the top of the head above the ridge) and
the frenulum (the ridge where the glans meets the shaft).
Often men will use lubricants like oil, vaseline, K-Y jelly, or
anything else that helps the penis glide through the hand.
They may move their pelvis up and down while they are masturbating. Some men enjoy thrusting their penis up against
something like a pillow, rather than using their hands. Some
men enjoy massaging their scrotom (balls), stroking their
chest, touching their nipples, their face, their thighs, or
inserting their finger in their anus for additional stimulation
during masturbation.

Women most often use their hands to manipulate their clitoris or to rub their entire vulva (all of the outside genitals).
Usually women use a circular motion to rub the clitoris.
Some women like to rub directly on it; others like lighter
stimulation, just brushing the top of it. Some women may
penetrate their vagina with their fingers. Other women enjoy
other sensations, like rubbing against a pillow or rubbing
their legs together, or feeling running water on their genitals.
Women may also enjoy stroking their breasts, touching their
nipples, touching their thighs or their face, or inserting fingers in their anus at the same time.

Masturbation with Sex Toys

Besides these organic methods for masturbating, using sex toys such as vibrators and dildos can be very exciting in masturbation. Mostly these are used by women, but men can also use them. Vibrators are either electric or battery operated. Some electric vibrators are designed as high-power vibrating massagers that could also be used on your shoulders, back, neck, or any body part. One of the most popular electric vibrators is the "Magic Wand" made by Hitachi (yes, the grill people make sex toys, too!). Most electric massagers are very large and are only for external stimulation, like clitoral stimulation. Some have attachments for penetration. Electric vibrators give off high-power vibrations, they are very sturdy, and, like any good electrical appliance, last for years and years.

Battery-operated vibrators are usually cylindrical, often shaped liked penises, so they can be used for penetration as well as external stimulation. These are less expensive than electric vibrators, portable, and less powerful, for people who like a gentler motion. (If a vibrator takes C batteries it will feel more powerful than if it takes AA's.) They usually are not too sturdy and do not last as long as electric vibrators. There are also battery-operated vibrators that are designed for use underwater, if you like to come in the tub or at the beach.

I am often asked if women can become addicted to using a vibrator. Women cannot become "addicted" in the true sense of the word; yet they can sometimes feel addicted to vibrators if they can no longer come without one. Many women like the electronic buzzing feeling of the vibrator so much that it makes it more difficult for them to have an orgasm without the vibrator. If this happens, a woman can make the choice either to enjoy the pleasure she receives from the vibrator, and not worry if she has trouble having an orgasm without it, or try to regain the pleasure she had from her former method of stimulation by stopping vibrator use altogether. Cut the cord (literally or metaphorically) if you feel "addicted" and you want to get over it. If you like using the vibrator, it's a good idea to maintain your ability to have an orgasm without a vibrator, just in case you ever want to, like maybe during intercourse.

As I mentioned, men sometimes like vibrators as well. Vibrators can be used on the outside of the penis, scrotum, or perineum (the area between the penis and anus), or a man may like to insert a vibrator into his anus. Most anal vibrators are smaller than vaginal vibrators; they also have a base so they don't slip all the way inside the anus.

Some vibrating toys are made exclusively for men—like the "Vibrating Vagina," a small plastic replica of a vagina that takes two AA batteries to get a man turned on. There are also vibrating "sleeves," which look like hollowed-out penises, that can be slipped over the penis.

There are other sex toys that can be used in masturbation as substitute penises. Dildos are used by women for vaginal or anal penetration and sometimes by men who like to feel anal penetration. If you want to be creative, you can use almost any smooth cylindrical object as a dildo.

▼ ▼

From manufactured dildos to cucumbers and bananas to candles and plastic bottles, you can put anything inside yourself that will turn you on.

▲ ▲

Just be sure that you follow a few simple rules if you put objects inside yourself: (1) do not use anything that can break, like glass; (2) do not use anything that is sharp; (3) do not use anything that is so small that it will be difficult to get out; and (4) put a condom on the object before you put it inside yourself. By using the condom you will not be letting bacteria from the foreign object get inside you.

Manufactured dildos are made of hard rubber, silicone, or vinyl. They come in a variety of colors, usually some variations in skin tones. Most dildos are between 5 inches and 9 inches long and one inch to two inches wide. They usually are shaped to represent penises, but there are some that are nonrepresentational shapes; some dildos are shaped and colored to look like bananas, people, dolphins, whales, and beavers (maybe you have to see them to believe them). There are even double-headed dildos so two people can use it at once. Dildos can also be placed in a harness that a woman can wear around her hips, giving her a substitute penis so she can penetrate another woman or a man. Some people like to warm up dildos so that they feel more lifelike. You can put a dildo in hot water. Or you can put one in the microwave—but be careful that the microwave does not overheat the dildo, you wouldn't want to burn yourself. You want it to feel lifelike, not painful.

Besides dildos and vibrators, there are many other types of sex toys. For example, ben-wah balls are small metal balls designed to rub against each other and provide stimulation when they are both inserted inside the vagina. Unfortunately, most women who try them are disappointed. Since the vagina has very few nerve endings inside it, most women cannot even feel the balls. Also, they are often difficult to remove, since the woman either has to use her vaginal muscles to push them out, or reach a finger inside to pick them out.

If you go to an adult/sex store, you can explore the aisles to find even more types of sex toys. You'll find things like blow-up dolls (and blow-up sheep), which are made for people to have sex with if they like doing it with a giant piece of plastic. These types of novelty toys are usually given as joke gifts and promptly thrown away.

Pornography: Magazines and Video

Maybe you remember when you were a little kid and *Playboy* was a really big deal. Maybe you'd peer across the counter at 7-Eleven to catch a glimpse of the cover girl. Probably when you were in elementary school some kid snatched his Dad's copy and brought it in for some private show-and-tell. Well, as an adult, you no longer have to sneak a peak at porn if it turns you on. I don't mean that you should be reading a porn magazine wide open on the subway, but certainly you can try to get rid of any anxiety that you may have about buying or reading pornography.

It's totally normal and healthy for people to enjoy fantasy material or to use it as a masturbation aid. People who like looking at sex or sexual poses to get aroused or have an orgasm will be turned on by porn magazines and videos.

▼ ▼

In order to get the most benefit from porn, keep in mind that what is going on in the images is only fantasy.

▲ ▲

The women in the magazine pictures do not look that way in real life: those pictures are touched up, airbrushed, and even altered with the help of computers. The actors in porn videos are professional performers, "sexual celebrities," who have sex for a living and who are following a script. Real-life sex almost never looks like the sex in the movies. Therefore, go ahead and enjoy pornography, but be sure not to base your sexual standards or expectations on those images.

Phone Sex

Instead of looking at sex in magazines and videos, some people like hearing sexual conversation to get aroused. Phone sex has been popular since the 1980s, when 900 numbers came about. For a substantial price, anyone can have a private, anonymous, sexually explicit conversation.

Different phone sex lines have different themes. Most are designed for heterosexual men, others for gay men, some for women. Some phone sex lines are only for S/M calls, or group sex, or busty women, or participants of a particular race or ethnicity. The list goes on and on. Interestingly, the caller never really knows what the phone sex operator looks like, since they only hear their voice. Remember that Aerosmith video, "Sweet Emotion"? Poor Billy thought he was getting off to some hot, stylish babe, when the phone sex operator was really a fat, hairy housewife who was ironing and holding her chubby baby.

▼ ▼ ▼ ▼ ▼ ▼ ▼ ▼ ▼ ▼ ▼ ▼ ▼ ▼ ▼ ▼ ▼

Phone sex is all about creating a fantasy.

▲ ▲ ▲ ▲ ▲ ▲ ▲ ▲ ▲ ▲ ▲ ▲ ▲ ▲ ▲ ▲ ▲

There are two types of professional phone sex, prerecorded messages and live phone sex. The live phone sex operators will ask you your fantasy and then talk it out with you, presumably until you have an orgasm. Usually the number that you dial spells out a word, like 1-900-Hot-Babe or 1-900-For-Puss. The prerecorded messages might sound something like this:

HI, I'm Roxy. Oooh, I'm so hot for you. Uh, can you tell how wet I am. I want you so bad. You'd feel so good dee-e-e-p inside me. Oooh, I'm touching myself. Oh it feels so-o-o good. Oooh. I'm coming. UH. Yes. Oooh. Ohhh. That felt so-o-o good. Only you could give me complete satisfaction. So please call me again really soon. And remember, it's only $3.95 for the first minute and 90 cents for each additional minute.

As Roxy mentioned, phone sex can be quite costly. Live phone sex usually costs even more. It is charged to your credit card or your phone bill. Be careful! Charges add up quickly when you are getting hot and heavy. Also, beware if you have roommates; they may see the charges on the phone bill, and you'll have to pay for and explain why you've made $500 worth of calls to Horny Sluts, Inc.!

Of course, if you want to talk dirty on the phone to your lover, you don't need to pay a cent. Phone sex with someone you know can be a great erotic thrill.

Fantasy

You certainly do not have to pay to get off on fantasy. There are people who get sexual pleasure simply from using their imaginations, even without using porn or sex toys. Fantasizing can be relaxing, exciting, arousing. You can fantasize anytime, anywhere. People fantasize about all kinds of things. Sometimes the fantasies are romantic; sometimes they are exotic.

Fantasies are great for your self-esteem. In your fantasies, you can dominate another person, or you can submit to the desires of another. You can be sexual with any person you choose: a rock star, your lover in real life, a friend, a professor, a stranger, or anyone.

▼ ▼

In your fantasies, you can be anyone you want to be, look and act any way you want.

▲ ▲

Fantasies can involve types of sex that you frequently enjoy or that you'd never want to try. For example, many people fantasize about raping or getting raped—they'd never want this to happen in real life, but it's perfectly fine (and "normal") in a fantasy. Fantasies are made up of imagination and creativity. It's OK to imagine anything!

If you think you might want to try some new sex act, but you're not sure, you can put that in your fantasies. See what it's like and try to gauge if you want to act it out. Just keep in mind that fantasies are often better than reality.

Some people who fantasize about their lovers when they are not there say that it helps them enhance their relationships. "It's like spending time with her, even though it's not reality," said twenty-six-year-old John. On the other hand, it is very common to fantasize about someone else when you are having sex with your partner. If you fantasize about someone else it does not mean that you want to have sex with someone else: You never have to act out or reveal your sexual fantasies! Some people find that fantasizing about being with another person during sex can increase their pleasure because it adds a new variation. Others find that it decreases their enjoyment of sex, because it distances them from their partner, or makes them feel guilty. If you get the most pleasure from being in the moment and only thinking about your partner during sex, then do not fantasize about anyone else. If you like fantasizing about other people, then enjoy it.

You may want to tell your partner about your fantasies. You can learn intimate things about each other, keeping in mind people do not always want to live out their sexual fantasies. However, sometimes fantasies are best kept to oneself—some lovers could feel hurt, jealous, and mistrustful, if, for example, you say that you fantasize about someone else or something risqué. "I once told a girl that I sometimes had fantasies about men. She freaked out and thought I was gay. I'm not gay at all. Fantasies are fantasies. It was a mistake to tell her. Other girls liked to hear about fantasies. She didn't," concluded twenty-four-year-old Craig.

All in all, sexual fantasy is a wonderful part of our sexuality. Sexual fantasies keep sexual imagination keen, and help increase sexual desire. There are even some women who say that they can have orgasms by fantasy alone—without even touching themselves. They call it "thinking off"!

Virtually Cybersex

If it turns you on to watch sex on your computer screen instead of on videos or in magazines, then computer programs that show sex may be for you. For example, there are CD-ROM programs for computers in which you can choose to see a picture of any number of models, undress them, and pose them. There are also CD-ROM strip poker games in which six women deal with anyone who wants to sit naked in front of their computer. Popular now are porn movies that have been transferred to CD-ROM. In these you can choose the order of the scenes on your computer. Yet don't be led to believe that you will be able to have an impact on what you actually see in the porn movie, or what the models do, or how much you'll see of the strip poker players. Like a computer game, the scenes are already programmed. All you do is choose the order of what you will see.

These things claim to be "interactive" or "virtual reality," because those are big buzzwords, but they are no more interactive than pushing the Fast Forward button on your VCR, or turning the page of a porn magazine. And until they offer attachments to place around the penis or in the vagina that would stimulate you while watch, it's not really virtual reality. Lacking "teledildonics," these types of materials are just another fun way to fantasize about nude images.

Getting Off On-Line: Computer Sex on the Internet

As soon as you have a modem for your computer and a membership to a computer network, it's easy to log on to computer "chat lines." In the world of cyberspace, you can meet all types of people who share your common interests. Unlike talking to a phone sex operator who's only talking dirty because it's part of the job, people who converse over the computer are doing it for fun, excitement, curiosity, or even to get off.

There are many different venues for on-line sex. Often the generic term "Internet" or the "Net" (which is actually a network of computer networks) is used to describe the system that links computers and allows people to talk to each other. But there are many other computer networks on the information highway: America Online, CompuServe, and Prodigy are the largest. Millions of people subscribe to these computer services, so at any given time, there are thousands of channels in operation and a great variety of topics that you can discuss over the computer-modem lines. About 70 percent of the so-called chat rooms are sexually oriented. (Of the non-sexual chat rooms, there are games like *Jeopardy!,* where you compete against other people answering *Jeopardy!* questions.)

The thousands of sexually oriented conversations each have titles to indicate their topic. You can see the list of topics, then decide which chats you will enter. Some deal with general sex topics, like group sex, S/M, and gay sex. Others deal with people looking to talk to others in their geographical area who share a highly specific sexual interest. You can also create a chat room of your own.

Once you choose the chat room you want to enter, you join a public conversation by giving yourself a log name different from your usual one, and entering your typed text. Instantaneously, your text is transmitted to everyone else who is reading the scroll of conversation in that category. You may address your comments to a particular person, or to the group in general. If you seem to be getting along especially well with someone in that public chat, you can ask if the person wants to create a private chat room so you can have a conversation that is not viewed by the rest of the people in the public space. When you create a title for your private chat room, it becomes a virtual place that is just for you two (or three or four if you're into group computer sex).

Some people wonder—or worry—if they really have privacy when they get kinky on the Internet. It is expected that when you create a private chat room, you have as much privacy as if you were talking to someone in a private phone conversation. If you trust your provider of the on-line service, then you will trust that no one is spying on you, just the same way that you would trust that the phone company is not listening in on your phone conversations. Also, you are not revealing your real name, since you are using a code name on-line. There are ways that your conversation could be traced to your computer, but this is rare. Honestly, the best protector of anonymity on the Net is indifference. If you don't care what other people think of the things you write, and other people don't care about the things that you write, then no one would go out of the way to try to trace you.

A big advantage of computer sex over professional phone sex is the low cost. Typically, computer services offer a package of on-line time with some hours free each month, and then the rest charged as a local phone call. So sex on the net is inexpensive, with typical costs ranging from only about $2.50 to $4.00 an hour.

Some people find that the drawback to computer sex is the tedium of typing. "I had to describe all of my actions. It was like, 'Now I'm unbuttoning the last button. Now I'm licking your nipple.' It was hard to get into it, thinking now I'm going to say this, now I'm going to say that. It was fun, but not a very erotic experience," explained twenty-five-year-old Evan.

People who enjoy this kind of "hot chat" the most have usually found a partner over the computer who is good at writing explicit erotic prose. (An advantage of professional phone sex over computer sex is that phone sex operators are trained what to say and how to say it. On a computer it's based on untrained people's ability to be creative and articulate.) In the best computer sex situations, the partners know which words turn the other on. Remember, if you are having sex over the computer, you are describing where you are putting which body parts. If the person you are typing to likes to use the word *cock* and you prefer *penis,* you'll have to agree on which words you'll use before it gets into the nitty-gritty of describing the sex act.

People who love getting off on-line do a lot of one-handed typing. "I would finger myself the whole time. I got good at typing with my left hand. It took a while to type out all the things I would think, but the anticipation only got me hornier."

Here's an example:

Enter the sex chat room called "Hot Tubs." See a scroll of conversation of people pretending to sit in a hot tub.

BIG BOY: Now I give you a backrub, Candy.

CANDY: Big Boy, scratch me where it really itches, if you know what I mean.

BIG BOY: Does that feel good, Candy? You are so sexy. I'd love to taste you to know if you are as sweet and sticky as candy.

CANDY: Hey, Big Boy, let's go private! I know you want a piece of Candy.

(In a private chat room a few sentences later.)

BIG BOY: Now I am going down on you. You do taste sweet.

CANDY: Oh, I feel like I'm going to come. Keep licking my clit.

BIG BOY: I am licking you harder. I'm licking your clit harder.

CANDY: Oh. I'm coming. Oh. Lick it. Lick it. Oh yes. Can you taste my sweet candy? Now can I make you come?

BIG BOY: Yeah. I'd like to put my dick in you now.

This continues until Big Boy writes that he has an orgasm. Then they both discuss how good their cigarettes taste. And finally, they log out.

Going to Adult Movie Theaters, Strip Clubs, or Prostitutes

While most people today prefer to stay home and watch sex on videos, some still like the old-fashioned experience of going to a theater to watch porn movies. Many men who go to XXX theaters usually feel that they have to get out of the house to watch porn movies, because they wouldn't want their family or roommates to know that they rented porn videos. Some men get turned on by the seedy feeling of an adult movie house. They may enjoy seeing other men watching them watch the movie as well. Sometimes two men will pick each other up at gay adult movie theaters, or there will be female prostitutes outside the theaters for straight men. Except for the rare case of Pee Wee Herman's arrest for masturbating "in public" at a XXX movie theater in Florida in 1991, going to these theaters is safe and legal.

Watching women strip at a strip bar or live peep show can give men the thrill of looking without the chance to touch. "I wouldn't want to have sex with anyone other than my wife, but I am always dying to see another pair of tits," said Michael, twenty-nine. For most men who enjoy going to strip clubs, it's about the fantasy. All of sudden after they walk in from the city streets, they are surrounded by beautiful women dancing. Yet men may soon find that as they adjust to the circumstances, their sexual arousal decreases.

"The worst part of the strip club is that after they strip the girls try to make conversation. It ruins the entire mood, because 99.9 percent of the time they have nothing to say," said twenty-seven-year-old Dave.

Some men who go to these places feel powerful because they think they are getting women to do anything for them sexually. Eric, twenty-four, said, "If I can get a woman to dance naked and sit on my lap for a few bucks then I feel like I am controlling her." Other men feel that strip clubs exploit them: he's the one who's laying out the $20 bills just to see nudity. Is it an even exchange? While the women are being treated as sex objects, the men are being stripped of their hard-earned cash.

Going to prostitutes or an escort service or a massage parlor that also gives hand jobs is another issue altogether, because it is illegal (except for certain places like the Mustang Ranch in Nevada). However, there are many men who still patronize prostitutes. As I explain more in the next section, there is a great difference between street prostitues and women from escort services who have sex for money. Men who want to have sex that has no emotional attachment and sex that may make them feel more powerful because they are paying for it will usually call high-priced escort services or go to massage parlors. Street prostitues usually work to service men who will help them buy drugs, or who don't care as much about protecting themselves from diseases, or who have very little money to spend on sex. These are the men who are more likely to get arrested for soliciting a prostitute.

Having Sex for Money: Prostitution and Stripping

At first, when Sydney on *Melrose Place* was into prostitution, she was a high-priced call girl who lived the good life. However, when Sydney was still short on cash, she had to turn to stripping, because, as *MP* viewers were told, once you take your clothes off for money, you won't be able to turn back to taking regular jobs. In a matter of a few episodes, Sydney had been transformed from a fancy call girl to a stripper, and then finally into a street prostitute who was getting beaten up for invading another pro's turf.

Viewers of *MP* know that the show is fiction (I mean who would ever believe that Andrew Shue would be interested in Courtney Thorne-Smith in real life?). Yet the characterization of Sydney has such a negative portrayal of the results of having sex for money that it made it look like anyone who is a prostitute or stripper is going to eventually destroy her life.

The truth is that it is mostly twentysomething women who have sex or strip for money, and they often go on to live normal lives in which they are neither beaten up by street prostitutes, nor do they have to stay in "the business" for the rest of their lives to make ends meet.

I am not trying to glamorize the jobs in which people use sex to make money. Certainly, the image of prostitution in *Pretty Woman* is not accurate, either. Some prostitues or escorts have severe psychological problems. It's illegal!

Yet the realities of stripping and prostitution is that many people—especially twentysomethings—can deal with taking off their clothes or having sex for money. Many of them live normal lives and continue with their normal lives during or after their job. These people who strip or are escorts do it for the money, enjoy it, and are careful about the work's effect on their physical and mental health. Rachel, a twenty-six-year-old graduate student in biochemistry, works in a peep show. "It's how I make enough to pay my rent. Financial aid in grad school sucks. My grants only pay for my research, not my rent. I have a great body, so I take advantage of it. I also like to feel powerful over the horny old men who can look but can't touch." Alex, a twenty-nine-year-old attorney who worked as a male escort, said that sex work was fulfilling to him: "I had always wanted to do it to affirm to myself that I still had it in me. Because I'm in such a traditional, conservative career, I felt like doing something wild on the side. Taking money for sex made me feel like a powerful, worldly, sexual man. I stopped doing it because I was afraid that if I got caught, my career would have been through."

Threesomes and Group Sex

It's common in monogamous relationships that one partner will have the desire to have a threesome. One of the attractions of having threesomes is the attention that two men can give one woman or two women can give one man. Also, the arousal that comes from watching your partner with someone else can be amazing for some people: "I always wanted to have sex with two women at once, to see their pussies rubbing together, to see two heads bobbing up and down on my dick. For my birthday, my girlfriend surprised me. She and another woman were sitting on my bed in lingerie. It was incredible, even better than my fantasies," said Chris, twenty-seven.

Even though sex does not always lead to love, emotions are still involved. If you have a threesome you are risking that you or your partner will fall in love with the other person. "I had a threesome with my boyfriend and his best friend. It was very good. The sex was better with my boyfriend's best friend. I asked my boyfriend if we could have the threesome again, and he said no because he knew how much I liked it. Then I started having an affair with his best friend. It was awful, because I fell in love with him," explained twenty-three-year-old Vicki. So if you are going to have a threesome, you have to take the risk of losing your partner. If you don't want to take that risk, you and your partner have to be able to detach yourselves emotionally and not be susceptible to the lust that results unless it stays in the context of the threesome.

Besides the occasional threesome, some couples are "swingers"— they look for other couples to have threesomes, or swap mates with another couple, or have a "foursome" with another couple, or have group sex with a lot of couples.

▼ ▼ ▼ ▼ ▼ ▼ ▼ ▼ ▼ ▼ ▼ ▼ ▼ ▼ ▼ ▼ ▼ ▼ ▼

The turn-on of group sex is often the heightened sensation of feeling many hands, tongues, breasts, feet, penises on you at once.

▲ ▲

Just image how great even a back massage could feel if there were ten hands instead of two. Of course, group sex sometimes feels risky or confusing. If you participate in group sex, you have to make sure that you can trust everyone involved to use birth control and to practice safer sex by using condoms, dental dams, or Saran Wrap.

Tantric Sex

Unlike some of the other sexual practices I've described, Tantric sex focuses on the connection between sex and spirituality. Tantric sex, or Tantra, draws upon Eastern philosophies and ancient sexual practices such as those of Buddhists, Hindus, and Taoists. Like yoga or meditation, it involves heightening all of the senses. The goal of Tantra is for two people to feel their individual energy connect up with the other person; then they connect their joint energy with the energy of the universe. Essentially they will become "one with each other and one with the universe."

▼ ▼

Couples who engage in Tantra get sexual stimulation from the energy exchange and the deep connection that they feel.

▲ ▲

Pleasure cannot be obtained unless the Self and all of the senses are in a state of accepting: the couple should be expecting the optimum sexual experience and surrender themselves completely to the experience, merging their bodies and their beings and becoming as close as possible. In a spiritual sense, the union between loving partners can be an experience where each can share their mutual interdependence. The sexy feelings come from the meditative, relaxed state.

In order to set the scene to achieve the heightened sensations, all of the five senses must be stimulated. For visual arousal, usually Tantra is practiced in the nude. If clothes are worn, they look romantic rather than aggressive. (Instead of wearing, for example, bustiers and leather, couples wear soft silky fabrics in pastels or gold colors.) Candles are used to provide a soft, mystical mood, and the lighting of the candles is symbolic of the experience. Lovers may light four candles: one representing the heart, one representing the mind, one representing the body, one representing the spirit. Incense stimulates the sense of smell. For sound, soft music is played, often New Age music. To stimulate the sense of taste, the couple may use wine or succulent fruits. As for touch, every body part will be stimulated as the couple begins the Tantric sex.

There are many different Tantric sexual positions. One starts by the two people stating their meaning for each other. They may say something like: "I honor you as an aspect of myself." Sitting cross-legged, face-to-face, they look into each other's eyes and hold each other's hands. They concentrate on this pose until they can feel energy flowing back and forth through their hands. After staying in this pose, they feel intoxicating sexual arousal flowing over their whole body from the closeness and connectedness with each other.

In sexual intercourse, the thrust is very slow during penetration—the man withdraws and reinserts his penis many times to prolong his orgasm. People doing Tantra usually hold back their orgasms for a long time. They would *never* think something like: "OK, let's get this over with, so I'm going to get in the best position that I know will help me have an orgasm." Rather they try to experience a full body orgasm. Some people describe the feeling as a calmer orgasm that focuses on all of the sensations.

The final outcome of Tantra is that it makes people feel a deep connectedness with their partner, often lasting for days after the sexual experience.

Foot Preferences

While Tantra focuses on spirit and whole body, this sexual practice concentrates on one body part—the feet. People with foot preferences get sexually aroused primarily by the sight, taste, or smell of their lovers' feet.

You've heard the expression "foot fetish" referring to someone who gets turned on by feet. I prefer to use the term "foot preference," since fetish is a pejorative that implies deviance.

A foot preference really is not all that odd if you think about it. In our society it's perfectly acceptable for a man to get turned on by looking at, touching, or licking a breast. We don't say that he has a "breast fetish." If we don't think that there's anything wrong with getting turned on by that body part, then why should we think there is anything wrong with a person getting turned on by any other single body part?

The foot is rich with nerve endings; it is a sensuous part of the body. But here in America we are trained to think negatively about our feet, that they're big and smelly and silly. In contrast, people with foot preferences find feet sexy. They may have an orgasm by feeling a tongue being drawn slowly between their toes or feeling their lover kiss the arch of their foot. Basically, any type of massage, washing, kissing, licking, or sucking may turn on someone who loves feet. Sometimes someone with a foot preference may fantasize about feet during masturbation, too.

▼ ▼

Foot preference can employ a lot of creativity and play. Imagine spending one hour just making love to your partner from the ankles down!

▲ ▲

Most people with foot preferences are men, desiring women's feet, but sometimes women are turned on by feet, too.

Transvestism

You've seen them on every talk show, but you may still wonder what transvestism is all about. The key to transvestism is transforming one's self to get aroused. A transvestite is someone who wears clothes of the opposite gender for sexual arousal.

"Trans" is from the Latin meaning cross, and "vest" means dress, yet the term cross-dressing has a slightly different meaning from transvestism. Cross-dressing is actually an umbrella term for anyone who wears clothes of the opposite gender for any reason, not just for pleasure, sexual arousal, or escape from traditional gender roles. Falling under the heading of cross-dressing would be anyone who dresses like the other gender for a lark, like if you dress up on Halloween—or for a job. For example, there are gay men, also called drag queens, who dress like women to entertain. Often they will dress like Judy Garland, Barbra Streisand, Joan Crawford, or other celebrities. Drag queens are not usually dressing for arousal—they usually are doing it for the money.

▼ ▼ ▼ ▼ ▼ ▼ ▼ ▼ ▼ ▼ ▼ ▼ ▼ ▼ ▼ ▼ ▼ ▼ ▼

Transvestites dress for sexual arousal or for a release from the traditional gender role.

▲ ▲ ▲ ▲ ▲ ▲ ▲ ▲ ▲ ▲ ▲ ▲ ▲ ▲ ▲ ▲ ▲ ▲ ▲

One final distinction: transvestites are not transsexuals. Transsexuals are people who feel that they should be in the body of the other gender, so they have sex-change operations. Transvestites have absolutely no desire to change their bodies, only their clothes.

Men who are transvestites may like dressing like a woman because they like the way it feels. It may make them more relaxed. If you saw the movie *Ed Wood*, you'll remember the scene where the director Ed Wood was having a particularly stressful day and the only way for him to chill out was to put on an angora sweater and a skirt. Transvestites might prefer to wear a skirt rather than a man's suit because it's much less confining and freer. Also, they might get turned on by feeling their penis or thighs or entire body brushing against the smooth fabric of feminine clothes. Some transvestites get the most turned on by feeling their skin against the women's lingerie they wear. Others get the most turned on when they succeed at "passing" for a woman in public; that arousal is from the sense of being allowed to be more feminine, more graceful, and being accepted in that role.

Transvestites may also be women. Yet since women have more freedom to wear masculine clothes anyway, transvestites are usually men.

One of the most common misconceptions about transvestites is that they are gay. Interestingly, most transvestites are heterosexual men. Only about 5 to 10 percent are gay, the same percentage as in the general public.

Sadomasochism (S/M)

When most people think of sadomasochism (S/M or S and M) all that comes to mind is leather, whips, chains, and handcuffs. S/M involves trust and communication. Sometimes it involves pain, but mostly it only involves power.

▼ ▼ ▼ ▼ ▼ ▼ ▼ ▼ ▼ ▼ ▼ ▼ ▼ ▼ ▼

S/M is a lot more than chains and pain. S/M deals with an exchange of power.

▲ ▲ ▲ ▲ ▲ ▲ ▲ ▲ ▲ ▲ ▲ ▲ ▲ ▲ ▲ ▲

To explain, I'll begin with definitions. In "S/M" the S stands for sadism; the M stands for masochism. The sadist is also called the "dominant," the "top," the "master." This is the person who is in control of the masochist, who can also be called the "submissive," the "bottom," or the "slave." Either the dominant or the submissive may be male or female.

Submissives get great pleasure from giving total control over to the dominant. Jake, a twenty-one-year-old submissive, says, "I'll let her do anything to me. I don't have to think about sex; she takes over." Dominants like twenty-three-year-old Marcia like taking control. She says, "I like constructing the scene, deciding what comes next. The order and the scripting is exciting."

S/M practicers usually dress to fit the role that they are taking on. The dominant may wear black leather or tight-fitting clothes made of rubber, lace—or any fabric that makes them look powerful—and sometimes clothes that reveal the breast, genitals, or butt. Submissives are sometimes nude while the dominant is clothed, thus giving a feeling of subservience and humiliation. Sometimes the submissive wears shabby clothes like an old white T-shirt or a burlap sack.

It takes a lot to understand the realities of S/M, because so many negative messages have been expressed about this practice, especially in movies such as *9½ Weeks, Blue Velvet, Bitter Moon,* and *Crimes of Passion,* which depicted violence and labeled it as S/M. S/M is not violent if it is done as it should be: with knowledge and agreement from both partners.

The key to an S/M relationship is consent. Both people have to discuss ahead of time if they are ready to engage in S/M sex. Once consent is established, the second step is scripting the scenario. S/Mers get explicit about exactly what they want their S/M scene to contain. Sometimes this involves sharing fantasies, like specifics about how they want to be touched or talked to. S/Mers also come up with a code word for *stop* to get around the problem of that part of the scenario that might involve the submissive saying, "No! Stop!" and not meaning it. Using the code word is the only way that one of them can stop the scene in the middle. Usually the couple chooses a one-syllable code word that sounds unique, like the name of a color or place. Without the code, as you can imagine, someone could get physically or emotionally hurt.

The irony is that with a clear way of communicating that "No means no," S/M is actually very safe. In fact, S/M may be even safer than traditional dating, where people take consent for granted. In traditional dating, unfortunately, "Stop" doesn't always mean *stop,* but the couple neglects to discuss this problem and date rape can result. In consensual S/M in which the couple obeys the given stop word, miscommunication and nonconsensual sex is practically impossible.

Sometimes S/M involves the consensual giving and receiving of pain and restraint. Some of the things that would be used to administer pain may be wire hangers, clothespins, metal clamps, hot wax, straight pins, wooden paddles, canes, leather whips, riding crops, or a cat-o-nine-tails (which is a short whip with lots of leather strips instead of just one). Objects used for restraint may be silk scarves, gags, blindfolds, ropes, rubber bands, handcuffs, chastity belts, or cock rings (which are leather or metal rings that fit around the base of the penis and scrotum). These S/M objects are usually purchased from adult/sex stores, or from hardware stores. No one should play with these dangerous objects unless they know exactly what they are doing. Practicing S/M that involves pain can be very dangerous unless the people know exactly how and where the body can take pain. This can be learned through an S/M organization or from other experienced S/Mers.

When S/M involves pain, there is a process that is usually followed to gain consent and script out the scene. First they agree upon the toys and equipment to use. Next, they agree upon the three components of the pain: intensity, duration, and rhythm. Usually the intensity and duration are inversely related: a short time is hard; a long time is light. For example, if they choose a whip, they might agree on five hard, short strokes administered in under five minutes. The rhythm is what adds to the arousal, the same way that the rhythm of intercourse or masturbation can help bring someone to orgasm.

People who engage in S/M make it clear that the pain is a "good" type of pain, unlike the unexpected pain of stubbing your toe, which they would still find unpleasant. Leroy, a twenty-six-year-old who gets turned on by being dominated, explains it this way: "It's like if you get into a bathtub when the water feels really hot at first; it's painful, and kind of stimulating. Your body gets used to the feeling and it's pleasurable." It also could be analogous to exercising hard, when it "hurts so good." All the nerves are awaiting intense sensation.

After the S/M scenario is played out the couple most often exhibits one of the deepest aspects of S/M: the caring. The couple often cuddles and talks about how the experience felt. It is difficult to do an S/M scene without having an intense connection, or love, because there is so much intimacy involved in it.

I must reemphasize that S/M should always be 100 percent consensual. Without explicit consent from your partner, using any type of S/M device, from the most benign, like a silk scarf as a blindfold, to the most dangerous, like a whip or metal clamps, is *extremely* dangerous and illegal. S/M must involve both partners having a lot of knowledge on the subject and true agreement, otherwise it is abuse, rape, and battering.

Finding Your Sexual Self

You can engage in any of these sexual activities or none. You do not have to pick one practice over another. You can dabble and even combine some component from any of the practices. You can fantasize about anything, and you can share the fantasy, act it out, or keep it to yourself. You may decide to try some of the sexual practices presented here, if you haven't already, or you may think up some of your own. Remember that your sexual choices do not need to be based on negativity or fear, since condoms can be easily integrated into any scenario in which you have a partner or partners.

▼ ▼ ▼ ▼ ▼ ▼ ▼ ▼ ▼ ▼ ▼ ▼ ▼ ▼ ▼ ▼
Sexuality is a wonderful, positive aspect of your individual personality.
▲ ▲ ▲ ▲ ▲ ▲ ▲ ▲ ▲ ▲ ▲ ▲ ▲ ▲ ▲ ▲

Look into yourself to explore your erotic potential: ask questions, observe, listen, read, explore. Celebrate sex by exploring the great diversity of sexuality. Allow your new knowledge of sexual diversity and erotic potential to be a boundless guide to your individual sexuality. How will you explore your own erotic potential?

CHAPTER 9

Sexual Healing
Resolving Sexual Difficulties

If It's Broken, Fix It

At some point in almost all people's lives, they experience a sexual problem. Sometimes the sexual difficulty can be so severe that sex feels more frustrating than pleasurable. If this happens to you, first you should try to resolve the problem by reading self-help information, such as what's in this chapter, and then if the problem persists you should see a sex therapist or medical doctor. There is no reason for you to go through life having problems with your sexuality, so don't shy away from the problem, figuring that it will work itself out over time. Instead, solve it, and start having a better sex life now.

The following sections describe the most common sexual problems and solutions for twentysomething women and men. If after reading them you feel you need more help resolving your problems, read the information at the end of the chapter about how you can find a good sex therapist. Then get help.

Resolving Women's Sexual Difficulties
INABILITY TO HAVE AN ORGASM

Inability to have orgasms is the number one sexual complaint among women in their twenties. Over 25 percent of college-age women report that they've never had an orgasm. Even now, in an era when women are supposedly more empowered about their sexuality, many still feel inhibited about learning how to please themselves. Others are trying to have orgasms but just don't know how to do it.

▼ ▼

If you have never had an orgasm, you must understand that you can have them and you will have them. You just need patience, time, and perseverance.

▲ ▲

If you aren't having orgasms, you could be afraid of intimacy, guilty about enjoying sex, tense, hostile toward your partner, or unable to give up control. If you are a woman with any of these issues who does not have orgasms, you would benefit from being in therapy to discuss the issues that may be interfering with your sexual response.

However, usually when women have difficulty achieving orgasm, the problem can be solved through learning more about their sexual response (the physical aspect of orgasm) and by letting go of any worries about being able to climax. The Catch-22 is that often when women can't come, they put so much pressure on themselves that they forget the pleasure of sex and psych themselves out of having an orgasm. Orgasms are a function of pleasure, so if you are tense or anxious then I can almost guarantee that it will not happen. To feel pleasure you must relax and let yourself go. This is not as easily done as it is said. As twenty-two-year-old Victoria explains, "Everybody would tell me that I should just relax. Well, I tried to relax; I tried to tense up; I tried everything, but I still never came."

Many women who have never had an orgasm are afraid to give up control. Even if these women try to come, they may still be subconsciously holding out because they are still trying to control their bodies. Sex is about letting go. During orgasm, you are totally out of control for a few moments; you might make sounds or motions during an orgasm that you would normally not make. In order to have orgasms, you must *accept* that to have the pleasure, you must take the risk of letting go of the control. Once you have achieved that acceptance, you should be able to relax and let yourself come.

If you've never had an orgasm maybe it's because you don't know what kind of physical stimulation you need. You might benefit from being in sex therapy to get proper instruction on exercises to teach yourself to have orgasms, but first try to do these exercises on your own. Remember, inability to have orgasms is common among young women, so don't automatically assume you have a major problem. Every woman is capable of having an orgasm. If you have never had one, you are not *in*orgasmic, you are *pre*orgasmic. You *will* have an orgasm: this is a fixable sexual problem!

The first step in learning how to have orgasms—before learning to come during sex with a partner—is to achieve them through masturbation. When you are learning how to have orgasms you will be focusing on getting your clitoris to perform the one function for which it is intended—pleasure. Locate your clitoris and become familiar with the way it feels, and how much pressure it takes to make it feel good. In women whose clitoris is located under the clitoral hood, it may be necessary to gently move the clitoral hood up a bit to expose the clitoris. If you are aroused, when you begin to rub your clitoris you should experience a pleasurable, relaxing feeling. Try rubbing it in a circular motion using your index finger or your index and middle fingers together. If it feels oversensitive, or starts to feel as though it aches a little to much, then apply a bit less pressure, or take a break for a second or two.

The whole time you do these exercises, you should try to stay aroused. You can increase the likelihood of having an orgasm if you think erotic thoughts. Try thinking about how good it feels when you are touching and kissing someone you want to have sex with until you feel turned on. Try watching a porn movie, if it will turn you on. Or try reading an erotic story in a porn magazine that describes the kind of sex you find exciting.

Even though you are stimulating your mind with erotic thoughts, keep focused on the feeling in your clitoris. If it feels good, but you feel you are staying at a plateau, then try to adjust to bring yourself over the edge to have the orgasm. Apply more pressure. Try masturbating in different positions, like on your stomach with your hand underneath you. Try inserting a finger from your other hand in your vagina to add to the stimulation. Overall, stay relaxed. Focus on the feelings inside your body, but don't try to force the orgasm to happen. Try to cross the threshold to orgasm by relaxing into it and getting into letting go. Also, it is important to keep breathing.

After a period of time, you should have an orgasm. It may be minutes or up to an hour of continuous contact, but at some point if you continue practicing it should happen. If it doesn't, you will inevitably get frustrated. If you do, try to calm down, clear your mind, and stop the exercise for that day; then try again another day. Don't give up. Stay dedicated to this as if it's a new project in your life. Play with these exercises every day for at least a half-hour if you truly want it to happen.

For many women, once they set their mind to it, they are successful at finding a way to have an orgasm. "I had tried everything, or so I thought. I just kept trying masturbating. It always felt good, but no orgasm. Then one night it worked. I think that that time I used more pressure than usual. I kind of got my fingers into the rubbing. I didn't put my fingers inside my vagina. That time the rubbing worked and I came. And I've been coming ever since," said Wendy, twenty-five. It can and will happen if you stick with it.

Many women find that if they have had difficulty having an orgasm then using a vibrator is most effective for coming the first time. (Choose a plug-in, electric vibrator, like the Hitachi Magic Wand, since the electric models have more power than the battery-operated ones.) Experiment with lying on your back and holding the vibrator on your clitoris or lying on your stomach with the vibrator underneath your pelvis, making direct contact with your clitoris. Relax, breathe, fantasize, move your pelvis gently, and make adjustments in your position and the vibrator's position until you feel the intensity of the feelings increase. Eventually, you should be able to have an orgasm. If you still have not come and are thinking of giving up these exercises, then see a sex therapist for more instruction.

It is common for women to have difficulty coming during intercourse, even if they come easily from masturbation or oral sex. This is because the motion that men and women need to have an orgasm is different. Most men need a back-and-forth motion, like the motion they would use during masturbation or during thrusting in intercourse, while most women need a more circular motion around the clitoris, like the motion she would use during masturbation. In order to have an orgasm from the clitoris during intercourse the woman may need to get into a position where she can rub against a man's pelvis while his penis is inside her. During intercourse, she should experiment with different positions. As Yolanda, twenty-four, found out: "I never could come during sex. Then I figured out that if I got on top and leaned down I could keep him inside me, at the same time that I rubbed my clit on him. Now I come every time I have sex." The best position for a woman to have an orgasm during intercourse often varies from partner to partner since all men's bodies are different. His height, weight, penis size, and position are all factors in the positions she will find to help her have orgasms.

Another way to stimulate the clitoris during intercourse is to get into a position where you can rub it with your fingers while he is thrusting. Don't be shy about "masturbating" yourself, thinking that you should be able to come from intercourse alone. Even if you can get to that point, sometimes you might want to speed things along by adding a little more clitoral stimulation.

Some women find that if they strengthen the muscles around their vagina, the pubococcygeus or PC muscles, then they feel more intense orgasms. Strengthening these muscles can make the vagina feel tighter around a man's penis. Because the PC muscles are the same muscles that can stop the flow of urine, you can locate them by recognizing what it feels like when the muscles contract. Then insert one finger into your vagina and try to contract the muscles around your finger. The muscles are all within your pelvis and vaginal areas, so you should not be feeling the muscles in your stomach or butt. In order to strengthen the PC muscle, you can do vaginal exercises called "Kegel Exercises." Exercise your vaginal muscle by contracting it twenty-five times in a row, twice a day, working up to fifty times in a row. Within a few weeks to a month you may notice that your vagina feels tighter and your orgasms feel stronger.

PAINFUL INTERCOURSE IN WOMEN

Painful intercourse, also called dyspareunia, is usually due to physical problems. In all cases, you should see a gynecologist to determine what is causing the pain and to remedy the problem.

If you want to try to determine the cause of the pain on your own, first figure out where the pain is located. If it is at the entrance to the vagina when the penis begins entry, the pain could be because your hymen is intact or remnants of your hymen remain. It is painful when a hymen breaks or stretches. You might want to have your gynecologist snip the hymen or the remnants of it. Pain at the entrance of the vagina could also be related to an infection in the Bartholin glands near the entrance of the vagina or from irritation or damage to the clitoris. You should see a gynecologist in all of these cases.

If the pain is inside the vagina, it may be related to an infection from a sexually transmitted disease, so you should have a gynecologist test you for STD's. Vaginal pain may also be related to an allergy to a new brand of condoms, creams, jellies, douches. To determine if this is the case, switch to another brand. If that doesn't immediately solve the problem, see a gynecologist, just in case there is another problem. Pain deeper inside the vagina could be related to a serious pelvic disorder, like cysts, tumors, or pelvic infections. Vaginal pain is rarely psychological, so if have it, you should definitely see a doctor. If your gynecologist can't find a medical cause for the pain, make an appointment with a sex therapist to see if you can uncover a less obvious psychological cause, such as a past sexual trauma or an aversion to sex.

VAGINISMUS

Vaginismus is a sexual dysfunction in which a woman's vaginal muscles in the outer third of her vagina involuntarily contract, making it difficult or impossible for a penis, and sometimes even something as thin as a finger or a tampon, to be inserted inside the vagina. Vaginismus usually has a psychological background. Often the woman is sexually repressed, afraid of men, or feels that sex is bad and dirty. Vaginismus may be the result of a bad experience with her sexuality, such as rape, sexual abuse, or a traumatic first sexual experience. In this case a woman's body "protects" her by contracting the muscles. This is an involuntary, subconscious reaction.

Causes of this sexual disorder are almost always psychological, and it is treated with a combination of talk therapy and physical therapy. If you have vaginismus and you go into sex therapy, your therapist will give you a series of exercises to do alone at home to begin conditioning your vaginal muscles to relax. Every day for a period of weeks or months, you will insert small plastic dilators into your vagina, using increasingly larger ones as time goes on. Eventually the muscles will be able to relax so a penis can be inserted without your muscles closing the vaginal entrance. The step-by-step conditioning will also help reduce your (conscious or unconscious) fears about having something inside your vagina. Besides the physical work with the dilators, you will benefit from talk therapy to discuss the issues that may have brought on your vaginismus and to help you understand that intercourse can be a pleasurable part of life.

Loss of Sexual Desire in Men or Women

If you are *sometimes* not interested in having sex when your partner is aroused, but you usually are, this is totally normal. If you are in a relationship, you may find that it is rare that two people have exactly the same desire for sex at the same time. Even if you want to awaken your desire, you may not be able to turn yourself on at will. For example, just because you usually get aroused by seeing your partner nude, you may not get excited seeing your partner nude if it's 6 A.M., you're half asleep, and sex is the furthest thing from your mind.

Usually it is easiest to postpone sex until you both feel desire at the same time. Try adjusting your schedules so that your sexual desire is more in sync. Try making time for sex when you know you will both want it. However, if your partner wants to have an orgasm and you do not feel desire, you can try to be part of the erotic experience without actually having intercourse or oral sex. In other words, your partner can masturbate while you watch or help. Or the partner with the higher sex drive can masturbate in private and can agree to have sex just on occasion. If you don't like these suggestions, and you still want your sex life to change, then you can both see a sex therapist about how you two can balance your differing levels of desire.

However, if one of you feels a complete loss of desire there may be a psychological reason or physical reason. You may lose desire if you are under stress from work or from any other aspect of your life, if you have gone through a recent trauma, if you feel depressed, or if you are unhappy in your relationship. You could lose interest because of a physical reason, such as hormone problems, illness, eating disorders, alcoholism, and drug abuse. If you can't pinpoint just what is preoccupying your subconscious, making your sex drive take a dive, a therapist may be able to help you discover what's interfering with your ability to get aroused. Remember, sexual attraction and arousal are very much tied to your feelings and thoughts. If you aren't getting aroused, don't just assume it's a "plumbing" problem. Talk it out with a therapist.

Resolving Men's Sexual Difficulties

PREMATURE EJACULATION

It is fairly common for twentysomething men to have orgasms during intercourse before they want to. Part of the reason why young men ejaculate prematurely is that they are still so excited by the sensation of sex. If a man almost always comes before he wants to, he needs to learn how to control when he will ejaculate.

Sex therapists are often reluctant to define just what "premature" means. Premature ejaculation may mean that a man comes after fewer than two minutes of intercourse or fewer than a dozen thrusts. It may also mean that he will ejaculate unintentionally during presex play, or as he is trying to penetrate the woman's vagina. Yet it is not advantageous for a man to try to time himself to see if he fits into a timed category of "premature ejaculator." A man is a premature ejaculator if he and his partner feel dissatisfied by his lack of control over how soon he will come, and the short length of time it takes for him to come during intercourse.

If a man comes before he wants to, he may have a very upsetting sexual experience because he feels guilty about "ending" before he could please his partner. Twenty-three-year-old Sam says, "I get so mad when it happens. I leave feeling like I'm not good enough and I never want to see the woman again." Often this problem reduces a man's self-esteem or makes him feel as if he's not masculine enough. Sometimes the partner is upset with him as well. This misunderstanding and anxiety can create a vicious cycle in that every time the man has sex he begins to worry that he will come too soon. He may even promise himself or his partner that this time will be different. Then, because he is worrying about it, his anxiety contributes to his problem and he still comes before he wants to.

In order to overcome premature ejaculation, first the man must learn that sex does not have to end in orgasm and does not always have to include intercourse. He can continue to have sex play with his lover after his orgasm. He can give his partner an orgasm before they have intercourse so he does not feel guilty over having his too soon. Yet it is important that rather than just making adjustments in who comes first he also learns how to control when he will come.

Some young men, like twenty-year-old John, try to change the things that they are thinking about during sex, in order to become less excited. "People told me to think about baseball. I guess I got too into the game—I lost my erection," says John. Turning off erotic thoughts during sex may help a guy last longer, but this is not an effective way to prevent premature ejaculation. First of all, like John, the man can lose his erection if he tries to turn himself off. Also, even if a man does not lose his erection from changing what he is thinking about during sex, by not allowing himself to think freely about erotic images during sex he is reducing intimacy with his partner. A man should not try to turn himself off during sex. The man's sexual problem is not that he is thinking erotic thoughts while having an erotic experience, but, in fact, that he is not thinking enough about what is going on in the moment.

When a man does not have control over when he ejaculates, he is often not focusing enough on how his body feels at each stage of excitement during intercourse. The man needs to learn how to focus on feeling the enjoyment of sex so he can get control of the feelings inside his body. By doing this, he will eventually be able to determine how he feels just before he is going to come so he can know how to reduce the physical stimulation and excitement when he wants to delay his orgasm. In particular, the man needs to learn what he feels like just before the "point of no return," when there is no way to stop the ejaculation. Eventually, he needs to be able to keep the feeling of pleasure strong without releasing and coming.

▼ ▼

The key to resolving premature ejaculation is for a man to feel in control of when he will ejaculate. Sex should be kept at a level where it is enjoyable but not out of control.

▲ ▲

If you ejaculate prematurely you may benefit from being in sex therapy (alone or with your partner). In sex therapy, you will get comprehensive instruction on how to get ejaculatory control. If you are dedicated to working on this issue you may be able to solve the problem without sex therapy. Through a series of exercises you can focus on getting control of your sexual responses, which will help you control when you ejaculate during intercourse.

First, start masturbating just like you usually do. Then, after you are fully erect and feeling very excited but have not yet reached the "point of no return," stop masturbating, wait a few seconds for your erection to subside a little bit, then start masturbating again. Continue this cycle of stopping and starting for about twenty minutes, then allow yourself to come.

After trying that activity about three times a week for two weeks, move on to the next step of this activity: work on being able to masturbate without stopping and starting. In other words, instead of stopping when you are very aroused, continue masturbating, but reduce the excitement so you do not come immediately. Try varying the amount of thrusting motions, relaxing your buttocks and pelvic muscles, and varying the tightness of your hand grip on your penis. This exercise should translate easily for use during intercourse. If you feel like you are getting too excited, you can thrust less or relax more during intercourse. This will help you maintain excitement for a longer period of time without coming. Lenny, a twenty-seven-year-old, found this was effective for him: "I don't come before I want to, because I relax my muscles instead of tightening up and *trying* to come."

During both of those exercises, it may be helpful to think about your arousal on a scale from 1 to 10:10 being the most aroused; 1 the least aroused. Then, through experimenting with the feeling during masturbation, you can figure out how to hover at about an 8, until you are ready to go to 10 and ejaculate. You can learn to enjoy sex while you are at an arousal point somewhere between 5 and 8, then let go and make it to the top, when you decide to let go and come.

You should be able to translate this skill of ejaculatory control from this masturbatory exercise to intercourse. If you still need more control over when you ejaculate during intercourse, you can try some more exercises while having sex with your partner. One of the most effective methods of controlling ejaculation during intercourse is called the "stop-start" technique. This is like the mastubatory exercise that I described in that the man stops intercourse when he gets very excited, just before he gets to the point of no return. You can stop thrusting, withdraw your penis until excitement subsides a little, then go back to thrusting and repeat the process. Some men can do this exercise without withdrawing their penis but by not moving or having the woman not move during intercourse.

To not interrupt sex quite as much as either of these exercises, you could try not to thrust so forcefully and to vary your position, moving around and stopping in a more casual way. For example, if you are on top and feel that if you keep thrusting you will come any second, then you can say to your lover, "Let's switch positions." Then you could withdraw your penis, and move to another position. When you insert your penis again and resume thrusting, the excitement will not be quite as high as it was before.

Another method, called the "squeeze technique" is the one that is most recommended by sex therapists. During intercourse, you can withdraw your penis when you feel too close to orgasm, and then either you or your partner can use a thumb and forefinger to squeeze the area just below the ridge of the head of the penis for a few seconds. This method disrupts sex more than the stop-start technique, yet is very effective. Sometimes it can also be effective if the person squeezes at the base of the penis. If just reading about these techniques is not helping you, then go to a sex therapist to talk about how you can get ejaculatory control.

INABILITY TO GET OR MAINTAIN ERECTIONS

It has been estimated that over half of the general population of men has had difficulty getting or maintaining an erection at some point in his life. Occasionally there are physical reasons why a man would not be able to get an erection, such as if he's on medication, drunk, ill, or has diabetes or circulatory problems. If a man frequently loses erections, or can never maintain an erection, he should see a doctor to find out if it is a medical reason. Most of the time, however, when a man has trouble getting an erection, it is not purely a physical problem. Sometimes he can't get hard because his mind is telling his body that he does not want to have sex.

To solve the problem, first it's important for you to determine if it's your mind or your body that is the culprit. To do this you need to consider if you never can get an erection, or if the problem is only that you occasionally lose erections. If you are telling yourself you never get erections, think about whether or not you get them in your sleep. It is normal for a man to get an erection every ninety minutes or so when he is asleep, and to wake up with an erection in the morning. If you never get erections at all, even in your sleep, then the chances are that you have a medical problem. If you normally get erections during sleep, when you wake up, or from masturbating or from any other sort of sexual arousal, then it is probably a psychological reason that makes you lose your erection during sex.

If there is no medical reason for your loss of erections, you can begin to examine possible psychological causes, such as stress, fatigue, guilt over having sex, or—the most common reason—performance anxiety. "I get limp with a new girlfriend the first few times we have sex. It's because I am scared that I won't be any good," said twenty-nine-year-old Richard, who has performance anxiety.

It is important for a man to realize that losing an erection does not mean that he is any less of a man. Matt, twenty-six, says, "I used to get so mad if I'd lose an erection that I'd bang on the walls and then stomp out of the bedroom. Now that I realize that it's just part of being a man, it happens less, and if it does I can get another one a few minutes later."

If all you can think about is the pressure on you to get hard and stay hard, then you may get caught in a continuous cycle of losing erections during intercourse. If you become so worried that you will lose your erection, then your fears and worries will make it a self-fulfilling prophecy. In order to avoid this, relax and try to realize that losing an erection every once in a while is usually no big deal. If you reduce stress, are not tired, are not intimidated or pressured by your partner, and feel very aroused, then eventually it is likely that you will regain the same ability to get erections. It definitely helps if you have an encouraging partner who tells you that it's OK if you lose your erection every once in a while. If the problem persists, you should see a sex therapist to help you uncover hidden reasons for the problem.

DIFFICULTY EJACULATING

There are several ejaculatory problems that men may experience. "Retarded ejaculation" means that it is difficult for a man to ejaculate during intercourse. Some men who have delayed ejaculation enjoy their problem at first, because it makes them and their partners feel like sex can "last for hours." Yet soon sex may become frustrating, since the man wants to come so much and cannot. This condition may have both a negative and positive effect on both partners. As twenty-five-year-old Marla explains, "It was great at first when he would take a long time to come, because we could have sex for hours. Then I hated it. Sometimes it hurt so badly because he'd keep going so he could try to come even when I was dry and wanted to stop."

A rarer problem is "retrograde ejaculation," a condition in which the man ejaculates but the ejaculate does not come out of the penis; instead it goes backward into the bladder. This is not dangerous, since the ejaculation will be released the next time the man urinates. Yet if you have this problem, you may want to talk to a doctor, just to be sure that there is not a more serious problem.

"Ejaculatory incompetence" means that a man does not ejaculate at all during intercourse. If these problems are related to a medical problem, then usually the man will not be able to ejaculate at all during any type of sexual activity, even masturbation. Most often men suffering from ejaculatory incompetence can ejaculate from masturbation but not during intercourse. This problem is most common in men under thirty. While ejaculatory incompetence is usually psychological, especially in young men, if you have this problem, you should consult a doctor to determine if the problem is a medical problem, perhaps a prostate problem, or related to diabetes or cancer. In the case of any type of ejaculatory problem, you should consider consulting a sex therapist to get to the root of the problem, and work on overcoming it.

PAINFUL INTERCOURSE IN MEN

If you feel pain during intercourse, it may be due to an allergy to using a certain kind of condom, or to spermicide such as nonoxynol-9, or to your lover's contraceptive foams, jellies, or douches. If this is the problem, you should use another type of condoms or spermicide or have your lover switch brands of contraceptive products.

In uncircumcised men, a tight foreskin that does not retract during erection may cause pain in the glans of the penis. Also, this sort of pain could be from an infection that developed around the foreskin due to uncleanliness. (An uncircumcised man should always clean the area under and around the foreskin and wash his penis with soap and water daily.) In the case of a problem with your foreskin, you should consult a doctor. Also, if you've ruled out an allergic reaction or a foreskin problem, you may be experiencing pain because you have a sexually transmitted disease or a more serious medical problem, like vascular problems or prostate problems, so definitely consult a doctor.

Finding a Sex Therapist for Men, Women, or Couples

If you cannot solve your sexual problem on your own, or you're impatient with the results of your own efforts to get back on track sexually, you might want to go to a sex therapist. Sex therapists are trained to help you resolve the basic issues that I covered in this chapter, plus they deal with issues of relationships, communication, identity, gender dysphoria, sexual orientation, and any other aspects of your personal life. (Sex therapists are not "sex surrogates"—people who have sex with you to try to resolve your problem. A legitimate, certified sex therapist talks you through exercises to resolve your sexual issues. They would never have sex with you.)

Sometimes people only need short-term therapy that lasts a few weeks; for example, premature ejaculation can usually be treated successfully in a few weeks. Other times, long-term therapy that lasts years is called for to help people deal with major psychological issues and to process how their past experiences and feelings have influenced their present, and how to shape their future.

Whether you are going into short-term or long-term therapy, it is extremely important that you feel confident and comfortable with the therapist you choose. You may have to do a little research to find a sex therapist you respect and trust. To find a good therapist in your area, you can either check the listings in your phone book, ask at a university, hospital, or health center, or ask friends for referrals (although I recommend that you do not go to the same therapist as a friend of yours because it adds a dynamic to the therapy that may make the therapy not as effective, perhaps because of an unconscious connection to the friend that will be present in therapy). The best source to find a certified sex therapist is the American Association of Sex Educators, Counselors and Therapists (AASECT). You can call them at (312) 644-0828, and for a small fee to cover printing and postage, AASECT will mail you a list of sex therapists in your area.

Once you find the names of therapists in your area, then your job is to interview them to find the one for you. Over the phone, the therapist should be glad to tell you his or her background, what degrees and certification he or she has, and if the therapist has an area of specialty. You should make sure that whomever you choose is a *certified* psychotherapist, psychologist, psychiatrist, family or marital counselor, or sex therapist. If you are starting therapy to treat a particular sexual problem, inquire about the therapist's special training in sex therapy or experience treating people with your specific problem.

If you feel comfortable enough talking with the therapist over the phone, set up a consultation. You may be nervous at your first consultation, but you should feel comfortable enough to talk openly with the therapist. If you go to a consultation with a new therapist and after your first session your gut feeling is that this therapist is not the one for you, go with that feeling, and then go to meet another therapist. You should not have to go to more than one or two before you find one who is good for you. But you do have the right to meet with a therapist, then decide to go to another one. Finding a therapist who is right for you is like starting any new relationship. You want to choose the best person for your current circumstance. The best therapy is the result of a good match between client and therapist.

CHAPTER 10

Playing It Safe

Birth Control, STD's, and Sexual Health

Female Sexual Health

WHY YOU NEED TO BE EXAMINED BY YOUR GYNECOLOGIST EVERY YEAR

It is crucial for women to regularly visit their gynecologist once a year for a breast examination, a Pap smear, and perhaps a sexually transmitted disease check. The doctor can detect cervical, ovarian, and breast cysts and cancers.

Women who are most prone to cervical cancer are those who were sexually active before the age of 18 and who have had multiple male sexual partners. Because there are rarely symptoms, when there are abnormal or cancerous cells on the cervix, it can only be detected by a Pap smear.

If you have never been to the gynecologist, then as soon as you finish reading the following sections, put this book down and pick up the phone book to call a gynecologist or health clinic to make an appointment.

WHAT WILL HAPPEN AT YOUR ANNUAL VISIT TO YOUR GYNECOLOGIST

The gynecological exam is quick and painless. It consists of three parts. First, the doctor will examine your breasts by looking and feeling for any lumps or discharge.

Then the doctor will have you lie down on the exam table for the second part of the visit: the vaginal-digital exam. During this part of the visit the doctor will insert her or his gloved, lubricated finger inside your vagina to feel for any abnormalities. The doctor will also push on your abdomen with a finger inside your vagina to feel your uterus.

During the third part of the exam, the doctor will insert a speculum inside your vagina. The speculum is a narrow metal instrument that holds the vagina open. While the speculum is holding the vagina open, the doctor will look at your cervix.

Then the doctor will try to detect cervical infections by performing a Pap smear. The doctor takes cells from the cervical walls by gently rubbing them with a long cotton swab. It doesn't hurt, since there are very few nerve endings near the cervix. The cells are smeared across a glass slide for examination under a microscope to look for abnormalities. If you think that you have been at risk for STD's, the doctor will also take samples from inside your vagina to run tests for specific STD's.

WHAT WILL HAPPEN AFTER THE VISIT

Within a week, you should receive the results of the tests. Negative results of your Pap test indicate that your cervix is healthy. Positive results may indicate "dysplasia"—abnormal cells covering the cervix. This most frequently develops in women between the ages of 25 to 35, although it may develop in women as early as their late teens or early twenties. If your test shows that you have abnormal cells, it is not cause for too much alarm. Dysplasia does not always develop into cancer, although, in some women, if left untreated, it can become cancerous.

It is also possible that the results of your Pap smear could show that you have early cancer or a growth of cancer cells on the top layer of the cervix. Although this develops most often in women between the ages of 30 and 40, it sometimes occurs in younger women. You will have follow-up visits with your doctor if your Pap smear is positive.

If your STD tests come back positive, then your doctor will either prescribe medication for you or ask that you return for another exam.

WHY YOU NEED TO PERFORM MONTHLY BREAST SELF-EXAMS

Breast cancer is the most common form of cancer in women in the United States, with over 140,000 cases diagnosed each year, that's more than 20 percent of women. More than 45,000 women die each year from breast cancer. While breast cancer affects people who are over 40 or 50 years old more frequently than people in their twenties, it is important to learn how to examine yourself for breast lumps.

Breast cancer is usually rather detectable, with symptoms such as lumps in the breast, nipple discharge, and changes in the shape of the breast. It is important to learn how to perform a breast self-exam, because, like most cancers, if it is detected early, breast cancer can be treated to prevent it from spreading, and frequently can be cured.

HOW TO PERFORM A MONTHLY BREAST SELF-EXAM

The exam consists of two parts. First you look at your breasts for any changes in them. Then you feel them for any lumps.

To begin examining your breasts, relax your arms on either side of your body. Look in the mirror for any change in the size, shape, or texture of your breasts. If you note any puckered or dimpled skin, or changes in the nipple such as scaling skin, or direction of the nipple, contact a doctor.

Next, hold your arms over your head to check for sores or dimpling under your breasts. Also, check to see whether your breasts move up and down together; they should.

Then place your hands on your hips, pressing in to tighten the chest muscles. Turn from side to side to view all areas of your breasts. Examine for dimpling or puckering of the skin. The skin should look smooth.

To examine your right breast for lumps, put your right hand behind your head, with the pads of the fingers of your left hand held flat and together, firmly pressing on the breast using small circular motions. Move in one finger-width, and continue in smaller and smaller circles until you have reached the nipple. Cover all areas including the breast tissue leading to the underarm area. Reverse the procedure for the left breast.

Gently squeeze each nipple checking for discharge. There should not be any discharge. Next, lie flat and place a pillow under your right shoulder. Put your right hand under your head. With your left hand, feel the right breast and armpit for lumps. Then place your left hand under your head and use your right hand to check your left breast and armpit.

If you do find a lump, or a change in consistency of the shape or skin of either breast, consult a doctor immediately.

You should become familiar with the feel of your breasts, since many women have lumpiness in their breasts that is normal and always present. What you should feel for during your self-exam is any lump that is hard, new, or different from what you usually feel in your breasts. If you have questions about what your breasts should "normally" feel like, or how to perform this self-exam more accurately, ask your doctor. This self-exam is not a substitute for yearly exams by your gynecologist, but it is necessary for early detection.

PREGNANCY

If you have missed your period, inexplicably gained weight, felt nausea and/or vomiting soon after engaging in sexual intercourse, you may be wondering if you are pregnant.

Other pregnancy indicators may include tender breasts, constipation, a constant need to urinate, color change in your nipples, hot flashes or an elevated body temperature, an increased sensitivity or repulsion to cigarette smoke, and fatigue or exhaustion.

While these symptoms don't necessarily indicate that you are pregnant, it is wise to take an early pregnancy test, which are available at supermarkets and drugstores.

Take-home pregnancy tests consist of a urine test to determine if it contains a high level of a hormone known as human chorionic gonadotropin, or HCG, which is released when conception has taken place. While these tests are usually accurate, some women have experienced false-negatives or false-positives, so you should follow up by seeing a doctor to confirm the results.

A doctor looks for several telltale physical signs of pregnancy that occur 6 to 7 weeks after your last menstrual period. After about 7 weeks into pregnancy, a pale violet coloration of the entrance to the vagina and the neck of the uterus may be evident. This is caused by blood engorgement in the vaginal area that may darken to blue, then to an almost blue-black tint as pregnancy progresses.

If you are pregnant and you were not planning to be, then you face a serious decision. Will you keep your child? Will you have an abortion? Will you give your child up for adoption? To explore the options, seek counseling from a nonbiased source. In other words, if you go to a prolife organization, like Birth Right, they will try to convince you to keep the child or put him or her up for adoption. Similarly, at some abortion clinics or Planned Parenthoods, you may feel influenced to have an abortion. Your decision should be based on your personal thoughts and feelings, not politics. If you need help making your decision, talk to people you can trust, or go to a neutral counselor or therapist.

▼ ▼
Don't get caught up in the politics of pro-life versus pro-choice when you are facing a real-life choice.
▲ ▲

Male Sexual Health

While most women know to check their breasts each month, few men know to check their genitals. Men may be prone to sexual health problems that early detection could prevent from being dangerous. For example, testicular cancer can be caught in its early stages if men practice a monthly self-examination. Also, men should inspect their genitals for changes to detect if they could have contracted a sexually transmitted disease. Maintaining good sexual health by being familiar with the way your body works can help you detect symptoms early enough to save your own life.

WHY MEN NEED TO CHECK THEIR TESTICLES EVERY MONTH

Testicular cancer is one of the most common cancers in men 20 to 35. If discovered early, it can be treated.

The first sign of testicular cancer is usually a slight enlargement of one of the testes and a change in its consistency. There is often a dull ache in the lower abdomen and groin, with a sensation of dragging and heaviness. Men who have an undescended or partially descended testicle are at higher risk of developing testicular cancer than others.

HOW TO PERFORM A MONTHLY TESTICULAR SELF-EXAM

It is possible to detect signs of testicular cancer early by performing a self-examination. All men should perform a monthly self-exam. The best time is after a warm bath or shower, when the scrotal skin is most relaxed.

Place your index and middle fingers of both hands on the underside of the testicle and your thumbs on the top. Gently roll each testicle gently between the thumb and fingers.

You should feel the epididymis, which is the structure at the back of the testicles where sperm collects. (If you are unsure where to find it, see the diagram in chapter 4.) Besides that structure, normal testicles should feel smooth. If you find any hard lumps or changes in consistency, see your doctor at once. Do not assume that you have cancer if you find a lump; sometimes a lump within the scrotum is a cyst or swollen vein. Only a doctor can tell you for sure.

WHAT WILL HAPPEN WHEN YOU VISIT A DOCTOR OR UROLOGIST?

The doctor will question you about your medical history, your family history of cancer, and symptoms you may be having, particularly regarding problems with urination. Then the doctor will conduct a physical exam.

First he will examine your testicles for any lumps or abnormalities, like you do in your monthly self-exam. Then he will conduct a digital-rectal exam to determine if you have any prostate problems, like whether the prostate is enlarged, has lumps, or has an abnormal texture. Because the prostate is in front of the rectum, the doctor can feel it by inserting a gloved, lubricated finger into the rectum. While prostate cancer usually does not develop in men who are in their twenties, an annual exam is a good precaution.

Playing It Safe

The following charts will help you make good choices. You will have a mindblowingly healthy sex life if you take care of yourself and play safely.

The Most Common Sexually Transmitted Diseases

DISEASE	WHAT IS IT?
Yeast Infection	Caused by overgrowth of normal vaginal or penile organisms. For women, can be caused by poor hygiene, antibiotics, birth control pills, pregnancy, or diabetes, as these disrupt the pH balance in the vagina. Can be spread through sex, but not really an STD.
Urinary Tract Infection	Infection from bacteria trapped inside the urethra. Common in women after they have sex multiple times with a new sexual partner, even if they are using condoms.
Crabs/Pubic Lice	Small crablike body lice in pubic hair. Extremely contagious. Commonly passed by sexual contact, or through bedsheets, towels, or clothes.
Chlamydia	Most common sexually transmitted disease. Bacteria that is transmitted through vaginal or anal sexual contact with an infected person. Oral sex with an infected partner may lead to a chlamydial throat infection.
Gonorrhea	A bacterial infection. May lead to severe inflammation of the urinary tract in men; in women, can result in inflammation of the reproductive organs and potentially lead to sterility, or spread to other parts of the body, resulting in arthritis and liver damage.

SYMPTOMS	HOW TO TREAT IT
In women: vaginal itching and thick white or yellowish vaginal discharge. In men: pain, itching, and discharge from the penis. Both men and women experience painful intercourse.	Treated with over-the-counter vaginal creams for women, topical creams for men. Often prevented in women by wearing cotton underpants; wiping from front to back; and avoiding pantyhose, tight jeans, wet bathing suits, feminine hygiene sprays, and douching.
In men and women: pain or burning sensation when urinating, and an urgency to urinate. Sometimes urine is cloudy or has an unpleasant odor.	Doctor can prescribe antibiotics to clear it up within one to ten days.
Severe itching. Appearance of tiny crablike lice in chest hair, armpit hair, pubic hair, eyelashes, or eyebrows.	Doctor prescribes topical medication. Clean linens, clothes, and towels. Try not to scratch. Anyone who has had intimate contact or has used the towels, clothes, or sheets of that person should also be treated.
Possibly asymptomatic. If symptoms are present they will be: For women, pain during urination, vaginal discharge, and lower abdominal pain; for men, burning sensation when urinating and penile discharge. Diagnosed by a doctor testing vaginal or penile secretions.	Doctor will prescribe antibiotic to clear the infection. Both partners should use the antibiotic, whether or not they are both symptomatic. It may take up to two weeks to clear up. During that time, infected partners must abstain from sexual activity.
May be asymptomatic. Symptoms may appear two to eight days after contact: itching on or around the sex organs, burning sensation when urinating, stomach pain, fever, and discharge. Diagnosed by a doctor testing vaginal or penile secretions.	Symptoms may disappear on their own, but can only be cured by taking antibiotics prescribed by a doctor.

DISEASE	WHAT IS IT?
Syphilis	Caused by a type of bacteria. In severe cases, attacks the nervous and cardiovascular systems.
Viral Hepatitis	A virus transmitted from sexual contact: hepatitis B and non-A, non-B hepatitis. (Other forms of hepatitis are caused by different viruses spread by contaminated water, food, and blood transfusions.)
Genital Warts/Human Papilloma Virus	Viral warts on the genital area transmitted through sexual contact.
Herpes	Genital herpes is one of two types of virus: Type-1 causes cold sores or fever blisters and can spread to the genitals through oral sex; Type-2 causes genital sores from intercourse and has been known to cause oral herpes. No cure, only treatments.
HIV and AIDS (Human Immuno-deficiency Virus and Acquired Immune Deficiency Syndrome)	A virus transmitted from infected semen, vaginal secretions, or blood getting into the bloodstream. HIV destroys a person's immune system and leads to diseases collectively labelled AIDS, which ultimately cause death.

SYMPTOMS	HOW TO TREAT IT
Symptoms usually appear within ten to ninety days after contact: painless chancre sore on the sex organs, rectum, and/or mouth. After one to five weeks, the sore usually disappears and a rash may appear. Symptoms disappear, yet disease is still present. Must be detected by a blood test.	A doctor will prescribe penicillin to cure it.
May be asymptomatic. May have a flulike reaction: fatigue, fever, chills, loss of appetite, achiness, tenderness in the abdomen, and jaundice. Diagnosed by a blood test.	No cure for viral hepatitis; doctor will prescribe medications for symptoms.
Small, painless, sometimes itchy, hard bumps that grow into warts on the genital area.	Warts must be removed by a doctor using acid, dry ice, lasers, or minor surgery. (Do *not* try to remove the warts on your own!) Virus stays in the body for a lifetime, yet symptoms may not reoccur. If warts do reoccur, they are again removed by a doctor.
Swelling, pain, itching, and burning at the place of infection, followed by reddening, tiny blisters that burst and form tender ulcers that crust and eventually heal. May include flulike symptoms. Outbreaks usually reoccur, sometimes for years.	Doctor prescribes antiviral medication Zorivax® (acyclovir) at the time of outbreak to heal the sores faster and to shorten the duration of the outbreak. Controlling stress, eating healthy, and exercising can limit the number of outbreaks.
HIV has no symptoms. Antibodies to the virus will show up in an HIV blood test. The first signs that HIV has become AIDS are when a person experiences night sweats, fatigue, noticeable weight loss, Kaposi's sarcoma (a rare type of skin cancer), or pneumonia.	There is no cure for HIV or AIDS, yet prescription medication, proper nutrition, exercise, and low stress may slow the virus. Each AIDS-related illness that occurs is treated as the illness requires.

How to Get Tested for HIV and What the Results Mean

If you think that you may have exposed yourself to the HIV virus and you want to find out for sure, then you should get tested for HIV. There are a number of reasons why some people should *not* get tested—for instance, if you think that you would be so devastated if you found out that you were HIV-positive that you would kill yourself. That is why, prior to HIV testing, any good testing site will do precounseling to find out if you should get tested. If the testing site does not have this kind of counseling, you might want to consider seeing a sexuality counselor or therapist beforehand, just to make sure that you understand the implications of getting tested.

You should only get tested at an anonymous testing site. Do not go to a regular doctor who takes your name and tells you that the results will be confidential. Once the doctor has your name and test results, you'll never know if it will truly be confidential. What if the doctor or his receptionist leaves your file out or lets your insurance company know you were tested? You could be denied insurance if you test positive. If others in your community find out from your doctor that you are HIV-positive or even that you got tested, you could be discriminated against: many people living with HIV and AIDS have lost their jobs or homes due to discrimination. At an anonymous testing site you will be asked to either give a fake name or you will be assigned a number. Also, to remain anonymous, if the test is not free, remember to pay in cash. I don't mean to make you paranoid, but with all the fear and misinformation about AIDS out there a lot of people are capable of being very cruel or unfair if they even suspect you have AIDS.

If you are getting tested with a partner, find a testing site that will allow you to be in the room when the clinician tells your partner the results, so there's no chance your partner will deceive you. Otherwise, the testing site may be able to put the results in writing, although this might be a problem if they don't have your real name.

Most cities have anonymous, free testing sites where you can get the results in about two weeks. There are also anonymous testing sites where you can pay a fee and get the results in two hours or one day or two days. You can check your local phone book for testing locations in your area, or call the Center for Disease Control National AIDS hotline to get information about testing sites in your area. The number is 1-800-342-AIDS.

Remember, the test for HIV actually is a test for your body's antibodies to the HIV virus, so you need to have had the virus for a period of months in order for your body to produce antibodies to it. There is no way to tell if you have HIV on the day that you were exposed to it. You need to wait about six months after your last possible exposure to the virus before it shows up as a positive result on an HIV test. (Sometimes HIV antibodies show up in tests sooner, perhaps in three months after you got the virus, but to be sure of the most accurate results, wait the full six months.)

The best way to be sure that you do not have HIV is to get tested, then abstain from sex or have very strict safer sex for six months, then get tested again. If you test negative the second time, then you do not have the virus.

The test itself is very accurate. At the test site, the clinician will draw a sample of your blood; then one or two tests on your blood sample will be run in the lab. If your blood tests positive for HIV in the first test (which is usually a test called the Elisa test), the lab immediately runs a second test to confirm the positive result (most often used is a test called the Western Blot yet sometimes other similar tests are used). If the second test is positive then you are HIV-positive. If the first test is negative then there is no second test, because the negative results of the first test are extremely accurate.

There are almost never cases of "false negative" or "false positive" results since the tests are highly accurate. In rare cases, antibodies to another virus in the body can trigger the test to come up with an "indeterminant result," meaning that you must get retested to find out the true results.

If you test negative for the virus, it does not mean that you will not be able to contract it in the future. Theoretically, if you test negative but have unprotected sex the next day you could get HIV. Therefore, if you test negative, try to stay that way. A negative test result is not a ticket to have unprotected sex.

If you test positive for the HIV virus but show no symptoms of AIDS-related diseases, then you may stay healthy, living with HIV for any amount of time from a day to over ten years. When someone has HIV they may look and feel just as healthy as they did before they had it. What it means to be HIV-positive is that your body contains a virus that is destroying your immune system, lowering the number of cells that you have to destroy diseases, and making it easy for you to get several diseases, collectively labeled as AIDS, such as pneumocystic pneumonia or Kaposi's sarcoma cancer. Once someone gets AIDS, the person may live for a number of years yet are usually plagued by one debilitating illness after another until one of the diseases eventually kills the person.

If you test HIV-positive but do not yet have AIDS, you must be sure to stay on a healthy diet, exercise, reduce stress, and take the preventative medication that your doctors recommend. Currently, there are some people who have been living with HIV for over ten years who have not contracted any AIDS diseases. Most people who receive a positive HIV test result get AIDS in about eight years and die about two years after that. Obviously, the outlook for HIV-positive people is bleak at the moment, but great strides are being taken toward finding a cure.

Birth Control

There is no such thing as a 100-percent-effective birth control method except for abstinence. There are, however, birth control methods that are very effective if used properly. If you do not want to get pregnant or get someone pregnant, you *must* use birth control every time you have sex. Never avoid birth control because you think it's too much trouble or because you think it will interfere too much with sex. To quote Roseanne Conner from the TV show *Roseanne,* when asked by her daughter Becky, "Doesn't birth control spoil the mood?" she responded, "Not as much as a screaming baby with a loaded diaper."

Selecting a method of birth control should be the responsibility of both partners, but because it is the woman who becomes pregnant, the choice is more often hers. In the best situations both partners agree on the method of birth control before having sex. If they do not agree, each must watch out for him or herself. If a man does not want to get a woman pregnant, he should always use condoms, even if the woman says she is using another method. If a woman does not want to get pregnant, she must always use birth control, even if her partner begs, "Just this once let's go without it."

Use only reliable methods of birth control, such as the ones in the following chart. Withdrawal or douching is about as effective as luck or prayer in preventing pregnancy.

To determine the best method for you, consider these issues: reliability, ease of use, messiness, sexual spontaneity, side effects, price, and how easy the birth control is to obtain from a drugstore or a doctor. Consult the following chart for details on each method. If you'd like more information, discuss birth control with a health practitioner, doctor, or registered nurse.

Birth Control Choices

CHOICES	WHAT IS IT?
The Pill	Taken daily, the birth control pill is composed of synthetic estrogen and progestin, similar to hormones produced by the ovaries.
The Condom	A condom is a latex or animal membrane sheath worn on the penis that will hold the semen when a man ejaculates. For AIDS prevention, use only latex condoms.
Vaginal Spermicides (foam, suppositories, creams, jellies, and film that contain sperm-killing chemicals)	Chemicals that kill sperm after the man ejaculates into the vagina. Spermicide is inserted into the vagina using a plastic applicator shortly before sexual intercourse.
Diaphragm and Cervical Cap	Rubber cups to be used together with vaginal spermicides. The diaphragm cup covers the cervix and, together with the spermicides, provides a chemical and physical barrier to sperm. The cervical cap is a thimble-shaped rubber cup fitted tightly over the cervix.
The Female Condom (Reality™)	A soft, loose-fitting polyurethane sheath that lines the vagina. Two flexible polyurethane rings are at either end of the sheath. One ring lies inside serving as an insertion mechanism and internal anchor; the other ring remains outside the vagina after insertion.

ADVANTAGES	DISADVANTAGES
The pill is 98 percent effective. No contraceptive needs to be inserted during sex. Regulates menstrual periods, lowers risk of ovarian and endometrial cancer.	Must be taken every day. Clinic or doctor visits necessary two times a year. Possible side effects first two to three cycles. No protection against STD's. Not recommended for smokers.
About 90 percent effective; when used with spermicidal foam, almost 98 percent effective. Low price. Easy to get at virtually any drugstore or grocery store. May help to control premature ejaculation and can enhance foreplay. Prevents STD and HIV transmission.	Some men don't like wearing condoms due to reduced sensitivity. Requires planning. May interrupt spontaneity. Some men lose erections with condoms. Condoms may break or slip off.
Used alone, spermicides are usually 80 percent effective. When used with condoms, about 98 percent effective. Inexpensive and available in almost all drugstores and supermarkets.	Must be inserted before every act of sexual intercourse. Tends to be messy. Not ideal for women who are uncomfortable touching themselves. May cause allergic reactions such as genital irritations.
With spermicidal jelly, diaphragms and cervical caps are 90 percent effective—and about 99 percent effective when used with a condom. Can be inserted up to six hours before intercourse, so allows for sexual spontaneity.	Cervical caps and diaphragms require doctor visits for fitting. Usage requires planning. Partner may feel the diaphragm rim during intercourse. Requires ability to insert fingers and device into vagina. May make women more prone to urinary tract infections.
Doesn't require fitting by a doctor. Available at most drugstores. Protects against STD's and pregnancy. Provides broader coverage than the male condom, protecting the labia, vagina, and penis. Polyurethane is stronger than the latex of regular condoms.	Some women have a problem inserting the female condom. One ring hangs outside the vagina, which can cause discomfort and/or self-consciousness.

CHOICES	WHAT IS IT?
Norplant	Hormones released from six thin, flexible capsules made of a soft rubberlike material surgically implanted under the skin of a woman's upper arm. Prevents pregnancy through ovulation inhibition and thickening of the cervical mucus.
Depo-Provera®	A hormone injection that is given by a doctor (or health clinic) once every three months.
The IUD	Intrauterine device. A plastic or copper device that is inserted into the uterus by a doctor. It prevents fertilization and implantation.
Fertility Awareness Method/Rhythm Method	Abstaining from sex on fertile "unsafe" days, often from days eight to twenty-one of a woman's menstrual cycle. Determined by using special "basal body" thermometer and abstaining when temperature is slightly lower or by examining vaginal mucus and abstaining when it is clear and slippery.
Sterilization	For men, sterilization is surgical vasectomy in which the vas deferens, the tubes that carry sperm, are cut and tied. In women, the most common is surgical tubal ligation in which the fallopian tubes are cut or blocked to prevent the union of sperm with the egg.

ADVANTAGES	DISADVANTAGES
About 99 percent effective. Lasts for up to five years. It allows for sexual spontaneity.	Severe side effects: violent nausea, irregular bleeding, and missed periods. Must be surgically removed, which can be costly and difficult. Not recommended for smokers.
At least 99 percent effective. No need to take or insert anything, just to visit the doctor four times a year. Cost is about the same per year as birth control pills. Makes sexual spontaneity possible.	Side effects include irregular menstrual bleeding and weight gain. Hormones may decrease the amount of minerals stored in bones, a risk factor that could lead to osteoporosis. Cannot be used by women who have a history of breast cancer, blood clots, liver disease, or stroke.
Always in place. Allows for sexual spontaneity.	Possible discomfort during insertion, heavier cramps and bleeding during periods, spotting during periods. May make users more susceptible to STD's. Must be replaced in one to five years.
Approved by the Catholic Church as a method of birth control. Useful to people who are opposed to other methods of birth control. Inexpensive; the only cost is for the special thermometer.	Not effective; may be as low as 60 percent effective. Requires dedication in keeping charts and records of changes in temperature and mucus. Enforced periods of abstinence and fear of the risk of getting pregnant may cause sexual problems.
Most effective method of birth control (except for total abstinence), approaching 100 percent effectiveness. Allows for sexual spontaneity. No birth control method needed for the rest of a person's lifetime. Covered by many medical insurance companies.	Not reversible, or difficult to reverse. May affect the person psychologically since he or she will never be able to have children. Since it does not protect from STD's, the person may still have to use condoms for disease prevention.

Postconception Methods of Birth Control

METHOD	WHAT IS IT?
The Morning-After Pill	Immediately after a woman has had unprotected intercourse (or within three days) she takes high doses of estrogen pills, often diethylstilbestrol or a combination of estrogen and progesterone, for five days to terminate the possible pregnancy.
RU-486	The so-called abortion pill is a series of hormone pills that cause contractions in the woman's uterus, causing her to expel a four-week- to seven-week-old embryo. Not yet available in the United States (commonly used in France).
Abortion	Abortion is the surgical removal of the uterine products of conception through one of several surgical techniques. Some techniques may be performed up to six months after conception.

ADVANTAGES	DISADVANTAGES
Provides an opportunity to avoid risk of unplanned pregnancy. Effectiveness is extremely high, about 99 percent. Used in cases when the woman did not expect to be at risk for conception, such as if she had been raped.	Morally unacceptable to some people. Within three days of unprotected intercourse, woman must make at least two visits to a doctor for an exam to receive the pills. Can cause severe side effects: nausea, vomiting, alterations in menstrual cycle. Not a routinely used method.
RU-486 is very effective, about 97 percent, and is not as invasive as other methods of abortion that require surgery.	Morally unacceptable to some people. May cause side effects, such as severe cramping and heavy bleeding, for up to two weeks after the embryo has been expelled. Long-term side effects are unknown.
Abortion provides an end to unplanned pregnancy and it is a legal and safe procedure when performed by a doctor or at a clinic. It is covered by many medical insurance policies.	Morally unacceptable to some people. Requires surgery plus additional medical office visits. Expensive. Rare but possible surgical complications such as hemorrhage or perforations of uterine wall. Emotionally taxing; patient may benefit from psychological counseling.

Final Words
Mindblowing Sex for Real People

Now you know everything about how to have mindblowing sex: how to make good decisions about sex, how to talk about sex, how to accept your body, how to find pleasure from many sexual positions, how to enjoy condoms, how to use all your senses to enhance sex, how to experiment with sexual diversity, how to resolve your sexual problems, and how to protect against pregnancy and STD's. You should be well on your way to great sexual health and immense sexual happiness. Yet, as I said at the beginning of this book, sex is a skill that you develop over time.

▼ ▼ ▼ ▼ ▼ ▼ ▼ ▼ ▼ ▼ ▼ ▼ ▼ ▼ ▼ ▼

Developing mindblowing sex is a process.

▲ ▲ ▲ ▲ ▲ ▲ ▲ ▲ ▲ ▲ ▲ ▲ ▲ ▲ ▲ ▲

The good news is that the journey to mindblowing sex can be almost as great as the arrival. It is unfortunate when twentysomethings don't strive sexually for the best. Jason, a twenty-one-year-old, said to me, "Sex is like pizza; I'll have it even if it's bad." How unnecessary! Sure, real people frequently compromise in their lives. But you do not need to settle for bad sex. You need to develop a sense of who you want to be sexually and how to get there, finding pleasure along the way.

Life as a twentysomething isn't about being pegged as a slacker or an Xer, it's about developing your real, adult identity. In order to come of age sexually, allow yourself to develop a sexual identity in which you always strive for mindblowing sex.

Make a sexual wish list of what you'd like to get out of sex. Strive for complete gratification. Modify your wish list as your priorities change. Pay attention to your progress in developing mindblowing sex. On the road to mindblowing sex, you may stop and ask, "Are we there yet?" With time, perseverance, and experience, you will have mindblowing sex, love, and relationships.

You are young and vibrant and capable of conquering the world—or at least capable of having a fantastic time. Enjoy your sexuality every step of the way, every day. Ultimately, mindblowing sex will be a reality.

HELPLINES

Free Information and Referrals About Sexuality

AIDS
Centers for Disease Control   1-800-342-AIDS
Sexually Transmitted Diseases
American Social Health Association   1-800-227-8922
Pregnancy, Contraception, Sexual Health
Planned Parenthood of the United States   1-800-230-PLAN
Child Sexual Abuse, Incest Counseling, and Referrals
I.O.F. Foresters National Child Abuse Hotline   1-800-4-A-CHILD
Urologic and Prostate Health
American Cancer Society   1-800-242-2383
**Breast Cancer, Ovarian Cancer, Prostate Cancer,
Testicular Cancer**
American Cancer Society   1-800-227-2345
Premenstrual Syndrome
P.M.S. Access   1-800-222-4PMS
Gay and Lesbian and Bisexual Services
Check your local phone book.
Rape Hotline
Check your local phone book.
Sex Therapy
For a list of certified therapists in your area call or write to:
American Association of Sex Educators, Counselors, Therapists
435 North Michigan Avenue, Suite 1717
Chicago, IL 60611   1-312-644-0828

INDEX

Abortion, 225, 240–41
Abstinence, 106–7, 175–76, 235
Accepting your body, 80–86
  improving your feelings, 84–85
  letting go during sex, 85–86
  men's concerns, 83–84
  women's concerns, 81–82
Acting sexy, 54–56
Adult movie theaters, 190
Adult/sex store, 181, 201
Aerosmith, 183
Affairs, 43–45
  extramarital, 34–36
  regret over, 46
Age differences, 32–34
AIDS (Acquired Immune Deficiency Syndrome), 2. *See also* HIV (Human Immunodeficiency Virus)
  condoms and (*see* Condoms)
  described, 230
  jaded view of, 120
  oral sex and, 94
  symptoms of, 231
  testing for, 232–34
  treatment of, 231
Alcohol, 20, 160–63
Allergies, 209, 218

American Association of Sex Educators, Counselors and Therapists (AASECT), 220
America Online, 187
Amyl nitrate, 162
Anal sex, 101–3
  communication and, 50
  for the first time, 102–3
  HIV transmission and, 113, 116–17
  oral-, 102
Anal vibrators, 180
Aphrodisiacs, 161–62
Arousal stage of sexual response cycle, 75, 76
Ashe, Arthur, 120
Astroglide, 129
Azmora, Pedro, 120

Backrub, 90
  instructions for, 153–55
Bartholin glands, 209
Basic Instinct, 3
Basinger, Kim, 149
Bearse, Amanda, 174
Bell, Andy, 174
Ben-wah balls, 181
Bernhard, Sandra, 174

Birth control, 45, 60–61, 235–41
    abortion, 240–41
    cervical cap, 236–37
    choices, 236–39
    condoms (*see* Condoms)
    Depo-Provera, 238–39
    diaphragm, 236–37
    female condom, 236–37
    fertility awareness method/
        rhythm method, 238–39
    ineffective, 75, 235
    IUD, 238–39
    morning-after pill, 240–41
    Norplant, 236–39
    the pill, 236–37
    RU-486, 240–41
    sterilization, 238–39
    vaginal spermicides, 236–37
Birth Right, 225
Bisexuals, 119, 170–75
    types of, 171
Bitter Moon, 200
Blood and HIV transmission,
    112–13
"Blowjob," 94
Blow-up dolls, 181
Blue Velvet, 200
Body language, 55–56
Bolero, 157
"Boner," 72
Boredom, 107
Boss, sex with your, 30
Bowie, David, 174
Bras, 148
Breast cancer, 223
Breasts, women's body image
    and, 81
Breast self-exam, monthly,
    223–24
Buddhists, 194
Bundy, Kelly, 3

Calvin Klein underwear, 148
Candles, 147, 195
Casual sex, 20–21, 26–28, 36

    regretting, 45
CD-ROM, 186
Centers for Disease Control, 139,
    141
    AIDS hotline, 233
Cervical cancer, 221
Cervical caps, 141, 142, 236–37
Cervix, 72, 117, 222
    abnormal cells covering the,
        222–23
Characters from television and
    movies, 165–66, 174
Chat rooms, 187–90
Cheating, 37, 38, 43–45
    extramarital affairs, 34–36
    HIV and, 143–44
Chlamydia, 117, 228–29
Choosing condoms, 122–28
    color, 126
    lambskin condoms, 128
    lubrication/spermicide, 127
    novelty condoms, 127–28
    packaging, 124
    receptacle tip, 124–25
    size, 125–26
    smell, 127
    taste, 127
    texture, 126–27
    thickness, 125
Circumcision, 73, 84, 218–19
Clerks, 61
Clinton, Bill, 177
Clitoral hood, 70, 205–6
Clitoris, 70, 83
    communication and, 50
    hand stimulation of, 100, 178
    masturbation and, 205–8
    orgasm and, 70, 77–78, 80, 97,
        207–8
Cocaine, 162
Cock rings, 201
Commitment
    condoms and, 143–44
    traditional sexual behavior
        and, 169

Communication, 47–68, 104
before sex, 63–64
bringing up the subject, 52
condoms and, 130–32
criticism, 51
difficulty with, 48–49
during sex, 64–66
feedback as, 51
flirting, 54–56
getting to the point, 51
honesty and, 50
"I love you," 66–68
for initiating sex, 58–59
keys to effective, 49–52
mixed messages, 50
new variations and, 66
nonverbal, 53–54
opening lines, 56–58
past sexual history, 59–63
sadomasochism and, 200
saying what you mean, 49, 54, 58
specificity, 50
stating your preferences, 51
talking it out, 47–48
thinking it out, 50–51
vocabulary and, 64
with, not at, your partner, 51–52
"yes" and "no," 53–55
Companionship and traditional sexual behavior, 169
Compatibility, 104, 105
CompuServe, 187
Computer programs, 186
Computer sex on the Internet, 186–90
Conception, 96
"Condom-ints," 137–38
Condoms, 109–44, 218
advantages of, 237
alternatives to, 140–43
anal sex and, 102
buying, 120–21
choosing (see Choosing condoms)
committed couples and, 143–44
communicating about, 130–32
complaints about, 109–10
dental dam, 114, 116, 136–37
described, 236
on dildos, 180–81
disadvantages of, 237
enjoying, 144
flavored, 127, 137–38, 159
funny ways to use, 138–39
HIV and, 111–17
how to use, 132–34
if it breaks during sex, 136
lubricating, 127, 128–29
preventing breakage, 135–36
protecting yourself with, 113–14
putting it on, 132–34
reasons for use of, 117
refusal to use, 140–43
STD's and, 60, 117
storing, 121–22
taking it off, 134–35
turning them inside out, 126–27
use of, every time, 117–20
for women, 139–40, 141, 236–37
Contraceptive products, allergies to, 218
Control, giving up, 205
Cornell University, 2–3
Costumes, 149
Coworkers, sex with, 20–21, 28–30
end of relationship, 21, 29–30
Cowper's gland, 74
Crabs, 228–29
Crawford, Cindy, 173
Crimes of America, 200
Criticism, 51
Cross-dressing, 197
Curtis, Jamie Lee, 149
Cybersex, 186
"Cyclic" bisexuals, 171
Cysts, 209

Date rape, 50, 53, 160, 200
"Deep throating," 94
Dental dam, 114, 116, 136–37
Depo-Provera, 238–39
Desire stage of sexual response cycle, 75
Diaphragm, 141, 142, 236–37
Digital-rectal exam, 227
Dildos, 179, 180–81
"Doggy style," 99–100
"Domestic partnership" laws, 175
"Double-bagging it," 126
Douche, 93, 136, 235
Drag queens, 197–98
Drugs, 160–63
Dumping your partner, 142–43
Duration of sex, 104–5
Dyspareunia, 209
Dysplasia, 222–23

Easy-E, 120
Ecstasy (drug), 162
Ed Wood, 198
Ejaculation, 78
  broken condom and, 136
  difficulty with, 217–18
  female, 77
  oral sex and, 94–95, 115
  premature (see Premature ejaculation)
  pulling out before, 114
  retarded, 217–18
  retrograde, 218
  slowing down, 98, 177
Ejaculatory incompetence, 218
Elbow Grease, 129
Elders, Dr. Joycelyn, 177
Elisa test, 233
Emotional element of sex, 7–8
  balancing other elements with, 9–11
  intellectual element and, 11–14
Emotionless sex, 30
Employee, sex with an, 30
End of relationship, 45

Epididymis, 74, 227
Erections, inability to get or maintain, 216–17
Erotic potential, 168
Erotic thoughts, 206, 213
Escort service, 191, 192–93
Etheridge, Melissa, 174
Everything but intercourse, 88–89
Exotica, 149
Exotic locations for sex, 150–51, 153
Experimentation, sexual, 41–42
  rating system for, 42–43
Eye contact, 56

"Face-fuck," 95
Face-to-face position, 99
False expectations, 23
Familiarity and traditional sexual behavior, 169
Fantasy, 184–86, 190
FDA (Food and Drug Administration), 127, 128
Feedback, 51
Feet, pointing of, 56
Female condom, 139–40, 141, 236–37
Fertility awareness method, 238–39
Fierstein, Harvey, 174
Finding your sexual self, 202
"Finger cots," 116
First sexual experience, 4–5
Flirting, 54–56
Food, 159–60
Foot preferences, 196–97
Foreplay, 89, 105
ForePlay, 129
Foreskin, 73, 218–19
Four "F's," 87
Four Weddings and a Funeral, 61
Frenulum, 72–73, 178
Frequency of sex, 106–7
Friends, sex with, 37–38
Fuck buddy, 36–37

Games with condoms, 138–39
Garcia, Jerry, 157
Gays, 119, 162, 170–75, 198
Geffen, David, 174
Genital warts, 117, 140, 230–31
Gere, Richard, 173
Gertz, Alison, 120
Glans, 72–73, 178, 218
Gold Circle metal condom pack-
    ages, 124
Gonorrhea, 117, 228–29
Grafenberg, Ernst, 77
Grant, Hugh, 61
Grateful Dead, 157
Group sex, 193–94
G-spot, 70, 77–78, 84
Gynecological examination,
    221–23
  after the visit, 222–23
  annual, 222
  need for, 221–22
Gynol II, 129

Harding, Tonya, 147
Helplines, 245
Hepatitis, 230–31
Herman, Pee Wee, 190
Heroin, 162
Herpes, 117, 140, 230–31
Hindus, 194
HIV (Human Immunodeficiency
    Virus). See also AIDS
    (Acquired Immune Defi-
    ciency Syndrome)
  condoms and (see Condoms)
  described, 230
  drugs and, 162
  female condoms and, 139
  jaded view of, 120
  lambskin condoms and, 128
  myth of population segmenta-
    tion and, 119
  plastic and, 137
  protecting yourself from,
    113–14

risk getting, 141
risks of, 111–13
spermicide and, l41, 142
symptoms of, 231
testing for, 141, 143–44, 232–34
transmission of, 111–13
treatment of, 231
HIV transmission quiz, 114–17
  anal sex, 116–17
  deep tongue-kissing, 114
  masturbating a partner, 116
  oral sex, 115–16
  pulling out before ejaculation,
    114
  vaginal intercourse, 115, 117
Homosexuality, 119, 162, 170–75,
    198
Honcho, 148
Honesty, 50
"Hot chat," 188–90
Human chorionic gonadotropin
    (HCG), 225
Human papilloma virus, 230–31
Hustler, 148
Hymen, 209

IKEA, 174
"I love you," 66–68
  responding to, 68
Incense, 195
Inconsistencies, 53–54
Information and referrals about
    sexuality, 245
Initiating sex, 105
Intellectual element of sex, 11–14
Intergenerational relationships,
    32–34
International Male catalogue, 148
Internet, 186–90
Intimacy and traditional sexual
    behavior, 169
IUD (intrauterine device),
    238–39
"I Want to Fuck You Like an Ani-
    mal," 157

Jackson, Michael, 173
Japanese condoms, 126
John, Elton, 174
Johnson, Magic, 120
Johnson, Dr. Virginia, 75

Kaplan, Dr. Helen Singer, 75
Kaposi's sarcoma, 234
Karen, 162
"Kegel Exercises," 208
Kinsey, Dr. Alfred, 170–71
Kissing, 90–91, 127
    HIV transmission and, 114
KY Jelly, 129

Labia majora, 70–71
Labia minora, 70–71
Lambskin condoms, 128
lang, k.d., 174
Last Tango in Paris, 129
Latex, 113–14, 116, 128
Lesbians, 170–75
Letting go during sex, 85–86,
    205
Lewis, 11
Lighting during sex, 147
Lingerie, 147–49
"Lipstick lesbianism," 173
Long-distance relationship, 31–32
Louganis, Greg, 174
Love, 22–23
    communicating, 66–68
    unrequited, 24–25
"Love Boat Syndrome," 40
Lowe, Rob, 147
LSD, 161
Lubricants, 127, 128–29, 178
Lust, 23–24, 38, 193
Lying, 24, 68
    about past sexual history,
        59–61, 118–20

MacDowell, Andie, 61
Madonna, 174
"Magic Wand," 179, 207

Magnum condoms, 123, 125
Male-superior position, 95–97
Man-on-top position, 95–97
Marathon sex, 104–5
Marijuana, 161
Married with Children, 174
Masks, 149
Massage, 90
    instructions for, 153–55
Massage parlor, 191
Masters, Dr. William, 75
Masturbation, 91, 106, 176–81
    health benefits of, 177
    HIV transmission and, 116
    inability to have an orgasm
        and, 204–8
    men, 178
    most positive reason for, 178
    mutual, 91
    negative messages about, 176
    noise during, 156
    orgasm and, 80, 177
    pornography and, 172
    premature ejaculation and,
        214–15
    "in public," 190
    with sex toys, 179–81
    taboo about, 177
    women, 178, 205–8
Maxx condoms, 123, 125
Meaningfulness of sex, 21–22
Media, 165–68, 174
Melrose Place, 174, 191–92
Men's sexual difficulties, resolv-
    ing, 211–19
    difficulty ejaculating, 217–18
    inability to get or maintain
        erections, 216–17
    loss of sexual desire, 210–11
    painful intercourse, 218–19
    premature ejaculation, 211–16
Men's sexual health, 226–27
    testicular self-exam, 226–27
    visit to a doctor or urologist,
        227

Menstruation and HIV transmission, 115, 116, 136
Mindblowing sex, 6–18
  achieving, 15–18
  balancing the elements of, 9–11
  emotional element of, 7–8
  intellectual element of, 11–14
  natural element of, 8
  personal creativity and pleasures of, 14–15
  technical element of, 8–9
Missionary position, 95–97
Mixed messages, avoiding, 50
Monogamy, 143–44, 169
Morning-after pill, 240–41
Morphine, 162
Most common sexually transmitted diseases, 228–31
Movement and sex, 103–4
MTV Music Awards, 173
Multiple orgasm, 79–80, 105
Music, 157, 195
Mustang Ranch, 191
Mutually monogamous relationship, 143–44

Naked, being, 84–85
Natural Born Killers, 68
Natural element of sex, 8
  balancing other elements with, 9–11
  intellectual element and, 11–14
  smells, 158
  sounds, 156–57
Navratilova, Martina, 174
Newborns, HIV transmission to, 112
New surroundings for sex, 150
9-½ Weeks, 149, 200
Nine Inch Nails, 157
Noise during sex, 155–57
"No means no," 53
Noninsertive sex, 89
Nonoxynol-9 spermicide, 127, 129, 136, 141, 142, 218

Nonverbal communication, 53–54
  body language, 55–56
"Nookie runs," 31
Norplant, 236–39
Novelty condoms, 127–28

Obsession perfume, 157
Oil-based lubricants, 128–29
One-night stands, 20–21, 26–28
"Only You," 157
Opening lines, 56–58
Oral-anal stimulation, 102
Oral sex, 76, 92–95
  communication and, 49, 65
  ejaculation and, 94–95
  for the first time, 92
  flavored condoms and, 127, 128, 159
  HIV transmission and, 94, 113, 114, 115–16
  mixing temperature during, 152–53
  safer, on a woman, 136–37
  sexual scripts and, 88
  "69," 95
Orgasm, 76–80, 145
  alcohol, drugs and, 161, 162
  clitoral, 70, 77–78, 80, 97, 207–8
  described, 76
  differences in intensity of, 76
  early sexual experiences and, 4–5
  ejaculation and, 78
  female, 70, 72, 77–80, 204–8
  inability to have an, 204–8
  male, 73, 74, 75, 78–79
  masturbation and, 80, 91
  multiple, 79–80, 105
  simultaneous, 79
  as stage in the sexual response cycle, 75
  Tantric sex and, 195–96
Outercourse, 89
Overweight body image, 81–82

Painful intercourse
   in men, 218–19
   in women, 209
Pap smear, 221, 222, 223
Peep show, 192
Pelvic infections, 209
Penis, 72–73
   HIV transmission and cuts on,
      113, 115, 116
   shape of, 84
   size of, 83–84
Penthouse, 148
Performance anxiety, 5, 216–17
Perineum, 75, 101
Personal creativity, 14–15
Petra, 27
Phone sex, 156, 182–84, 189
   live, 183, 184
   prerecorded, 183
Photographing your sexual expe-
      rience, 146, 147
Pill, the, 131, 236–37
Planned Parenthood, 225
Plastic and HIV transmission, 137
Plateau stage of sexual response
      cycle, 75, 76
Platters, the, 157
Playboy, 182
Playgirl, 148
Playing it safe, 227–31
Pleasure Plus condoms, 125
Pneumocystic pneumonia, 234
"Point of no return," 213, 214, 215
Polaroid photographs, 146
Poor body image. See Accepting
      your body
Poppers, 162
Pornography, 182, 190
Positions for intercourse, 95–101
   changing, 152
   man on top, 95–97
   rear entry, 99–100
   side by side, 98–99
   sitting, 99
   standing, 100–101

woman on top, 97–98
Postconception methods of birth
      control, 240–41
Power, relationships and, 30, 34,
      35, 191, 192–93
Precum (preejaculatory fluid),
      74–75
   HIV transmissions and, 114,
      115, 116, 117
Pregnancy, 60–61, 139, 225–26
   indicators of, 225
   unintended, 117
Premature ejaculation, 96
   condoms and, 125
   resolving, 211–16
PrePair, 129
Presley, Lisa Marie, 173
Pretty Woman, 192
Prince, 3
Probe, 129
Prodigy, 187
Professor, sex with a, 30
Prostate, 74
Prostate gland, 75
   stimulation of, 101
Prostitutes, 191–92
Psychedelic drugs, 161
Pubic lice, 228–29
Pubococcygeus (PC) muscles,
      208

Quaaludes, 162
Quickie sex, 104, 105

Rape fantasy, 184–85
Ravel, Maurice, 157
Reality condom, 139, 236–37
Real world of sex, 1–18
   mindblowing sex (see Mind-
      blowing sex)
   redirecting sexuality, 1–6
Rear-entry position, 99–100
Reasons for having sex, 21
Rectum, 75
Redecorating your bedroom, 150

Redirecting the sexuality of our generation, 1–6
Refractory period, 78, 79
Regretting a decision, 45–46
Rejection, 35, 37
    fear of, 58, 105
    moving on and, 24–25
Reputation at work, 29
Resolution stage of sexual response cycle, 75, 76
Retarded ejaculation, 217–18
Retrograde ejaculation, 218
Rhythm and tempo of sex, 103–4
Rhythm method, 238–39
Ribbed condoms, 126
Richards, Michael, 149
Rimming, 102
Role plays with condoms, 138–39
Roseanne, 174, 235
RU-486, 240–41
Rubber gloves, 114, 116

Sadomasochism (S/M), 199–202
    caring and, 201–2
    code words and, 200
    consent and, 200, 201
    dominants, 199
    pain and, 200–201
    scripting the scenario and, 200, 201
    submissives, 199
Safer sex, 120. *See also* Condoms
Saran Wrap, 114, 116, 137
Saying sexy things during sex, 155
Schwarzenegger, Arnold, 149
Scrotum, 72, 73–74, 178
Security and traditional sexual behavior, 169
Seinfeld, 149
Semen, 78
    HIV transmission and, 112–13, 116, 117
    taste of, 94
Seminal vesicles, 74

Senses to enhance sex, using your, 145–63
    drugs or alcohol and, 160–63
    smell, 157–58
    sound, 155–57
    taste, 159–60
    touch, 152–55
    turning on to, 145
    vision, 146–51
"Sequential bisexuals," 171
Serial monogamy, 40
Serious committed relationship, 39–40
Sex drives, unequal, 65–66
Sex surrogates, 219
Sex therapists, 219–20
Sexual addiction, 106
Sexual desire, loss of, 210–11
Sexual diversity, 165–202
    abstinence, 175–76
    accepting your sexual orientation, 170–75
    adult movie theaters, 190
    computer sex on the Internet, 186–90
    cybersex, 186
    fantasy, 184–86
    finding your sexual self, 202
    foot preferences, 196–97
    freedom to practice any type of sex, 167–69
    group sex, 193–94
    ideas about, 165–66
    masturbation, 176–81
    myths about, 166–67
    phone sex, 182–84
    pornography, 182
    prostitutes, 191–93
    sadomasochism, 199–202
    sex toys, 179–81
    strip clubs, 190–91
    strippers, 191–92
    tantric sex, 194–96
    threesomes, 193–94
    traditional sex, 169–70

Sexual diversity (*cont.*)
   transvestism, 197–99
Sexual guidelines, 28. *See also*
      Who should you have sex
      with?
   regretting a decision and, 45
   setting, 19–20
   sticking to, 20–21
Sexual healing, 203–20
   finding a sex therapist, 219–20
   loss of sexual desire, 210–11
   men's sexual difficulties (*see*
      Men's sexual difficulties,
      resolving)
   women's sexual difficulties
      (*see* Women's sexual difficul-
      ties, resolving)
Sexual health. *See* Men's sexual
      health; Women's sexual
      health
Sexual history
   lying about, 59–61, 118–20
   talking about, 59–63
Sexually transmitted diseases
      (STD's), 117, 209, 219. *See
      also* AIDS (Acquired Immune
      Deficiency Syndrome); HIV
      (Human Immunodeficiency
      Virus)
   cervix and, 72
   chlamydia, 228–29
   crabs/pubic lice, 228–29
   genital warts/human papilloma
      virus, 230–31
   gonorrhea, 228–29
   herpes, 230–31
   lying about, 59–60
   preventing (*see* Condoms)
   syphilis, 230–31
   testing for, 222, 223
   urinary tract infection,
      228–29
   viral hepatitis, 230–31
   yeast infection, 228–29
Sexual orientation, 170–75

Sexual plumbing, 69–75
Sexual politics, 3
Sexual response cycle, 75–76
Sexual scripts, 87
   changes in, 88
   traditional, 87–88
Sharing needles and HIV trans-
      mission, 112, 119
Side-by-side position, 98–99
Silent sex, 155, 156
Simultaneous orgasm, 79
Sitting position, 99
"Situational" bisexuals, 171
"69," 95
SK 70, 127
Smell to enhance sex, 157–58, 195
Smiling, 56
Smith, Patti, 157
Snap decisions, 20–21
Snugger condoms, 126
Social acceptability and tradi-
      tional sexual behavior, 169
Sound to enhance sex, 155–57,
      195
Speaking the same language, 64
Specificity, 50
Sperm, 74–75
Spermicide, 127, 129, 136, 141,
      142, 218, 236–37
"Spoon position," 100
"Squeeze technique," 215
Standing sex, 100–101
Stating your preference, 51
Statutory rape, 34
Sterilization, 238–39
Stern, Howard, 3
"Stop-start" technique, 215
Strip clubs, 190–91
Stripping, 191–92
Strip show, 149
Studded condoms, 126
Student, sex with a, 30
"Sweet Emotion," 183
"Swingers," 194
Syphilis, 117, 230–31

Taboos, 173–74, 177
Tantric sex (Tantra), 194–96
Taoists, 194
Taste
    to enhance sex, 159–60, 195
    flavored condoms, 127, 137–38
Technical element of sex, 8–9
    balancing other elements with, 9–11
    intellectual element and, 11–14
Telephones
    long-distance relationships and, 32
    phone sex (*see* Phone sex)
Television, 165–66, 174
Temperature during sex, 152–53
Testes, 73–74
Testicular cancer, 74, 226
Testicular self-exam, 226–27
Testosterone, 74
"Thinking off," 186
Threesomes, 193
Times (London), 173
Tongue-kissing and HIV transmission, 114
"Totally erotic activities that people enjoy without having intercourse," 88–95
    exploring each other's genitals, 91
    kissing, 90–91
    masturbation, 91
    oral sex, 92–95
    touching, 89–90
Touching, 89–90
    each other's genitals, 91
    to enhance sex, 152–55, 195
"Traditional sex," 169–70
"Transitory" bisexuals, 171
Transsexuals, 198
Transvestism, 197–98
Trojen-Enz Large condoms, 125
True Lies, 149
Trust and traditional sexual behavior, 169

Tumors, 209
2 Live Crew, 3

Uncircumcised men, 73, 84, 218–19
Underwear, sexy, 147–49
University of Pennsylvania, 3
Unrequited love, 24–25
Urethra, 75
Urinary tract infection, 228–29
Uterus, 72, 117, 222

Vagina, 71, 77, 113, 222
    blowing into the, 93
    contraction of, 71–72
    dilators of, 210
    HIV transmission and, 114, 117
    lips of, 70–71
    muscles around, 208
    penis size and, 83
    taste of, 93
Vaginal-digital exam, 222
Vaginal lubrication, 71
Vaginal secretions and HIV transmission, 112–13, 115, 116
Vaginismus, 209–10
Values, 142–43
Vas deferens, 74
Vasectomy, 74
"Vibrating Vagina," 180
Vibrators, 179–80
    inability to have an orgasm and, 207
Victoria's Secret catalogue, 148
Videotaping your sexual experience, 146–47
Viral hepatitis, 230–31
Visual experience of sex, 146–51, 195
Vocabulary, 64
Vulva, 69, 178

Waiting time before having sex, 25–26

Water-based lubricants, 128, 129
Western Blot test, 233
Wet, 129
White, Ryan, 120
Who should you have sex with?,
     28
  affairs with married people,
     34–36
  age differences and, 32–34
  boss, 30
  coworkers, 28–30
  employee, 30
  friends, 37–38
  fuck buddy, 36–37
  long-distance relationship,
     31–32
  professor, 30
  serious committed relation-
     ship and, 39–41
  student, 30

Williams, Robin, 162
Withdrawal, 75, 235
Woman-on-top position, 97–98
Women's sexual difficulties,
     resolving, 204–10
  inability to have an orgasm,
     204–8
  loss of sexual desire, 210–11
  painful intercourse, 209
  vaginismus, 209–10
Women's sexual health, 221–26
  gynecological examination,
     221–23
  monthly breast self-exam,
     223–24
  pregnancy, 225–26
Wonderbra, 148

Yeast infection, 228–29
"Yes" and "no," 53–55